*Auteur/Provocateur*
The Films of Denys Arcand

**Recent Titles in
Contributions to the Study of Popular Culture**

"Mr. B" Or Comforting Thoughts About the Bison: A Critical Biography of Robert Benchley
*Wes D. Gehring*

Religion and Sport: The Meeting of Sacred and Profane
*Charles S. Prebish*

Songs of Love and Death: The Classical American Horror Film of the 1930s
*Michael Sevastakis*

Hollywood as Mirror: Changing Views of "Outsiders" and "Enemies" in American Movies
*Robert Brent Toplin, editor*

Radical Visions: American Film Renaissance, 1967-1976
*Glenn Man*

Stanley Kubrick: A Narrative and Stylistic Analysis
*Mario Falsetto*

Ethnicity and Sport in North American History and Culture
*George Eisen and David Wiggins, editors*

The Neutral Ground: The André Affair and the Background of Cooper's *The Spy*
*Bruce A. Rosenberg*

Post-Franco, Postmodern: The Films of Pedro Almodóvar
*Kathleen M. Vernon and Barbara Morris, editors*

Populism and the Capra Legacy
*Wes D. Gehring*

Dark Alchemy: The Films of Jan Švankmajer
*Peter Hames, editor*

# Auteur/Provocateur

## The Films of Denys Arcand

*Edited by*
André Loiselle and Brian McIlroy

Contributions to the Study of Popular Culture,
Number 45

GREENWOOD PRESS
WESTPORT, CONNECTICUT

Published in the United States and Canada by
Greenwood Press, 88 Post Road West, Westport, CT 06881
An imprint of Greenwood Publishing Group, Inc.

English language editions, except the United States and Canada,
published by Flicks Books, England

First published 1995

Library of Congress Cataloging-in-Publication Data

Auteur/provocateur: the films of Denys Arcand / edited by André
   Loiselle and Brian McIlroy.
      p.    cm. -- (Contributions to the study of popular culture.
   ISSN 0198-9871: no. 45)
      Filmography: p.
      Includes bibliographical references and index.
      ISBN 0-313-29672-3 (alk. paper)
      1. Arcand, Denys. 1941-   --Criticism and interpretation.
   I. Loiselle, André. II. McIlroy, Brian. III. Series.
   PN1998.3.A735A88   1995
   791.43'0233'092--dc20                                    95-3998

© individual contributors 1995

All rights reserved. No part of this publication may be reproduced, stored in a retrieval system or transmitted in any form or by any means: electronic, electrostatic, magnetic tape, mechanical, photocopying, recording or otherwise, without prior permission in writing from the publishers.

A paperback edition of *Auteur/Provocateur* is available from the Praeger Publishers imprint of Greenwood Publishing Group, Inc. (ISBN 0-275-95297-5)

Library of Congress Catalog Card Number: 95-3998

ISBN: 0-313-29672-3
ISSN: 0198-9871

Printed in Great Britain.

# Contents

| | |
|---|---|
| Acknowledgements | vi |
| List of illustrations | vii |
| Introduction<br>*André Loiselle* and *Brian McIlroy* | 1 |
| Alone and with others: Denys Arcand's destiny within the Quebec cinematic and cultural context<br>*Pierre Véronneau* | 10 |
| Sound design and music as *tragédie en musique*: the documentary practice of Denys Arcand<br>*Réal La Rochelle* | 32 |
| A cinema of radical incompatibilities: Arcand's early fiction films<br>*Gene Walz* | 52 |
| Gender relations in *The Decline of the American Empire*<br>*Denise Pérusse* | 69 |
| Arcand's double-twist allegory: *Jesus of Montreal*<br>*Bart Testa* | 90 |
| No big picture: Arcand and his US critics<br>*Peter Wilkins* | 113 |
| "I only know where I come from, not where I am going": a conversation with Denys Arcand<br>*André Loiselle* | 136 |
| Denys Arcand: filmography<br>*Compiled by André Loiselle* | 162 |
| Denys Arcand: selected bibliography<br>*Compiled by Brian McIlroy* | 170 |
| Index | 183 |
| Notes on contributors | 194 |

# Acknowledgements

This book could not have been written without the help of many people. Foremost among these are, of course, our contributors Denys Arcand, Pierre Véronneau, Réal La Rochelle, Gene Walz, Denise Pérusse, Bart Testa and Peter Wilkins. For help with photographs, stills and other materials, we would like to thank Valérie Allard at Max Films, Alain Gauthier at the Cinémathèque Québécoise, and the Stills, Posters & Designs Department of the British Film Institute. For translations, we are indebted to Joëlle Bourjolly, Fred A Reed and Caroline Sévigny. Generous support was gratefully received from Avigail Eisenberg, Gail Oelkers and the faculty and staff of the Department of Theatre and Film at the University of British Columbia.

André Loiselle · Brian McIlroy
University of British Columbia
*February 1995*

# List of illustrations

Full captions for illustrations which follow page 120. All names read from left to right.

- *Denys Arcand*.
- *Réjeanne Padovani*: Margot MacKinnon as Stella Desaulniers.
- *On est au coton*: textile worker.
- *Love and Human Remains*: Joanne Vannicola as Jerri, Thomas Gibson as David, and Ruth Marshall as Candy.
- *Seul ou avec d'autres*.
- *Le Confort et l'indifférence*: René Lévesque, leader of the sovereignist Parti québécois and Premier of Quebec (1976-85), with his wife, Corinne Côté.
- *Québec: Duplessis et après...*: Robert Bourassa, leader of the provincial Liberal Party and Premier of Quebec (1970-76, and 1985-) campaigning in 1970. (Bourassa resigned as Premier in 1993.)
- *Le Déclin de l'empire américain*: Louise Portal as Diane, Dominique Michel as Dominique, Dorothée Berryman as Louise, and Geneviève Rioux as Danielle.
- *Le Déclin de l'empire américain*: Louise Portal, Gabriel Arcand as Mario, and Yves Jacques as Claude.
- *Jésus de Montréal*: Johanne-Marie Tremblay as Constance Lazure, Rémy Girard as Martin Durocher, Robert Lepage as René Sylvestre, and Catherine Wilkening as Mireille Fontaine.
- *Jésus de Montréal*: Lothaire Bluteau as Daniel Coulombe, and Catherine Wilkening.
- *Jésus de Montréal*: Rémy Girard and Robert Lepage.
- *Jésus de Montréal*: Catherine Wilkening, Lothaire Bluteau and Johanne-Marie Tremblay.
- *Gina*: Céline Lomez as Gina.

André dedicates this book to Naomi, Éliane, Sylvie and Odette

Brian dedicates this book to Valerie

# Introduction

## André Loiselle and Brian McIlroy

With the unexpected triumph of *Le Déclin de l'empire américain* (*The Decline of the American Empire*) at the Cannes Film Festival in 1986, and the international success of *Jésus de Montréal* (*Jesus of Montreal*) three years later, Denys Arcand has risen from relative obscurity outside Quebec to the rank of Canada's most widely acclaimed filmmaker – with the possible exception of David Cronenberg. However, Arcand's contribution to world cinema is not limited to his two hits of the 1980s. Indeed, these films only brought broader recognition to a cinéaste whose career spans thirty years and includes a number of significant productions worthy of academic scrutiny. The purpose of this book is precisely to offer a critical overview of the work of a director who has moved in and out of the spotlight over the decades, but who has never ceased to make intelligent and challenging films.

From his controversial documentary, *On est au coton* [*We're Fed Up*, 1970], censored by the National Film Board for its "subversive" description of the textile industry in Quebec, to *Réjeanne Padovani* (1973), a fiction film shifting from operatic beauty to graphic violence in its depiction of bourgeois corruption, and *Le Confort et l'indifférence* (*Comfort and Indifference*, 1981), a brilliant analysis of the failure of the nationalist dream that underlies the entire Quebec culture, Arcand has always produced works whose caustic expositions of society's contradictions leave no one indifferent. His whole canon, including *The Decline of the American Empire* and *Jesus of Montreal*, has been the subject of either dithyrambic praises or vehement condemnations, according to the critics' position in relation to the issues examined by the cinéaste. Although it is too early to evaluate the impact of his most recent offering, *Love and Human Remains* (1993), which deals with the search for love in a chaotic urban environment, there is little doubt that it will trigger as many contradictory reactions as Arcand's previous films.

This volume attempts to account for the conflicting responses which Arcand's films have generated since the very beginning of his career in the 1960s, by bringing together scholars who hold different opinions about his relationship to his material, and about his status in national and international contexts. The following six essays comprise a mosaic of opposing viewpoints and compose something of a dialogic or polyphonic commentary on Arcand's career and work, thereby echoing the debates surrounding each of his films.

In addition, the dialogic arrangement of the book also seeks to parallel Arcand's own intellectual approach to his subject-matter. Clearly, one of Arcand's preferred cinematic practices is the construction of dialogic structures through the juxtaposition of contradictory and irreconcilable elements at every level of a film's diegesis. Unlike many filmmakers, Arcand does not resort to juxtapositions and parallels for the purpose of bringing his films to a climactic synthesis. Rather, he uses parallelism to expose contradictions and similarities, but never carries the dynamic through to a unifying resolution. Thus, adjectives such as "dialogic" or "polyphonic" are more appropriate to describe Arcand's work than the usual term "dialectic" because, as Anne Herrmann explains, "unlike the dialectic, which seeks to transcend oppositions by means of a synthetic third term, the dialogic resists the reconciliation of opposites by insisting on the reciprocity of two or more antagonistic voices".[1] This avoidance of the comfortable stability of the dialectical synthesis is exactly what characterizes Arcand's work as a whole. Similarly, this volume does not close the debate on the cinéaste with a synthetical conclusion that we, the editors, could have written. The collection of texts ends with Arcand's own comments on himself, thus adding another voice to the dialogue.

Arcand's fascination with comparison, juxtaposition and parallelism springs from his education as a historian at the Université de Montréal, where he came to believe that one historical phenomenon has meaning only when considered in relation to other phenomena. Arcand's particular brand of historicism is evident in the short documentaries which he made for the NFB, having been hired in the early 1960s as the designated historian of the French unit. For instance, in *Champlain* (1964) Arcand constantly moves back and forth between the early 17th century, when Samuel de Champlain was enthusiastically trying to establish a colony in New France, and 1964, when the Quebec people had still not achieved the "vie douce et tranquille", of which their ancestors had dreamed.[2]

As Arcand learned and mastered the techniques of documentary filmmaking throughout the 1960s and the early 1970s, his films became increasingly complex, but always conserved the same basic structure. In his 1972 feature-length documentary *Québec: Duplessis et après...* (*Quebec: Duplessis and After...*) on the 1970 provincial election, Arcand draws parallels between contemporary politics, the politics of former Quebec Premier, Maurice Duplessis from the 1930s through to the 1950s, and the traditional nationalist aspirations of the French-Canadian people as identified by Lord Durham in his 1839 *Report on the Affairs of British North America*.[3] By exposing the surprising similarities between and among the Durham Report, Duplessis's nationalistic orations and the 1970 campaign speeches of the Provincial Liberal Party and the separatist Parti québécois, the filmmaker disrupts comfortable assumptions about the "evolution" of political thought in Quebec, and questions the validity of the endless nationalist debate.

Similarly, Arcand's fiction films of the 1970s and 1980s very clearly display this dialogic inclination. His first fiction, *La Maudite Galette* [*The Damned Dough*, 1971], describes a milieu of alienated proletarians who resort to crime to make a quick buck, without knowing how to use the money once they have acquired it. Throughout the film Arcand divides the working class into parallel sub-classes that prey on one another but never envision the possibility of uniting against an extra-diegetic common enemy.

His second fiction film, *Réjeanne Padovani*, offers a more complex orchestration of the various voices that cover the discursive field. Here Arcand manifests his dialogic imagination by adopting an upstairs-downstairs structure that shows us corrupt businessmen, lawyers and politicians enjoying champagne on the first floor, and their bodyguards guzzling beer in the basement. The two initial groups are sub-divided further as the issue of gender comes into play. In both clans, men are in charge, while women function as mere servants or sexual objects.

On only one occasion in the film do all cliques come together. The force that temporarily manages to bridge the gap and challenges the dehumanizing mechanisms of a degenerate capitalistic system is the lyrical beauty of opera. As a diva sings an aria from Gluck's *Orfeo ed Euridice* (*Orpheus and Eurydice*, 1762) for the entertainment of the entrepreneur-cum-mafioso Vincent Padovani and his guests, the subordinate group literally climb upstairs, to the level of the masters, to catch a glimpse of the private performance. For a brief moment there seems to be a way of resolving differences. But as soon as the song is over, all resume their respective functions, and the reign of abuse, violence and discrimination recommences with no end in sight.

*Réjeanne Padovani* hints at Arcand's tendency to search for reconciliation in the realm of the lyrical arts. But the cinéaste's urge to question the possibility of ever achieving synthetical harmony within society still prevails. His next film, *Gina* (1975), offers the bleakest example of his lack of faith in dialectical resolution. Based on the incidents surrounding Arcand's shooting of his 1970 documentary *On est au coton*, the plot of *Gina* revolves around the title character, a stripper giving shows in a small-town hotel, where there resides a crew of would-be Marxist filmmakers who are shooting a denunciative documentary on the textile industry. Having been gang-raped by snowmobilers after one of her shows, Gina requests her agent and his thugs to take revenge on the rapists. Simultaneously, the producing company of the documentary (sarcastically called the National *Cinema Board*), fearing reprisals from the textile corporation, terminates the shooting and calls the filmmakers back to Montreal.

On the surface, the film crew, the stripper and the textile workers share a common lot, as they are all persecuted by the establishment. But again Arcand refuses to fabricate a synthetical conclusion that would see the oppressed uniting against the oppressors. Rather, the potential cohesion dissolves as each faction chooses a different way of coming to terms with their circumstances: Gina escapes to Mexico, having overseen the carnage of the rapists; the filmmakers forego their Marxist vocation and agree to shoot a commercial film; and the workers resume their daily routine. Arcand's refusal of closure is nowhere more evident than in *Gina*.

As the only work in Arcand's canon that bears a strong autobiographical mark, *Gina* also represents a turning point in the director's career. Following this process of self-questioning on the effective role of the cinéaste in Quebec, Arcand moved away from personal fiction films and, for the next ten years, worked only on documentaries, television shows and impersonal commercial films. Those ten years were crucial, however, in Arcand's evolution as a filmmaker, as he strived to perfect his craft and become a competent film technician. Thus, when he returned to his personal cinematic practice in 1986, with *The Decline of the American Empire*, he was better equipped technically to convey his particular vision of the world.

In essence *The Decline of the American Empire* is quite similar to the earlier fiction films, as it also adopts a dialogic structure that contrasts a variety of voices. Set in post-Referendum Quebec (that is, in the context of a society that had recently foregone its very public attempt to secure independence from Canada), the film explores the contrasting discourses of women and men on the most private of subjects: sexuality.[4] A masterful montage of sequences, in the first part of the film, counterpoints the respective sex-related anecdotes of the women, working out at the gym, and of the men, cooking a meal for their female friends.

The second half of the film begins with a physical combination of the two parallel lines of action, as both groups meet for dinner. However, this reunion of bodies in the same room, like the sexual act, does not manage to bridge the gap between the two sides. Although they discuss at length, they do not communicate. The problem of the male/female dichotomy is epitomized in the relationship between Rémy and Louise. After more than a decade of married life, Louise learns, late in the film, that Rémy has slept with all his female friends and many others. What follows is an awkward domestic argument that settles nothing and leaves the characters (and the audience) hanging between separation and reconciliation.

Where *The Decline* ends, *Jesus of Montreal* begins. As Arcand explains: "*Jesus of Montreal* is the continuation of *The Decline*. Once everybody has slept with everybody else, what does it all add up to? Where are we? Where are we going? Thus, when I start on *Jesus of Montreal*, it is the continuation. Here's someone who will try to give meaning to all this".[5] *Jesus of Montreal* tells the story of Daniel Coulombe, a young actor hired to play the role of Jesus in a passion-play produced by the Oratoire St-Joseph. Once again, Arcand's dialogism is apparent. At the level of the narrative of the film, the dual structure contrasts two conceptions of art: on the one hand, the actors involved in the production of the play, who are wholly dedicated to their craft; and, on the other hand, the media and the authorities of the Oratoire, who see art as a commodity.

The conflict between the true artists led by Daniel, and the corruptors of art led by Father Leclerc and a lawyer called Cardinal, is ingeniously allegorized by Arcand as he sets parallels between events in the life of Jesus, and Daniel's struggle to remain true to his art. However, the similarities between Jesus and Daniel do not constitute the core of Arcand's discourse. Rather, Arcand's basic concern is that Daniel is an artist. It is at that level that the main dialogic – between Jesus and Daniel – operates. Arcand's point by establishing certain parallels between Jesus and Daniel is, in fact, to emphasize the essential differences between their respective projects.

Jesus of Nazareth's project of salvation is rooted in spirituality, whereas that of Jesus of Montreal focuses on the here-and-now of the collective aesthetic experience. The historical Jesus urges his disciples to see him as the channel through which their souls will pass into another world. Daniel Coulombe, on the other hand, asks his followers to rediscover the virtues of the unifying humanist venture, and simply become involved in the creative process. The passion-play, as a collective creation that brings a sense of purpose to both the actors and the spectators, is but the first step towards a rediscovery of the power of art to bring human beings together. In *Jesus of Montreal*, for the first time since *Réjeanne Padovani*, art seems to offer an alternative to the dialogic chasm. Whether in the form of the passion-play or Pergolesi's *Stabat Mater*, heard at the beginning and at the end of the film, lyrical art appears to emerge as a possible solution to human contradictions.

But nothing in Arcand's films is ever quite as simple as it seems. Indeed, it could be argued that *Jesus of Montreal* resists reconciliation as much as his previous films. Following the accidental death of Daniel during a performance, and the rather dubious metaphor of the humanist resurrection as "organ transplant", Arcand adds a few scenes which undermine the apparent transcendental character of the film. In one of these scenes, the satanical lawyer (Cardinal), persuades three of Daniel's four disciples to partake in the foundation of the "Daniel Coulombe Theatre". In his demonic way, the lawyer argues convincingly that experimental art and commercial success can be harmonized. Thus, he provides an extremely ironic synthesis to the film's conflict. By having one character refuse the lawyer's offer and walk away as empty and unfulfilled as she was at the beginning of the film, Arcand forces both the optimist and the cynic to question their interpretation of the film. Without negating the positive effect that Daniel has had on his followers, Arcand once again resists the reconciliation of opposites and reasserts his socio-historical dialogism.

Many of the issues raised above are expanded upon at length by our contributors. In "Alone and with others: Denys Arcand's destiny within the Quebec cinematic and cultural context", Pierre Véronneau opens our collection of essays with a historical overview of Quebec cinema and documentary practice following the establishment of the National Film Board in 1939. Denys Arcand has played a pivotal role in the development of our perception of Quebec cinema, and this essay charts chronologically the work of a powerful cinéaste, from his early documentaries up to and including his recent fiction feature films. To Véronneau, the key words for Arcand in his critical investigation of contemporary and past Quebec society are "re-evaluation" and "paradox". Concentrating on the director's fascination with history and political processes, Véronneau argues that Arcand may be compared with Jean Renoir, who "wanted to change the world while maintaining his distance from those who were the agents of this change". Arcand has thus marked out a place for the intellectual filmmaker/commentator.

"Sound design and music as *tragédie en musique*: the documentary practice of Denys Arcand" by Réal La Rochelle combines the voice of Arcand – in a series of dialogues with the author – with an appreciative survey and analysis of the filmmaker's early short works and his three major feature documentaries, *On est au coton*, *Quebec: Duplessis and After...* and *Comfort and Indifference*, all in terms of their employment of sound and music. It reveals that Arcand's aesthetic relies heavily on his subtle merging of sound and visuals, an observation which has rarely been made before in assessments of the director's work. Arcand was largely self-trained in sound use at the NFB, and La Rochelle reveals how in the feature films, including the most recent work, *Love and Human Remains*, this love of melding sound and music with visuals continues to be a strong aspect of Arcand's œuvre.

The focus in Gene Walz's "A cinema of radical incompatibilities: Arcand's early fiction films" is on the lesser known *La Maudite Galette*, *Réjeanne Padovani* and *Gina*. Walz's close analyses of these films suggest that Arcand may be considered alongside Godard and Renoir in the tradition of European art cinema. Of particular interest are the innovative technical developments emerging in these early fiction films, such as the Godardian "planimetric" style in *La Maudite Galette*. Although Arcand and Godard eventually took different paths, Walz points to the "normally incompatible opposites" which Arcand invariably combines: "the straightforward and the parodic; the naïve and the cynical; social commentary and generic escapism". For Walz, "Arcand's world is almost unrelentingly Darwinian".

Denise Pérusse's "Gender relations in *The Decline of the American Empire*" is a major consideration of Arcand's first international success. Pérusse argues that the film's main thesis is that the search for individual rights, including personal happiness, in our late capitalist society has overcome traditional, liberal notions of collective rights. One of the ways of showing how this society has decayed, according to Pérusse, is the "layering of clichés", which conveys the failed idealism of the film's largely complacent baby boomers. Pérusse analyses the "characters" as purveyors of these clichés and of this general malaise, and argues that the most telling indictment of this dead milieu is the abject failure of workable cross-gender relationships, which Arcand mercilessly spotlights.

The filmmaker's next major international success is subjected to an exhaustive and challenging critique in Bart Testa's "Arcand's double-twist allegory: *Jesus of Montreal*". Testa examines the structure of Arcand's film, concentrating on the use of ellipsis and his "diagrammatic narrativity". In his tracing of the Christological allegory, Testa brings out the complexities of Arcand's "correspondences" and their contemporary relevance. Testa forcefully puts the case that "Arcand executes a crucial displacement in the allegory away from the religious towards the artistic". But Testa also sees that the aura of politics is never far from the surface of Arcand's film work. He sees a "double-twist", whereby politics takes over from art "when the film passes beyond allegorizing the ministry to allegorizing the Passion".

The final essay, Peter Wilkins's "No big picture: Arcand and his US critics", provides a larger context in which to discuss the concerns of both *The Decline of the American Empire* and *Jesus of Montreal*. Wilkins is fascinated that at last an opportunity has presented itself to look at the "reversal in the flow of culture" between the United States and Canada. Normally, Canadians are resigned to US culture bombarding television and cinema screens, and news-stands. Wilkins probes the reaction of American critics to a specifically Canadian product – two successful Quebec films. The often confused and myopic response, discovered in his survey, helps to raise the questions of Arcand's filmic irony and of why his films, in a postmodern sense, "assert their visibility by refusing consumption". Wilkins wonders if this "resistance" may be useful to English Canada and its filmmakers, particularly through recognising Arcand's commitment to a place "on the outskirts of the empire".

The publication of this book follows the general release of Arcand's latest film, *Love and Human Remains*, adapted by Brad Fraser from his play *Unidentified Human Remains and the True Nature of Love* (1989). Our volume comes as a timely retrospective on Arcand's work, for this most recent production marks another turning point in his career. In addition to being the first film, in over twenty years, that Arcand has directed without having written (or co-written) the screenplay, *Love and Human Remains* is also his first "Canadian" feature, as opposed to the strictly "Quebec" projects on which he had worked previously. Indeed, the film was co-produced by a company from Ontario and, while it was shot in Montreal, post-production took place in Toronto, where the film also premièred in September 1993.

More important, however, is the fact that *Love and Human Remains* is Arcand's first feature in English. Although the director insists that the only reason for his making the film in English was to respect the integrity of Fraser's original text, it is difficult not to speculate on the filmmaker's ambition to join the mainstream of the lucrative American movie industry. Furthermore, the story-line of the film, which revolves around young, attractive urbanites looking for love in all the wrong places, and the topical backdrop of serial killings give *Love and Human Remains* a commercial edge absent from the majority of Arcand's previous works.

But Arcand has already demonstrated – especially with *Gina*, his biggest popular success of the 1970s – that a commercial style does not preclude sagacious insight into the more abstruse modes of societal operation. It is not unlikely that *Love and Human Remains* will prove to be as representative of the 1990s as *The Decline of the American Empire* was of the 1980s.

*Notes*

[1] Anne Herrmann, *The Dialogic and Difference* (New York: Columbia University Press, 1989): 15.

[2] Quoted from *Champlain*. "A gentle and peaceful life".

[3] Maurice Duplessis, who was Premier of Quebec between 1936 and 1959, with a short interruption during the war, is associated with a period of religious and political repression in the province. The Duplessis era, also known as "the Great Darkness", came to an end with Duplessis's death in 1959 and was followed by a phase of modernization and reform, labelled "the Quiet Revolution". Lord Durham wrote his *Report on the Affairs of British*

*North America* in the wake of the 1837-38 insurrection, during which a group of French Canadians vainly resorted to violence to bring about changes in the structure of the colonial Government.

[4] In 1980 the separatist government of the Parti québécois, under the leadership of René Lévesque held a Referendum on sovereignty-association – a doctrine that advocates the political independence of Quebec while retaining certain economic ties with Canada. 60% of the population of Quebec voted against independence, thus negating twenty years of nationalist claims. Throughout the remainder of the 1980s the issue of Quebec nationalism was buried. The 1990s, however, have seen a resurgence of nationalism in Quebec.

[5] Translated from the French: "Si bien que, *Jésus de Montréal* est la poursuite du *Déclin*. Une fois que tout le monde a couché avec tout le monde, qu'est-ce que cela signifie? Où en sommes-nous? Où allons-nous? Donc quand j'aborde *Jésus de Montréal*, c'est la suite. Voici quelqu'un qui va tenter de donner un sens à tout cela." See Léo Bonneville, "Interview Denys Arcand", *Séquences* 140 (June 1989): 15.

# Alone and with others: Denys Arcand's destiny within the Quebec cinematic and cultural context

*Pierre Véronneau*

TRANSLATED FROM THE FRENCH BY JOËLLE BOURJOLLY

> I find that too much is written about our cinema. Basically, we don't have cinema, we have film literature .... As far as I am concerned, I can't help thinking there is something unwholesome about it all. But let us admit, so as not to be too hard on the filmmakers, that wholesomeness is rare in Quebec. (Denys Arcand)[1]

1963 – the year in which Denys Arcand began directing his first documentary – is commonly regarded as marking the inception of modern Quebec cinema, with such landmark productions as *Pour la suite du monde* (*The Moontrap*) by Pierre Perrault and Michel Brault, and *A tout prendre* (*Take It All*) by Claude Jutra. However, it must be remembered that with the creation of the National Film Board (NFB) in Canada in 1939, French-speaking filmmakers had already begun to address the needs of the francophone public.

For a number of years, Quebec cinema grew mainly within a federal (Canadian) institution dominated by anglophones. Endangered as a group, the francophone filmmakers fought for their existence. In 1952 they were inadvertently aided in their struggle by the arrival of television, for which NFB films were required for transmission. They were also bolstered by the move of the NFB's headquarters to Montreal four years later. During the same period, feature production was developing as an industry. Studios were built and films were made, beginning in 1944 with *Le Père Chopin* [*Father Chopin*] by Fédor Ozep, and ending, 18 films later in 1954, with *L'Esprit du mal* [*The Evil Spirit*] by Jean-Yves Bigras. Melodrama was the keynote of the films of that era, which presented a rich social portrait of contemporary French-Canadian society: traditional and dominated by Catholic values and conservatism.

From the mid-1950s and for the next ten years, Quebec society underwent a process of social and economic modernization – later called the "Quiet Revolution" – which was characterized by the national awakening of Quebecers. Filmmakers were not immune to this nationalist call to arms. At the NFB the francophone filmmakers, originally formed as a small cell, became a tighter group which called itself the "French Team" and fought for an autonomous French production unit, which they achieved in 1964. From the origins of this group sprang the documentary movement in Quebec. They began to challenge certain aspects of conservative ideology diffused by Quebec élites, and to propose new ways of seeing and doing things. Technically, they experimented with light cameras and sound equipment, like their English colleagues of the Candid-Eye movement (Roman Kroitor, Wolf Koenig, Terence Macartney-Filgate), so that they could get closer to the people. (The Candid-Eye movement was characterized by its use of on-the-spot interviews and an unassuming voice-over.) When the conservative Government was defeated in 1960 and the Quiet Revolution began officially, these filmmakers wholly endorsed its main ideas, especially its reformism and nationalism. They wanted to record the real speech of the people and refused the traditional authoritative voice-over commentary.

Many of the French Team were attracted by the *cinéma direct* style (which incorporated elements of the Candid-Eye but relied less on interviews). However, some were unhappy at the NFB since they were not allowed to shoot features and to express themselves freely. Some were separatists and wanted to deal openly with this issue in their films, while others were radicals who wanted to criticise Quebec's social system. The establishment of a film industry, somewhat encouraged by television production, was an attractive challenge for yet another group. For these reasons, some directors decided to quit the NFB and pursue their own goals. Jutra, Pierre Patry (*Trouble-fête* [*Trouble Makers*], 1964) and Claude Fournier (*20 ans express* [*Twenty Year Express*] series, 1967) are shining examples.

Even though the NFB was criticised, it was nevertheless a place of opportunity where filmmakers could explore the documentary, deal with cultural issues and discuss socio-historical questions. It was in this context that Denys Arcand joined the NFB. In the foreword of a special issue of *Copie Zéro* dedicated to Arcand, I wrote briefly about the intelligent and fascinating work that emerged from this director who embraced all that was both mainstream and marginal about Quebec cinema. This text will attempt to explain that paradox.

In 1959 Arcand, then an 18-year-old college student, collaborated with his colleague Stéphane Venne on a short film, *A l'Est d'Eaton* [*East of Eaton's*]. While at university two years later, they produced a feature film (based on their personal experiences) for the Association générale des étudiants de l'Université de Montréal (AGEUM) with the help of fellow history student Denis Héroux.[2] Thus, Arcand, like so many of his peers in the years to come, began his career by making a student film.

*Seul ou avec d'autres* [*Alone or with Others*, 1962]

*Seul ou avec d'autres* portrays the ups and downs of collegiate life for a first-year university student. The action centres around the daily activities of a young female protagonist. Although they were novices, the student team boldly solicited the help of NFB professionals who, much to their surprise, accepted the challenge.[3] These were the virtuosos who had perfected the *cinéma direct* technique – light camera, synchronous sound – and who now for the first time applied their skills to a feature film. Thus, *Seul ou avec d'autres* marked the first collective effort not only of two generations of filmmakers, but also of two styles of writing and filming.[4] Even though the resulting work was disorderly, future projects would prove more cohesive.

Despite its clumsiness, loosely-woven plot and semi-professional touch, the film's emphasis on realism gives it the appearance of an impressionist documentary on the social science milieu of the early 1960s. It is not easy to distinguish Arcand's individual work in this project. The casual attitude and social criticism are attributable more to the generation than to the directors. There is nevertheless one scene which pinpoints Arcand's preoccupations: the discussion with Professor Guy Rocher, Director of the Sociology Department. He explains that Quebec has always been a withdrawn society, always choosing the regional rather than the universal; this phenomenon was also found in universities. He even criticises the educational system which does not encourage the development of individual thinking – the one thing Arcand tries to focus on.

During this time a group of intellectuals at the Université de Montréal proposed an analysis of Quebec history and society. This influenced Arcand, and he became interested in the views of Maurice Séguin and his colleagues.[5] They felt that the impact of English occupation on Quebecers in 1760 had left them isolated on the fringes of the United States, and had forced them to develop survival strategies to validate their existence. All Arcand's work explores this dimension of Quebec's history and mentality. Rather than dwell on personalities, he describes "the consequences of men's actions and the close rapport they have with the present society and their implications for future societies".[6]

Although he maintains that two years of history studies (obtaining his undergraduate degree, the "licence" in 1961) did not make a historian of him, it is obvious that this discipline was the basis for his intellectual development. Arcand still shows a marked interest for this method and for those who practise it. He does not shy away from making reference to historians (from Tacitus and Machiavelli to Maurice Séguin and Michel Brunet); he is inspired by their thinking. His culture draws him back to history and almost all his films bear witness to profound historical research. He spontaneously views his subjects from a historical angle – he historicizes them. His first films are a testimony to this approach.

The first short historical films (1964-65)

Armed with feature film experience and the encouragement of the NFB filmmakers with whom he collaborated, Arcand, then 21 years old, submitted a script entitled *Samuel de Champlain, une réévaluation* to the NFB during the summer of 1962. At that particular time, the NFB had a series of historical films in preparation, entitled "The History Makers". Since it was trying to strengthen the francophone contribution to the industry, Arcand's proposal was easily accepted. The freshman director entered an institution that was fully active at the cinematographic, formal and organisational levels, and his project did not shock his peers.

It may be said that the common theme which would resound throughout the remainder of his work was then already contained in one word: re-evaluation. The French explorer and geographer Samuel de Champlain scouted New France and founded Quebec in 1608. He eventually attained a mythical status in Quebec history. With *Champlain* (1964), Arcand proposed to demolish the myth that was so dear to Quebec's national identity. In his script he questions the colonization of New France, which he characterizes as "an artificial country built contrary to the laws of history".[7] During the anti-colonialist struggle for national liberation of the 1960s, this questioning was not surprising, yet astonishing at the same time.[8] Even if it translates into a revised history, stamped by Marxist thought, *Champlain* stands apart from the Quebecer nationalist awakening of the 1960s, which proclaimed the importance of the survival of the francophone people.

In my opinion, this attitude expresses the essential elements of Arcand's thought. He refuses to reduce reality to mere terms that can be represented in a simple and malleable equation. Interdependence and complexity generate a discursive and narrative structure in him that is quite paradoxical. In this way Arcand not only departs from commonly accepted opinions, but also validates both true and false propositions. This thinking creates an uncertainty in relation to the action.[9] We can attribute contradictory arguments to him because the structure of his films does not represent a singular perspective. Faithful to his vision of history, Arcand suggests a course that resembles more a labyrinth than a simplification. His cinema feeds on paradox rather than on certainty.

One may assume that the NFB authorities were wary of a director so disrespectful of official history, particularly since the work to be entrusted to him on the eve of the Canadian Centennial (1967) was aimed at teaching people to love Canadian history. The film encountered some difficulties. Arcand edited his script and modified his commentary, but managed nevertheless to slip in some personal points of view. The film's reception was so controversial that the NFB commissioned an editor (Réjane Charpentier) to make an abridged version, entitled *Québec 1603*, mainly using footage of Frédéric Back's drawings. This film's perspective was the exact opposite of Arcand's, and therefore it should not be considered as one of his films.

He enjoyed less freedom on the two short films which followed *Champlain – Les Montréalistes* (*Ville-Marie*) and *La Route de l'Ouest* (*The Westward Road*, both 1965) – for which he was supplied with very specific scenarios. In order to state his opinions, he resorted to cinematic discourse, making his most eloquent points through editing. Thus, in *Ville-Marie* the dichotomies of past/present, construction/destruction and religion/death alternately suggest that ancient values inevitably crumble and that we should not venerate a dead universe. Arcand's first three "professional" films contain the seeds of what will later be considered his trademarks: pessimism (in his view of history) and cynicism. I do not subscribe to this characterization, which limits the director's thinking, which is marked, I believe, at the crossroads of uncertainty and paradox. It is true, however, that Arcand's melancholic humour bluntly attacks the entire system and offers neither a solution nor a model. These first historical films were disturbing because they did not follow the traditional concept of history. He was not interested in one character in particular, but described how people's actions have a close rapport with the society in which they live and the subsequent impact for future societies.

So Arcand succeeded by avoiding the quagmire and maintaining his sharp, observing eye. This by no means facilitated his task and he could not do as he pleased. Passionately in love with his profession but not inclined towards compromise, he would rather accept making banal films on assignment than sit idly waiting.[10] *Montréal un jour d'été* (*Montreal on a Summer Day*, 1965), *Volleyball* (1966) and *Parcs atlantiques* (*Atlantic Parks*, 1967) offered him the opportunity to practise making documentaries, just as he would later make commercials. Aside from the obvious financial benefit, he acquired experience working with technicians and familiarized himself with new equipment. One may consider the six short films, with their imperfect, down-to-earth style (which was different from the usual *cinéma direct* style) as Arcand's apprenticeship, since there was no other way to learn about filmmaking in Quebec. Arcand, who tends not to flatter himself, has already categorized his consigned films as insignificant.

## On est au coton [*We're Fed Up*, 1970]

The arrival of a new management team at the NFB in 1967 and the creation of a Programme Committee gave more power and decision-making to the filmmakers.[11] The NFB was now open to films with a social orientation, and in 1968 Arcand proposed to shoot a documentary on the textile industry in Quebec, which he thought could bring to light the limits of technological and managerial thought then prevalent in North America. He called his film *On est au coton*, a popular expression meaning "we are fed up" and referring to textiles in its use of the word "coton" ("cotton").

Workers in the textile industry are among the lowest paid in Quebec and are subjected to wretched labour conditions. Arcand and his team expected to find the workers in a state of rebellion comparable to their own. In reality, it was the opposite. The filmmakers eventually understood that they were "making a film, not about rebellion, but about resignation".[12] In choosing to acknowledge this fact, Arcand set the militant politicians against him, specifically the Marxist-Leninists who blamed him for not taking a clear class stand in not making a propaganda film. Commenting on the reaction he said:

> I always had difficulties with militants. They are always extremely serious people; one should not make light of their cause. Unfortunately for me I love to laugh ... Laughter has a diabolical ring, it is a fundamental rejection of the human condition. It exposes all those who have a pretty high opinion of themselves, and God knows there are a lot of them![13]

In fact, Arcand distrusts dogmatism and refuses simple solutions, and for that reason he may be said to have an ambiguous point of view. To him reality is complex, and each situation has many facets; roles and identities become mixed and confused, and life itself is ambiguous. The picture he paints of the situation in the textile industry, the union disputes he recalls (going as far as allowing an ex-communist supervisor to speak) and the quality of life he depicts were sufficiently harsh to scare both the employers who appeared in the film and the NFB authorities, who insisted on making cuts. For them the film lacked objectivity in describing the industry. Originally intended to be 173 minutes, the film was reduced to 159 minutes, but these cuts were still not sufficient. The censorship ordered by the NFB delayed the release of the film until 1976.

This censorship brought Arcand closer to his colleagues, who were subjected to the same treatment: Jacques Leduc with *Cap d'espoir* (*Cape Hope*, 1969), Perrault with *Un pays sans bon sens!* (*Wake up, mes bons amis*, 1970) and Gilles Groulx with *24 heures ou plus* (*24 Hours or*

More, 1976). *On est au coton* remains the most famous banned film; this degree of censorship is exceptional in itself, and also revealing, since it exposes the series of mutilations often suffered by NFB productions. The film stands out from the documentaries of the "Groupe de recherches sociales" (Social Research Group) and of the series "Challenge for Change/Société nouvelle", both of which demonstrate in the final analysis that the economic and social system in which we live can be reformed.[14] Arcand neither offers solutions (for which he was criticised by the left-wing) nor charms anyone. His description of the world of workers is crude, at times fierce and alienating, and does not rally the spectator to action. Although the film is a reminder of the textile union disputes, it also denounces the imperialist American presence and its domination of Quebec. It demonstrated that the laws of the state protect the companies and favour the exploitation of workers. Because it reveals to the spectator the dialectic between analysis and reality, *On est au coton*, together with Arthur Lamothe's *Le mépris n'aura qu'un temps* [*Contempt Will Last But a Time*, 1969] will remain one of Quebec's greatest political films.

## *Québec: Duplessis et après...* (*Quebec: Duplessis and After...*, 1972)

Despite the turn of events taken by *On est au coton* and even though the film was not yet completed, the NFB agreed to underwrite Arcand's new project. He wanted to capitalize on the forthcoming provincial political campaign of 1970 – which promised to be turbulent – in order to depict the political scene in Quebec.[15] At that time the Union nationale was running the government.[16] The Liberals, after a surprising defeat by the Union nationale in 1966, now presented a new leader, Robert Bourassa.[17] The Parti québécois, a nationalist party established in 1968 that promoted the political sovereignty of Quebec while proposing to retain an economic association with Canada, took up the challenge in the political arena under the leadership of René Lévesque. The Social Credit, a rightist populist party which already had members elected in the federal House of Commons, attempted to win seats into the National Assembly of Quebec. This exceptional conjuncture fascinated Arcand because it highlighted the diversity of the political currents crossing Quebec. It also allowed him to analyse the mechanisms of political power in the province and, more precisely, the mechanisms involved in the ascension to power. He studied three areas – rural, semi-urban and urban/worker – to discover the many nuances buried in electoral processes. Since he did not have access to party leaders, he mainly followed minor candidates. He was impressed by these candidates' speeches, and he hypothesized that there was no historical discontinuity between 1936 (the year that Maurice Duplessis's

Union nationale first gained power), 1955 (the apogee of Duplessism) and 1970.

Contrary to the belief of many historians, the Quiet Revolution struck Arcand as a relatively superficial phenomenon, because the basic structure of society remained relatively stable despite the changes affecting Quebec. According to him, Duplessis personified, or was the bearer of all the doctrines that could put the province into motion. That is why Arcand did not hesitate to use Duplessis's old speeches (through cross-cuts) in his editing, comparing them with contemporary speeches, going so far as juxtaposing René Lévesque's picture with Duplessis's words. He was criticised for suggesting that the nationalism of previous years was the same as today. Arcand would later be quoted as saying: "The film suggests the idea that in the process of deep cultural and economic structural modifications, the appearance and disappearance of various political parties, as well as the rise and fall of charismatic 'personalities' are just superficial phenomena that can only play a subordinate role in the historical evolution of a people".[18]

Once again his point of view, ambiguous though it may be, is developed through his editing, influenced by Eisenstein's concept of the "montage of attractions". As in *On est au coton* he makes reference to two extra-diegetic texts in order to establish the historical perspective. The first is the *Durham Report*, excerpts of which one of the actors delivers.[19] The second is *Le petit catéchisme des électeurs*, a parody on the "little" Catholic catechism book produced in 1936 by the Union nationale, used to promote its programme and denounce the corrupt Liberal Party. These two texts place this film under the twin stars of conquest and subservience, cynicism and lies, and enhance its provocative aspect. It is important to point out that at the time Arcand was finishing the fictional part of his shooting, the October Crisis exploded.[20]

The crisis resulted in setting the radical nationalist factions against both the reformist nationalists and the pro-federalists, who preached law and order.[21] This turmoil in the Canadian political arena forced Arcand to take this conjuncture into consideration in the general organisation of his film. He had to refrain from making certain statements but he suggested – through editing – several unmistakable interpretations determined by the current socio-political context. *Quebec: Duplessis and After...* was not released until 1972. Arcand never concealed his radical opinions, leftist nationalism and taste for a liberty bordering on anarchy.[22] He also does not believe in objectivity and refuses to propagandize. The film was debated as much among the federalists as it was among the sovereignists.

## La Maudite Galette [*The Damned Dough*, 1971]

Finally accepting producer and filmmaker Jean Pierre Lefebvre's repeated offers to venture into fiction, Arcand prepared a script with writer Jacques Benoit, entitled *La Maudite Galette*, which he shot and completed in 1971. Speaking of this particular stage of his career, Arcand stated: "The preceding documentaries led me into such an ideological and political impasse that I was reduced to incoherent babbling. It is a film on lesser-men, rejects of humanity, who practically no longer express themselves, but survive on hold-ups, guns and theft. Everyone gets killed in the end."[23] In this fictional film, like the two that would follow, Arcand examines the dregs of Quebec society. It seems that this world fascinates him, as if he sees a deeper metaphor for Quebec itself: a decrepit and decadent country in which he places no hope.[24]

The film depicts the story of a poor family, the kind of rejects of the capitalist world who do not hesitate to employ petty criminals and resort to torture and crime in order to extort a large sum of money (the "dough") from their uncle. Seemingly a detective story, if not a film noir, this portrait of Quebecer misery, set against a backdrop of gangsterism, does not fully subscribe to the rules of the genre. For example, Arcand's cinematic expression does not follow the quick tempo needed to build suspense. He also paints miserable characters with whom the spectator cannot identify. Through his portrayal of the alienated condition of Quebecers, who endure rather than speak out, Arcand provokes a malaise and leaves his spectator with no hope and no way out. His black humour, dry tone and harsh caricature bear the mark of brutal cynicism, the more so since Arcand does not judge his characters. He is content to present them and watch them, and is more interested in the living conditions than the human inter-relations. Some were disgusted by the film, which they found too complacent towards these villainous people. But the majority proclaimed enthusiasm for a film which became a social commentary, a cinema with punch.

*La Maudite Galette* was screened in Cannes in 1972, at the same time as Gilles Carle's *La vraie nature de Bernadette* [*The True Nature of Bernadette*]; both films were well-received. Although Carle was somewhat known and Arcand not at all, the success of both films forced critics to re-examine their opinion of Quebec cinema, which up to that point was perceived primarily through the lyrical documentary work of Pierre Perrault. Reflecting the consensus from both sides of the Atlantic, one critic wrote:

> Hustling things on, with actors who act as if they are not acting, this *Maudite Galette* proves in its own way that Canadian directors know how to keep an eye open, the right

one too .... The film begins as a comedy of manners, realistic, even sordid. Then, imperceptibly, the tone rises. The merely vulgar becomes macabre. The family quarrels degenerate into slaughter, and all this without losing its humour.[25]

## Réjeanne Padovani (1973)

Encouraged by the success of *La Maudite Galette*, Arcand teamed up again with Lefebvre and Benoit for another fictional film, *Réjeanne Padovani*. The majority of this film takes place in one evening where a developer, who has links with the underworld, invites the Mayor of the city and the Minister of Public Works to dinner. Arcand delights in describing, with an indifference that borders on contempt, the complicity between these groups and the hypocrisy of their values. He claims to have prepared the film by studying the decay and fall of the Roman Empire and by reading Suetonius. In that epoch, like the one described in the film, there was an unmotivated society (or rather one motivated by futile gain), living in the comfort of its "bread and circus games". The society of Quebec, and that of Montreal in particular, woke up one morning surrounded by a destroyed environment, controlled by profiteers walking hand in hand with Power, whose "hands are always dirty", as Sartre would say.

A number of films may be cited in order to understand the purpose behind this film: *La Règle du jeu* (*The Rules of the Game*, 1939) by Jean Renoir; *Le Charme discret de la bourgeoisie* (*The Discreet Charm of the Bourgeoisie*, 1972) by Luis Buñuel; and *Le mani sulla città* (*Hands Over the City*, 1963) by Francesco Rosi. Arcand exposes many things that should upset the spectator – corruption, crime, etc. – but since, as he sees it, there really is no class struggle in Quebec, only exploiters and exploitees happy with their fate, there is no point in trying to change it. That is why Arcand's cinema simply underlines the contradictions; he criticises but does not offer solutions. It is political cinema minus the militant dimension. The irony of this scenario is that the militants presented in the film, leftist journalists and members of a citizen's committee, are victims of police repression, the same police that rubs shoulders with organised crime and politicians. As in his previous film, Arcand does not concentrate on effects, camera movement or fancy editing; he does not think of himself as Costa-Gavras. He prefers efficiency in his narrative structure. He offers the spectator a quasi-tragedy which respects, as closely as possible, the rule of the three unities: a single place (Padovani's house); a single time (an evening); and a single action (the harmony of the reception that is jeopardized by Réjeanne Padovani's arrival, justifying her elimination). He presents a harsh tragedy where neighbouring worlds depend on each other:

upstairs, men with power ("stars", it might be recalled, of *Quebec: Duplessis and After...*); downstairs, those who serve them.

Presented at Cannes in 1973, the film was a success and Arcand became celebrated in France. The public liked his charisma and intelligence, and his work received critical acclaim: "Arcand is a moralist of the highest class, that of Juvenal and Voltaire", wrote Jean Rochereau.[26] The filmmaker could now command respect on the international scene; with all doors wide open to him, he could easily prepare his next film.

## *Gina* (1975)

There is an unquestionable autobiographical dimension to this film, where two stories intertwine. The first is about a team of filmmakers shooting a documentary on the textile industry. They run into obstacles put up by company executives and the National Cinema Board (this diegesis refers to the story of *On est au coton*).[27] The second is Gina's story, about an exotic dancer who is raped by a gang of snowmobile drivers; she will be avenged by her protector's henchmen. This time Arcand dazzles us with his writing, especially towards the end of the film, when the tensed-up violence finally explodes, in true Hollywood style (he was later accused of having sold out aesthetically). He also abandons almost all humour. The world he describes, which is solely oriented towards sex and violence, is more hopeless than in preceding films. He acknowledges the social decay of Quebec and nothing gives him hope, not even the young worker, who is exploited like the dancer and condemned to cheap labour and subservience.

If Arcand interjects his personal history into the film, it is not because of vague complacency, but as an explanation of where Quebec cinema stood at that time. The filmmakers he presents are conscientious and dedicated people, whose impotence is painfully obvious. Their governmental employer can stop their work as it pleases; they cannot contribute to the awareness and liberation of the young worker (and, by extension, the working class); and they are unable to shield Gina from the fatuity of the snowmobile gang – only the bouncers manage to do so. This is why in the last scene the crew is seen filming a "commercial" police story. It is as if he is saying, "For lack of anything better, let 'true' cinema be entertaining at least". This conclusion is not the least of the paradoxes evident in the film, which confused some of Arcand's followers.[28] So he set aside the cinema for a few years, and instead leaned towards television.[29]

It must be remembered that the second half of the 1970s and the early 1980s were an inauspicious time for Quebec cinema. Although it is said that the years 1967-75 were the golden age, the decline of

Quebec cinema paradoxically coincides with the rise to power of the Parti québécois in 1976. Is it because the nationalist wave that sustained Quebec cinema had fallen? On this point Michel Euvrard has written: "When the tide is low, the beach is littered with unattained objectives, of illusions – quiet or not .... It is a transitional cinema for a country moving once again, and more than ever, towards uncertainty."[30] I have commented elsewhere on this critical pessimism and my appreciation of Arcand's work in the 1980s is not foreign to my evaluation.[31]

*Le Confort et l'indifférence* [*Comfort and Indifference*, 1981]

All Arcand's previous work proves that he is a man who has a "Quebec-ache", just as one has a heartache or a bellyache. Strangely, it is not by masochism that he speaks of his country and his society. It is the call to duty of the historian lying dormant in him that compels him to do it. In this way his documentaries are more than just sketches; they are frescoes. Arcand could not refrain from filming the Referendum campaign of 1980 on the sovereignty of Quebec. The film brought back into the foreground the local political issues that the films of the late 1970s tended to avoid.

For many weeks Arcand followed the representatives of both groups, the 'OUI' and the 'NON', and allowed each side a chance to speak. He already knew the outcome when he began to edit the film: the 'NON' had triumphed. As with *Quebec: Duplessis and After...*, the result of the event determined the structure of the film and the interpretation. The shock of the Referendum's result was catastrophic to a number of intellectuals and probably also to Arcand. The editing of the film lasted a year, during which time Arcand tried to find a humorous way to convey a reality that pained him deeply. He adopted a mocking tone, insolent or frankly amusing, using satirical and often brilliant editing. He does not hesitate to treat those he is filming in an unrestrained manner, dissecting the demagogy and narrow-mindedness of many of the protagonists; he caricatures to saturation the cast of political men and condemns their misleading aphorisms. The film uses terms with heavy connotations, such as "country", "nation", "money", "security" and "liberty". The film mercilessly confronts the spectator with his own imagination. Once more he resorts to a practice which is found in all his documentaries: the intervention of a non-diegetic "commentary". Here it is Machiavelli, incarnated by an actor (Jean Pierre Ronfard) in costume who recites passages from *Il principe* (*The Prince*, 1513). According to Arcand, Machiavelli holds an outsider's point of view on the debate.[32] Depending on the scene, the "Prince" could be Canadian Prime Minister Pierre E Trudeau, Montreal Mayor Jean Drapeau or Quebec Premier René Lévesque. This distanced point of view, achieving a kind of Brechtian detachment, could be assimilated into that of the historian Arcand pretends to be. Perhaps he wants to stir up Quebecer pride by presenting them with such an image that they would want to affirm themselves as a people. Basing his argument mainly on editing (dialectic between the images, dialectic facts/ Machiavelli), Arcand, to paraphrase Godard, politically makes political cinema; he uses films to dismantle the codes of the representation and the ideologies that manufacture social consent.

Some believe that the documentary tradition hindered the evolution of fiction filmmaking in Quebec because it inhibited the freedom of film directors who were trying to adhere to reality; they also feel that it impeded their training and dramatic talent. Arcand nevertheless managed to bridge the two forms, even though *La Maudite Galette*, like many other Quebecer films of this period, retained the observational perspective of a documentary. From *Réjeanne Padovani* onwards, he showed greater skill at dramaturgy, making his characters more complex, even if they served as support in his depiction of a particular milieu. Then *Gina* allowed him to focus his interest on some characters as characters and to use, where necessary, a faster, more mobile style. Taking a phenomenological approach, he let people's actions speak for themselves. His return to documentaries is a testimony to this experience. He does not minimise filmic expression in order to attain this unrealistic, hypothetical adequacy; he just maintains a safe distance from it, which is why his critical freedom is so effective and why his cinema is definitely *civic* cinema.

It might have been expected that *Comfort and Indifference* would be Arcand's most controversial film. Never again would his position come under such attack; to some people his criticism seemed to take on a combative stance. "A vengeance from an intellectual wanting to insult the little people who said NON .... The director specifically chose to show the cowardice of a people .... He is saying to the people they are stupid and cowardly, and he thinks he is brave", said Lise Bissonnette in the newspaper of which she would become editor-in-chief several years later.[33] She predicts success for the film in petits bourgeois circles and denounces Arcand's remarks quoted in the press release, to the effect that the "Quebecers are so spoiled by the crumbs of American wealth one cannot hope for much from them".[34] This image of the Quebecer struck the attention of an English-speaking reporter who said that "Quebecers are a complacent lot of louts who love colour TVs, crass materialism and are indifferent to noble visions of self-sacrifice, heroic risk and independence."[35] Subscribing to Lise Bissonnette's opinion, he concludes that the film is a "cheap, condescending, ivory tower view of Quebecers". Another journalist active on the transcultural scene, Fulvio Caccia, adopts a different and more original point of view from the image of Quebecers projected in this film:

> This immense national patchwork is similar to our political reality: interminable and confused. It is to break this narcissistic circularity that Machiavelli is introduced. But the dice are loaded .... Arcand and his collaborators missed a great opportunity to explore this problem more deeply by not confronting the ambivalent and two-faced personality of the Quebecer. A more discerning look at the history of Quebec could have shed some light on this double cultural heritage which constantly steers cinematography and politics towards melodrama. In retreating behind the observer's objectivity – those who refuse to be implicated – the director could only restore to Quebecers the inverted image of their own self-seduction. It is the mirror of Narcissus.[36]

This opinion serves to criticise Arcand on his sacred ground: history. *Comfort and Indifference* brings to a close the political cycle inaugurated by *Quebec: Duplessis and After...* and continued with the *Duplessis* television series, which he scripted in the late 1970s, and marks the end – temporarily, it is hoped – of Arcand's documentary career.

Perspective

In an imitation of the crew in *Gina*, Arcand then made a commercial film, *Le Crime d'Ovide Plouffe* (*The Crime of Ovide Plouffe*, 1984). For his own sanity he afterwards took a break to prepare for his brilliant comeback: *Le Déclin de l'empire américain* (*The Decline of the American Empire*, 1986). I shall not deal with this film, nor that which followed, *Jésus de Montréal* (*Jesus of Montreal*, 1989), since they are thoroughly examined elsewhere in this book. What observations can be drawn from this analysis of Arcand's films, which will also allow us insight into his future work?

From the three short historical films to *Jesus of Montreal*, Arcand uses an analogous, discursive structure. He alternates the past and the present, and compares and cross-checks them. In other words, he historicizes the present (even to a great extent in his fiction films). History informs reality, and reality becomes relative. In this perspective the present loses its weight, limits and certainty. Some may have thought that for Arcand history was predetermined and that he subscribed to a cyclical model. On the contrary, I believe that his thinking is marked by historical indeterminism. Even if all the cards were dealt, history would not necessarily repeat itself. Having the past in mind, Arcand suggests that one can understand and master the present, recognise its agents and their doctrines, and guide one's actions accordingly. One constant that appears in his work is the refusal of amnesia, even though we live in a society that tends too often to seal off the past and the depth and complexity of things, a society which "manufactures consent", which disinforms.[37] For Arcand, facts and events carry all the weight of history and there is no better remedy for forgetfulness and no better aid to intelligence than the reconstruction of history (forgotten or repressed), and the reminder of the origin of things.

Arcand's interest in history is not that of a memorialist or a chronicler, but that of a person who can extract from it material for comprehension and reflection. He refuses to validate an interpretation simply because it has made itself more visible or more manifest, or knows how to impose itself on the media. He would not be one to say that he belongs to the "lyrical generation", simply because François Ricard's book, *La génération lyrique*, was fashionable in Quebec in 1992.[38] Although he was part of the Marxist and sovereignist movement, he was always critical of it. When asked in an interview to what he attributed his independent thinking, he answered that "no theory, no idealism, no analysis ever totally convinced me".[39] That for him is the characteristic of the intellectual, especially of the committed intellectual. As French essayist Pierre Bourdieu has written:

> The intellectual is a paradoxical being who cannot be perceived as such as long as you grasp him through the classical alternative of autonomy and commitment, pure culture and politics. This, because he historically constituted himself as such, with and by surpassing this opposition .... He exists and subsists for as long as, on one hand, an intellectual and autonomous world exists and subsists (meaning independent of religious, political, and economic powers, etc.) of which he respects the specific laws; and on the other hand, the specific authority in this universe works in favour of autonomy and is engaged in political battles.[40]

This does not quite correspond to the model established by Sartre, but comes close to Arcand's specific practice in the cultural field. He does not yield his ideology to predetermined, conformist rhetoric; he attempts to unveil what underlies or predetermines it. He confronts, and that is why there is no "Arcandian" discourse. It is by careful deconstruction that he touches on ethical and political responsibility. A director who becomes irresponsible says, "After me, the heavens can fall". This is not the case with Arcand. If it is true that being cultivated is asking questions and not giving answers, then Arcand is a very cultivated director.[41]

This is why Arcand was always sensitive to mediocrity, particularly that of men of power (for example, the politicians of *Réjeanne Padovani* and the advertising creators in *Jesus of Montreal*), while being more indulgent towards ordinary people, whom he tends to present in a positive light. He is knowing of those who placate the world and refuses to do it himself. In *Jesus of Montreal* this is very explicit. Arcand points to the mass media that make intelligent people acquire idiotic reflexes. He aims especially at advertising because in large part it finances the means of communication; it also curtails freedom of expression and anaesthetizes the social body. It is not innocently that Arcand describes this world. To those who only see emptiness, playfulness, humour and harmlessness, Arcand reminds them that advertising exerts a power that has repercussions on economic, moral and social levels. In fragmenting the entire field of the media, in chopping all that it touches, advertising prevents the expression of a full and cohesive ideology (which itself leaves room for thought) by filling in the cracks where one could reflect.

Neither is it innocent to pair advertising with television. Television can show everything that is visible, but at the same time make invisible that which is essential (such as the relationship between things and facts). Appealing to intellectuals, it appears to offer a forum, but in fact it prevents them from participating effectively and excludes them from public debate. Television has acquired a firm grip on the population and plays the role of social therapist; it has, by its tentacular presence, the capacity to grasp everyone. By the format it has adopted, the time-frame that constrains it and the pseudo-balance of viewpoints it must offer, television has stunted analysis. Even worse is the advent of "reality shows" that make us believe television is documenting the present in depth. Arcand praises a non-superficial way to view reality. He takes the opposite course of the glib pseudo-analysts (those who practise small-time sociology or indulge in a *Reader's Digest* philosophy, or film buffs who fancy themselves as critics), who confuse inquiry, perspective and reflection with sensationalism of politics, exploitation and human misery. For example, soap operas seem to mirror all contemporary preoccupations (AIDS, racism, pollution, ecology, incest, broken families, unemployment, etc.) but actually gloss over them with artificial drama or artificially dramatic situations. When television does show solutions, they are often of an individual nature, requiring little collective action or human solidarity. Arcand always avoids proposing elementary solutions. He highlights and presents arguments; he does not solve them. He is not a militant filmmaker. Militant filmmakers portray a non-analytical or pseudo-analytical relation to reality. They favour poetic formats, practise a single-minded cinema, abandon social reflection and reject collective perspectives – all instances where the capacity for analysis remains dormant. Arcand's films, on the contrary, show characters who do question, and he includes a willingness for analysis in the form itself (witness his editing) and in his overall aim.

Conclusion

Some filmmakers have tried to be agents of reflection on the history of Quebecers (Perrault, Groulx, Lefebvre); others aimed without hesitation at fitting into the North American film entertainment industry (Héroux, Carle, Fournier). In his documentary practice Arcand attempts, without compromise, to make films on the political conscience of Quebecers. In *On est au coton* he analyses the condition of the working class and presents the zero conscience level in this circle. In *Quebec: Duplessis and After...* he draws up a report on the political condition of Quebec to demonstrate that political morality and conscience have hardly changed, and that the effects of the Quiet Revolution have been overestimated. In *Comfort and Indifference* he shows that the political fate of Quebecers remains in disarray. In his first three fiction films, he showcased the lower depths of Quebec society, reeking of pessimism. But his later fiction films broke out of this darkness and the criticism became wiser and more serene.

In the 1990s an atmosphere of despondency reigns. Many are affected by the pervasive defeatism. The illusions of 1968 have collapsed and the disenchantment offers fertile ground for the affirmation of the élitist autonomy of intellectuals. Historically this has given rise to art for art's sake, as opposed to bourgeois art and social art. This is not the case with Arcand. A recent publication by the French writer Serge Halimi bears the title "Sisyphe est fatigué". One wonders if Arcand would be an exhausted Sisyphus? After having pushed his cinematic boulder up the ramps of Mount Conscience, after having established the relative "uselessness" of such an enterprise, Arcand, assuming his doubts, refusals, irrationality and feelings, refocuses his work on the ethic of the individual without completely ignoring social causalities and the systems which exploit the individual, as seen in *Jesus of Montreal* (advertising and religion). The most notable filmmaker who followed a similar road was Jean Renoir, who exchanged political conscience for the moral of pleasure. Like Arcand, Renoir wanted to change the world while maintaining his distance from those who were the agents of this change (political men, parties, militant or union organisations, etc.).

Although there are many manifestations that make reference to a disillusioned generation, Arcand paints a portrait of these people without ideals, without adopting this point of view himself, because he was never one of those who devoted themselves wholeheartedly to a cause. Even in the face of those with whom he could have had some affinity, he would keep a distance (he was reproached, for instance, on the subject of nationalism in *Quebec: Duplessis and After...*).

For not having raised too much hope for change, Arcand does not have to mourn his convictions and actions. He is not one of the poets of deception, thrown off balance by the economic and moral crisis of the West. If some went from an era of "morality and responsibility" to one of irresponsibility or, more precisely, to one focused on the individual who gets out of an awkward situation, who is looking out for his or her immediate interests, who mistrusts commitments and social causes, who becomes cynical when faced by politics, this is not Arcand and he comments on the attitudes of this group in *The Decline* and *Jesus of Montreal*. From the era of certainty to the "era of emptiness" (to paraphrase Gilles Lipovetsky's *L'ère du vide*), the transition for him is not brutal and quick. Somewhat of an agnostic, Arcand is an excellent witness of the uncertainty that our era creates, and he resorts to paradox to keep us informed. That his appreciations are in harmony with the quality of his cinematic expression demonstrates that, at all the stages in his active life, he has been one of the most important Quebec filmmakers.

*Notes*

[1] Denys Arcand, "Speaking of Canadian Film", in André Pâquet (ed), *How to make or not to make a Canadian Film* (Montreal: Cinémathèque canadienne, 1967): 17.

[2] At this time in Montreal there were two English universities, McGill and Sir George Williams, and one French university, Université de Montréal. Denis Héroux was to become a well-known director and producer.

[3] These were cameraman Michel Brault, Marcel Carrière on sound, and Gilles Groulx for editing – three experienced filmmakers whose work is closely associated with the *cinéma direct* tradition.

[4] This undertaking pleased everyone so much that the AGEUM did an encore with *Jusqu'au cou* [*Up to the Neck*, 1964] with Denis Héroux (director), Denys Arcand (co-writer), Michel Brault and Jean-Claude Labrecque (camera), Marcel Carrière and Werner Nold (sound), and Stéphane Venne (music).

[5] One of whom was Professor Michel Brunet. It is one of his books, *Notre passé, le présent et nous*, that Mario gives to Diane in *The Decline of the American Empire* (1986).

[6] "En quoi les actions des hommes ont un rapport étroit avec la société dans

laquelle ils vivent et quelles en sont les implications pour les sociétés futures". Denys Arcand, "Denys Arcand: la conscience politique des Québécois".

Interview conducted by Nicole Charest, "Cinq cinéastes québécois, cinq façons de voir la vie et le cinéma", *Perspectives* 22 (December 1973): 8.

[7] "Pays artificiel bâti contre les lois de l'histoire".

[8] In an article entitled "Des évidences", appearing in the Marxist review *Parti Pris* 7 (April 1964), Arcand speaks of colonized Quebecers and concludes: "Le destin du cinéma québécois est collé au destin du Canada français .... Une production artistique nationale n'est méritée que par un peuple debout .... Maintenant que des Québécois se sont levés et mis en marche à grands risques, il est vrai que chez les cinéastes on soupçonne des velléités de révoltes pelliculaires". ("The fate of Quebec cinema is inseparable from the fate of French Canada .... A national artistic production is only earned by people who are on their feet .... Now that Quebecers have risen and moved forwards at great risk, it is true that filmmakers are suspected of mounting a filmic revolution".)

[9] He was reproached for this in his "militant" films and it has been used to explain his heightened emphasis on the individual in his more recent work.

[10] Although a permanent staff member at the NFB, he resigned in 1966.

[11] The departure of the director of French production, Pierre Juneau, in 1966, and the arrival of a new commissioner, Hugo McPherson, in 1967.

[12] "En train de faire ... un film non pas sur la révolte, mais sur la résignation". Denys Arcand, quoted in Réal La Rochelle et al, *Denys Arcand* (Montreal: Conseil québécois pour la diffusion du cinéma, 1971): 19.

[13] Translated from the French: "J'ai toujours eu quelques difficultés avec les militants. Les militants sont toujours des gens extrêmement sérieux; il ne faut pas plaisanter avec leur cause. Malheureusement pour moi, j'aime bien rire .... Le rire a quelque chose de diabolique, c'est un refus fondamental de la condition humaine. Il remet profondément en cause tous ceux qui ont une belle opinion d'eux-mêmes. Et Dieu sait qu'ils sont nombreux!" "Entretien. Conversation autour d'un plaisir solitaire" by Pierre Jutras, Réal La Rochelle and Pierre Véronneau, *Copie Zéro* 34-35 (December 1987-March 1988): 9.

[14] The main documentaries of the group are *Saint-Jérôme* (1968) by Fernand Dansereau, *L'école des autres* [*The School of Others*, 1968] by Michel Régnier and *La p'tite Bourgogne* [*Little Burgundy*, 1968] by Maurice Bulbulian. On "Challenge for Change", one may consult Louise Carrière's master's thesis in sociology, *La série de films Société nouvelle dans un Québec en changement, 1969-1979* (Université du Québec à Montréal, 1983), 305 pp.

[15] The film was to be part of a series dedicated to four "great" personages of Quebec history: Brother André (a saintly figure in Quebec), Maurice Richard (hockey player), Willie Lamothe (country and western singer) and Maurice Duplessis (Quebec Premier 1936-39; 1944-59).

[16] Founded in 1935 by Maurice Duplessis, this party came to power before the war, was defeated in 1939, regained power in 1944 and maintained it until 1960. Duplessis was master of his party and of Quebec electoral habits. A traditionalist, he played the conservative nationalist card and promoted autonomy for the Province; opposed to the labour movement and supported by the Roman Catholic Church, Duplessis kept Quebec in an archaic state that was described as "the Great Darkness". After his death in 1959, the party had difficulty holding together and was defeated in 1960 by the Quebec Liberal Party, under the leadership of Jean Lesage. Thus began the era of modernization and recovery called "the Quiet Revolution".

[17] The Liberals under Robert Bourassa won the 1970 election and were re-elected in 1974. Defeated in 1976 by René Lévesque and the Parti québécois, Bourassa left politics for almost a decade. Voted back into office in 1985, he remained Premier of Quebec until he announced his resignation in 1993.

[18] Translated from the French: "Le film propose l'idée que dans la modification profonde des structures économiques et culturelles, l'apparition et la disparition de divers partis politiques de même que la montée ou la chute de 'personnalités' charismatiques ne sont que des phénomènes superficiels qui ne peuvent modifier qu'accessoirement l'évolution historique d'un peuple." (quotation from a text distributed at the film's release in June 1972). Even if Arcand thus suggests that classes and class struggles are the motor that drives history, we can believe that, in practice, the film overturns the Marxist perspective because it shows that politics can only function like theatre, as a staging of individuals.

[19] Lord Durham was named Governor General of Canada after the 1837 uprising against the British, which was savagely suppressed by the British Army. Among the measures he advocated to solve definitively the colony's problems, we find the assimilation of French Canadians, which hastened the union of Upper and Lower Canada. His famous *Report on the Affairs of British North America*, dated 4 February 1839, speaks of relations between the French and English nations, and of the manner in which to treat the "conquered race".

[20] A small cell of the Front de Libération du Québec (FLQ) terrorist movement kidnapped a British diplomat in October 1970. Several days later a Quebec minister was also detained. The Canadian Government, under Trudeau, claiming fear of an insurrection, invoked the War Measures Act and sent the army to Quebec. The minister was killed; the terrorists arrested and others exiled. The October Crisis left its mark on Quebec political life and inspired several films. See Pierre Véronneau, "Les événements d'Octobre au cinéma", *Québec Studies* 11 (autumn 1990/winter 1991): 29-36.

[21] This includes the Mayor of Montreal, Jean Drapeau, whose re-election a few weeks after the Crisis to the detriment of the radical nationalist Front d'Action Politique, benefited from the general political shift to the right.

[22] Witness his link with the Marxist review *Parti Pris*.

[23] Translated from the French: "Les films documentaires précédents m'avaient conduit dans une telle impasse idéologique et politique que j'en étais réduit à des balbutiements incohérents. C'est un film sur des sous-hommes, des restants d'humanité, du monde qui s'expriment quasiment plus, qui vivent de hold-ups, de guns, de vols. Tout le monde se tue à la fin." Quoted in *Denys Arcand*: 28.

[24] Parallels have been drawn between the world depicted by Arcand and that of writer Michel Tremblay. I do not perceive the same bitterness in Tremblay who, born into a working class family, confesses a great sympathy for all his characters.

[25] Translated from the French: "Mené tambour battant par des comédiens qui jouent comme s'ils ne jouaient pas, cette *Maudite Galette* prouve à sa façon que les réalisateurs canadiens savent ouvrir l'œil. Et le bon .... Le film démarre dans la comédie de mœurs, réaliste, sordide même. Puis, insensiblement, le ton monte. Le crasseux vire au macabre. La querelle familiale tourne à la boucherie, et cela, sans que l'humour perde un instant ses billes." Henry Rabine, *La croix* 16 October 1972.

[26] "Arcand est un moraliste de la classe supérieure, celle des Juvénal et des Voltaire". *La croix* 16 December 1973.

[27] In *Gina* Arcand changes the name of the National Film Board to the National *Cinema* Board.

[28] Another paradox is presented by the fact that his next work was a short film made for the labour movement: *La Lutte des travailleurs d'hôpitaux* (*The Struggle of Hospital Workers*, 1976).

[29] Arcand had already scripted a series, *Minute, papillon* in 1967-68; he does not consider it a personal project. This is not the case with the television series *Duplessis* (1978), which recalls the career of Maurice Duplessis and examines through fiction the political situation of the time. It often returns the question, asked in *Quebec: Duplessis and After...*, to the personality debate, which is perhaps the unavoidable lot of televised fiction. Later he directed a few episodes of *Empire Inc.*, a television series focusing on big business in anglophone Quebec.

[30] Translated from the French: "Quand la mer se retire, elle découvre une grève jonchée d'objectifs non-atteints, d'illusions tranquilles ou pas ... C'est un cinéma de transition pour un pays de nouveau et plus que jamais incertain". Michel Euvrard, "Quand la mer se retire", in Louise Carrière (ed), "Aujourd'hui le cinéma québécois", *CinémAction* (Paris) 40 (November 1986): 27-34.

[31] "Les années 80: le sextant défaille", in "Focus on Quebec Cinema in the 1980s", *Québec Studies* 9 (autumn 1989/winter 1990): 1-8.

[32] In *On est au coton* he uses a similar device by punctuating the film with intertitles taken from the work of Marcuse to "explain" *a posteriori* the evolution of North American society and the way in which the capitalist system takes over its citizens.

[33] Translated from the French: "Une vengeance d'intellectuel en mal d'insulter le petit peuple qui a dit NON ... Le cinéaste a surtout choisi de montrer la lâcheté d'un peuple ... On dit au peuple qu'il est stupide et lâche, et on se croit courageux." "La vengeance et le mépris", *Le Devoir* 30 January 1982.

[34] "Québécois sont tellement pourris par les miettes des richesses des États-Unis qu'on ne peut plus rien en espérer".

[35] Nick Auf der Maur, "Referendum film pretentious bore", *The Gazette* 10 February 1982.

[36] Translated from the French: "Cet immense patchwork national est semblable à notre réalité politique: interminable et confuse. C'est pour briser cette circularité narcissique que Machiavel est introduit. Mais les dés sont pipés .... Arcand et ses collaborateurs ont raté une belle occasion d'explorer plus à fond le problème en confrontant la personnalité ambivalente et gémellaire des Québécois. Un retour judicieux sur l'histoire québécoise aurait contribué à jeter une lumière accrue sur ce double héritage culturel qui fait constamment déraper la cinématographie et la politique d'ici vers le mélodrame. En se retranchant derrière l'objectivité de l'observateur – qui refuse de s'impliquer – les cinéastes ne pouvaient que restituer aux Québécois l'image inversée de leur propre auto-séduction. C'est le miroir de Narcisse." "Le miroir de Narcisse", *Virus* February 1982.

[37] The expression is borrowed from Peter Wintonick and Mark Achbar's film, *Manufacturing Consent: Noam Chomsky and the Media* (1992).

[38] Although when asked, "Depuis *Le Déclin*, on a l'impression qu'enfin tu laisses parler ton lyrisme", he replied, "C'est vrai ... L'époque est comme ça. L'âge que j'ai y fait aussi quelque chose." ("Since *Le Déclin*, we have the impression you are giving voice to your poetic expression." / "It's true. A sign of the times. My age also has something to do with it.") *Copie Zéro* 34-35: 10.

[39] "Aucune théorie, aucun idéalisme, aucune analyse ne m'a jamais totalement convaincu". *Copie Zéro* 34-35: 9.

[40] Translated from the French: "L'intellectuel est un être paradoxal, que l'on ne peut pas penser comme tel aussi longtemps qu'on l'appréhende au travers de l'alternative classique de l'autonomie et de l'engagement, de la culture pure et de la politique. Cela, parce qu'il s'est constitué, historiquement, dans et par le dépassement de cette opposition .... Il n'existe et ne subsiste que pour autant que, d'une part, existe et subsiste un monde intellectuel autonome (c'est-à-dire indépendant des pouvoirs religieux, politiques, économiques, etc.) dont il respecte les lois spécifiques, et que, d'autre part, l'autorité spécifique qui s'élabore dans cet univers à la faveur de l'autonomie est engagée dans des luttes politiques." Pierre Bourdieu, "Pour une internationale des intellectuels", *Politis, la revue* 1 (winter 1992): 9.

[41] This does not prevent him from also liking to speak the truth, especially when institutions disguise historical facts (witness Champlain's pedophilia or Duplessis's alcoholism).

# Sound design and music as *tragédie en musique*[1]: the documentary practice of Denys Arcand

Réal La Rochelle
TRANSLATED FROM THE FRENCH BY FRED A REED

> Do we wish to cross the sea?
> Where leads this great passion
> which in us surpasses all others?
> Why do we fly toward
> that point at which
> all suns set and flicker out?[2]
> Nietzsche, quoted in *La Route de l'Ouest*

When Denys Arcand's feature-length film *On est au coton* [*We're Fed Up*, 1970] embarked on its five-year clandestine career before its official release in 1976 (thanks to newly-available lightweight video technology), Quebec's militant political counterculture was quick to hail it as a working-class documentary/manifesto akin to Vertov's *Kino-Eye*, or perhaps as a piece of Quebec "May '68" agit-prop. It was neither of these; nevertheless, Sydney Newman, Commissioner of Canada's National Film Board, denounced it. NFB policy was to "defend capitalism" and Newman, like the Left, had taken Arcand's film for a red flag, a Maoist tract.[3]

This was only one of the interlocking paradoxes surrounding a film which found itself assigned to censorial purgatory in the vaults of the NFB (only to be released six years later), while at the same time enjoying wide underground circulation. If *On est au coton* had been taken for what it really is, a *tragédie en musique* whose subject is textile workers and the ineluctable shut-down of their dust-clogged 19th century mills, there would have been no censorship – and no widespread covert distribution. The film would have delighted a handful of the avant-garde cinema's happy few, or the rare disciples of an audiovisual treatment inspired by contemporary *musique concrète*. It would have been eruditely dissected as a kind of synthesis of Walter Ruttmann's radio Hörspiel *Wochende* (*Weekend*, 1930) and the 1927 film classic *Berlin: Die Sinfonie einer Großstadt* (*Berlin: Symphony of a Great City*), perhaps even as a contemporary filmed opera of the kind of which NFB composer Maurice Blackburn dreamed when he created his Atelier de Conception Sonore (Sound Workshop) which was active during the 1970s.

An industrial symphony

Archaic textile mills in stark blacks and whites/machine noise broken sharply by silence. Again and again, the same pattern. Faint ambient voices hissing like the winter wind; women whispering in front of a punch clock. 19th century photographs of exiled Quebec textile workers – children included – in the United States/long silence. A hoarse, wracking spasm of coughing/a dust-coated crucifix nailed to a mill wall. Shots of soundless knitting looms/abrupt sound cut to noise cross-fading to echo/again, silence...

Such is the audiovisual counterpoint which Denys Arcand employs time and time again in the first part of the film, almost as if to draw attention to its experimental style and structure. Particularly compelling is his treatment of voices: weak, timid, resigned, the oppressed voices of working men and women – including those of the two protagonists, Carmen and Bertrand – recorded in muffled spaces like Catholic confessionals; the staged appearance by professional trade unionist Madeleine Parent reading a court decision (under the conservative Duplessis régime) against the "seditious conspiracy" of the labour movement; Arcand himself in voice-over describing the censored sequences; the convulsive hacking cough of a worker now seen in forced retirement, displaying his cruel affliction for the camera in shame, almost pleading for forgiveness. Finally, a recurring leitmotif is woven into the two and a half-hour film: the machine-gun bursts of an IBM electric typewriter replacing voice-over commentary, as it hammers out quotations from Herbert Marcuse in capital letters, including a last, terrifying aphorism: "THE MACHINE IS THE MOST EFFICIENT POLITICAL INSTRUMENT".[4]

The only "music" in *On est au coton* occurs in the epilogue: during a sequence depicting a reception given by Quebec's Lieutenant Governor, a brass band plays. The pompous ensemble turns the assembled politicians, police officers and press agents invited for a few hours of meaningless small talk into objects of derision, transforming the entire sequence into a "human comedy" straight out of Balzac.

The same band is heard a few seconds later against the scene of a crowd walking down the street, with inserts of a beggar and close-ups of Carmen, also walking. Then suddenly: abrupt cut to silence over the macabre hulk of an empty mill. Fade in to the weak voice of a mill worker, in echo, "we gave them everything we had... me, I loved my job...". Back to the deafening roar of machinery. Link cut to the IBM machine-gun: "the machine is the most...".

First dialogue[5]

*Question:* Denys Arcand, when one views *On est au coton* as a rhythmic restructuring of images and sound, it is much more compelling as a lyrical poem than as a documentary or objective report.
*Arcand:* The film is, first and foremost, the subjective vision of my own discovery of the world of labour. I've never made anything but extremely personal films, and I've never made any claims for authenticity beyond my own, including the way I look at history.

*Question:* In your film the mill closing is like an act of fate — inevitable. But no one wants to believe it, neither the union leaders such as Madeleine Parent, nor the workers, nor the Quebec Government and its experts.
*Arcand:* This blindness is a tragedy, most of all for the workers who are victims of fate, who play it out in their day-to-day routine, in their blood, in their lives...

*Question:* One might argue that the visuals and some of the live sound point to a journalistic investigation into mill closings, but the soundtrack, with its rigorously structured alternations of noise and silence, with its confidential, intimate treatment of voices, belies this impression.
*Arcand:* One of the textile workers' fundamental problems is the infernal, indescribable roar of the mills. Noise is a recurring theme in the film. I wish I had had modern THX technology to convey just how unbearable it really is. The decibel levels are so high that the noise cannot be absorbed by the ear; it invades the body through every pore. We were working under the severe limitations of 16mm optical sound, which I found quite unsatisfactory. So I decided to use clear-cut alternations and brutal cuts, to set up unexpected counterpoint between noise and silence, between noise and voices speaking in a confidential tone, and so on. I ended up handling the sound and musical sequences as if they were *musique concrète*.

*Question:* So it would not be an exaggeration to call *On est au coton* a truly musical film, a contemporary musical film. As Michel Fano calls it, a kind of *audiovisual opera*?[6]
*Arcand:* Not in the slightest.

*Tragédie en musique*

Although there is little doubt that the dramaturgical matrix of Arcand's films can be traced back to Greco-Latin tragic tradition, as reformulated in the French tragedy of Racine and Corneille, it also draws on composite models such as the plays of Shakespeare and Molière (*Tartuffe* and *Don Juan*), where tragedy successfully integrates comedy, and even farce. The tragic form, which in conceptual terms reaches back to Sophocles or even further, to *The Book of Job*, establishes as its first premise that death is both imminent and inevitable: the concept of "fatum". According to Borneque and Cauët's *Dictionnaire latin-français du baccalauréat*, which was an integral part of the Quebec classical college curriculum in the 1950s, when Arcand was a student, "fatum" could be translated as oracle, destiny, cruel fate, misfortune, death and cadaver.

In tragedy we know from the beginning that the end point is death. The only "vital" question which remains is: how will the end point be reached? In the classical French culture of the 17th century, tragedy was acted in rhythmic, declamatory parlando. These were the foundations upon which Lully, Charpentier and, later, Rameau were to construct and consolidate French opera as *tragédie en musique*. Arcand's films are broken down into rhythmic cells in which the soundtrack is treated as music. The effect is a curious intermingling which elicits both fascination and disquiet. The form of modern *tragédie en musique* is itself rare: modern opera (whether in audiovisual or purely audio form) does not derive from as ancient or archaic a model as tragedy, but rather from romantic drama.

In fact, all Arcand's principal films, from his first experimental feature-length documentaries, *On est au coton* and *Québec: Duplessis et après...* (*Quebec: Duplessis and After...*, 1972) – including his caustic *Le Confort et l'indifférence* (*Comfort and Indifference*, 1981) – to his main "fictions", above all *Réjeanne Padovani* (1973), *Gina* (1975), *Le Déclin de l'empire américain* (*The Decline of the American Empire*, 1986), *Jésus de Montréal* (*Jesus of Montreal*, 1989) and *Love and Human Remains* (1993), can be defined as *tragédies en musique*.

Close examination of the feature-length "documentary" films is essential, for in them Arcand's dramaturgical matrix is never as apparent as in his "fictions", even though the filmmaker stresses in the third dialogue below that there is no distinction between these so-called genres. By illustrating how these feature-length "documentaries" work as *tragédie en musique* we may better understand the originality of the filmmaker at work in a form which, at first glance, would seem utterly conventional. The same process leads us directly to the source of Arcand's method, style and writing: his first historical short films – *Champlain* (1964), *Les Montréalistes* (*Ville-Marie*, 1965) and *La Route de l'Ouest* (*The Westward Road*, 1965) – as fresh today as the day they were shot and audacious in their postmodernity, form a trilogy of great lyrical beauty.

Second dialogue

> *Question:* The credits do not indicate who was actually responsible for the sound editing and design of your first films.
> *Arcand:* We did not even use terms such as these in the 1960s and 1970s. In fact, right up until *The Decline*, I always took a direct hand in both the picture and sound editing process for all my films, working alongside NFB editors such as Werner Nold, Pierre Bernier and Monique Fortier. I edited *Réjeanne* with Marguerite Duparc; *Gina* I did single-handed! In every case, I took an active part in both sound and picture editing.

> *Question:* Where did you get the idea of designing sound and music in this way, like a collage, without reference to the kind of live sound which seems to depend on direct audiovisual linkage?
> *Arcand:* My first films, all my films in fact, had nothing to do with live sound; they were something totally different. My short films in particular. Back then I was fascinated by the NFB Sound Effects Library. I would spend hours listening to one sound loop after another; they were all painstakingly catalogued. The section I liked best was the "winds"; I used a lot of those winds. If you were to ask me from whom I learned this method of free sound collage, this blending of voices off and image, I guess I would have to call myself a disciple of Gilles Groulx; he and I met many times to discuss film and music.[7] I do not recall having talked with him specifically about sound design, but something must have rubbed off on me.
> 
>   I had become quite familiar with composers of *musique concrète*, such as Pierre Schaeffer and Pierre Henry, and listened to a lot of modern music which always struck me as film music, music which, ever since Schoenberg, seems ontologically inseparable from cinema.
>   Then, too, I made a point of using specific voices. For instance, there was Gisèle Trépanier, the actress I worked with at the Université de Montréal theatre workshop. Her voice was gentle and assertive at the same time, yet it had an almost timeless quality which could convey intimacy, and yet break with the notorious "objectifying" off-camera voices of the

conventional documentary. As I had already done in my first short, very personal films, we recorded Gisèle's voice with the microphone right up against her mouth, which conveyed the intimacy of the spoken part and the subjectivity of the viewpoint.

*Question:* The voice recording seems suspended in a cage of silence, a kind of sound cloister, a troubling vacuum...
*Arcand:* We worked long and hard on the reverberation, the echo of these intimate voices. Since we had none of the electronic instruments available today, we had to use the NFB elevator shaft!

"The machine is the most efficient political instrument"

Marcuse's aphorism is a fitting epigram for each of Arcand's experimental documentaries. Machines-as-objects, machines-as-noise whose timbres and rhythms are resonant with ideological and political overtones. The machinery of the muskets of French colonization in *Champlain* overlaps into the noise of the contemporary urban environment recorded in and around the seedy businesses which have borrowed the name of the Governor of New France; and the machinery of demolition cranes and urban commerce in *Ville-Marie*. Finally, electoral "machines": the 1970 provincial election in *Quebec: Duplessis and After...*, and the 1980 Referendum in *Comfort and Indifference*; in both are heard cheering and shouting, patriotic songs and partisan chanting, military bands, and voices bellowing "O Canada", the Canadian national anthem.

Arcand employs these Varèsian mechanics, to the full extent of their sound-effect aggressiveness, in counterpoint with oppressive silences, with the whispered voices of history, with baroque or classical music. In *Champlain* the tragedy of the first French colony and the Indian wars is underscored by Purcell's theme from *The Music for the Funeral of Queen Mary*. This was several years before Kubrick was to employ the same melody, performed on a Moog synthesizer, in *A Clockwork Orange* (1971).

*Champlain* already contains the basic components of an original audiovisual collage style, a style which brings old and new into collision: the colonialist lyricism of 17th century texts with the Mohawks of today, and Champlain's icy reverie at the founding of Quebec with the ethnocentric consumerism of the present. These meet in an incessant whipsaw movement spanning three centuries, in which the tragedy of the brilliant cartographer, the doomed construction of a New France and the rape of the American Indians by a politico-mystic bulldozer all combine to reveal Arcand's cultural and political vision of Quebec, in the pragmatic, phlegmatic manner of a Roman epicurean.

This vision is expanded upon in *Ville-Marie*, the pinnacle of Arcand's short films and one of the greatest ever made in Quebec. The film came under sharp attack when it was released at the Montreal International Film Festival in 1965, from both pro-Church intellectuals and certain self-righteous thinkers, including the film magazine *Séquences*, which assailed it in an article by Father Henri-Paul Sénéchal. "Denys Arcand", wrote Father Sénéchal, "a director who takes himself for an historian" presents "the mystical epic of the founding of Montreal...in a grotesque, mocking manner which focuses only on the sordid". The film is "a far-fetched interpretation of French-Canadian history", part and parcel of "the tendency which seeks masochistically to besmirch our past".[8]

Nevertheless, Arcand has the courage and lucidity to show that the heartfelt though mystical desire of Montreal's French founders to establish, against all logic, a city dedicated to the Mother of God, had ended in tragedy for those who conceived it, for the colonists themselves and for the indigenous people. It had in fact been transformed into its opposite. The startling metropolis which is Montreal, after consolidating its military defences, was to draw its nourishment from commerce and industry. Slowly it interred its ambition to become a "city of God", culminating in the modern-day demolition of its churches.

It should come as no surprise to find the filmmaker intermixing the "Hallelujah" chorus or "Chantons à Dieu" with musket shots, the noises of demolition and explosion, and contrasting these sounds with their antithesis, the sepulchral silence of the graves of the sisters of the Congregation of Notre-Dame over which float the voices of nuns (reading authentic texts), exhorting themselves to "mortify the flesh by chains of iron and by other lacerations". Religious madness, concludes Arcand, is another tragedy of New France, already so ill-begun by Champlain at the settlement which was to become Quebec.

*The Westward Road* is an in-depth examination of the relativity of history, of the certainties it reveals and of the more numerous doubts it bears. Lost in the mists of the past, the great migrations towards the American West become for Arcand a vein rich in ethnic tragedy, where flashes of illumination and restless scrutiny simultaneously interpenetrate and coexist.

The great adventures of history – the Oriental migrations which brought the American Indian peoples to the Western hemisphere; the voyages of the white friars of Ireland to Iceland; that of the Vikings towards Greenland; and finally the southern European expansion towards Latin America, New France and New England – are also, suggests Arcand, through the use of blackouts, silences, phantom drum rolls and the whistling of the sea wind, those by which "dreamers choose their fantasies, the footpaths of their legends", just as the mythical figure of Wotan or the monumental boat-shaped tomb remnants spring from the archaeological depths of Viking culture.

"Verily, we can no longer remember these men", speaks the historian in voice-over in the film. Ironically counterposing Cartesian doubt against the biblical, historicist authority of the word "verily", the assertion adroitly sets research against intuition, the certainty of the artifact against the inherent mystery of the information it contains. In the same way, Arcand intertwines the historian's lecture with old organ music, ancient Scandinavian and Gaelic chanting from the Folkways Records archives, or choral works of the Renaissance, one of which laments, over and over again, "Naught but death do I desire..."

Consistently, the filmmaker connects his solitude in the face of history with contemporary events: rocket launchings; military and police helicopters; tourists visiting the New York World's Fair in 1964; or a model of the "Santa Maria" of 1492. Today, like yesterday, the great quests of the adventurous are undertaken for commerce, for money, with "Bible and sword". It should come as no surprise that we also (even then!) encounter Machiavelli – whose presence almost twenty years later, in *Comfort and Indifference*, had come to dominate Arcand's *tragédies en musique*. The trail westward was blazed, we hear him saying, by "audacious, innocent and cruel men who believed, like Machiavelli, that men neither could nor must be faithful to the Prince who can neither defend nor repress them".[9]

In the space of two short years at the National Film Board Denys Arcand, in his first trilogy, established the tightly knit structure which he was later to develop in the feature-length format: musical tragedy as formal matrix; the coexistence of past and present; the glacial movement of historical fact providing root nourishment for the epiphenomena of superficial actuality; and the relativity of human history set against the history of the universe, attested by the quotation from Nietzsche, spoken against the dark silence of the soundtrack which ends *The Westward Road*.

Two political machines

The trilogy of short documentaries scrutinized the French colonial past in North America the better to illuminate current trends in Quebec national culture. Moving in an opposite direction, but drawing on the same sources, Arcand focuses his critical attention on two principal political events of the decade 1970-80 in the light of history and of its extremely deliberate movement.

The provincial election of 1970, which saw the sovereignist Parti québécois (PQ) spring from the ruins of the Catholic nationalism of Maurice Duplessis's Union nationale and the shadow of the federalist Liberals, provided the stimulus for *Quebec: Duplessis and After*.... Ten years later came *Comfort and Indifference*, dealing with the 1980 Referendum (called by the PQ which had by then assumed power) on sovereignty-association between Quebec and Canada. Here the filmmaker puts the finishing touches to the most startlingly insightful political fresco ever produced by the Quebec cinema.

The two films, in which penetrating *readings* on the tragedy of the conquest of New France by the British military illuminate the burning immediacy of current events, present at the same time a clinical depiction of the two Liberal pan-Canadian ideological machines, one based in Ottawa (the federal Liberal Party), the other in Quebec (the provincial Liberal Party). The two combine to carry out the sacrificial slaughter of the Agnus Dei of Quebec sovereignism on the altar of the ironclad law of the modern-day "Prince", as Machiavelli so adroitly puts it in *Comfort and Indifference*, in which a real, flesh and blood Machiavelli, portrayed by actor Jean Pierre Ronfard, is ensconced in an office high at the top of Place Ville Marie, the Montreal skyscraper designed by architect I M Pei.

Once again, through a clever collage of sound and visuals, Arcand moves from the speeches of each electoral campaign to the historical texts; small steps in the day-to-day chronicle of events are set against the long cycles of ethnography; from the shouts of politicians to the whispering of ancient voices in the silence; from the banal, pathetic gestures of the moment to the secular tragedy of a "people without history and without literature...poorly educated and immobile" but "which must not be taken lightly".[10] This manner of writing makes it possible for Arcand to transcend what at first glance seems to be mere reporting, and to fashion from it *tragédies en musique* for our time.

Machiavelli: "It is easier to conserve old values than to invent new ones".[11]

If ever there existed films which, during the rise of the Parti québécois in the 1970s and 1980s, irritated the nationalists and their sympathizers, these were two of them. Some critics made strenuous and vocal objections, others never forgave Arcand – notwithstanding his empathy for the cause of a sovereign Quebec – for having drawn a parallel between René Lévesque and former Premier Maurice Duplessis in the first film; or even worse, for having demonstrated, in the second, the inability of the 'OUI' forces, in their naïvety and weakness in the face of the Prince (Trudeau, the British crown, the Canadian army...), to win the

1980 Referendum campaign; or, to cast the allegory in a minor key, for having shown the innocence of St John the Baptist's lamb in the face of the British-Canadian lion.[12]

For Arcand the two political campaigns only confirmed Quebec's status as a conquered people, and illustrated the century-long stability of the political machines whose function, from Duplessis to the Parti québécois, from the Social Credit Party to Robert Bourassa's Liberals, was only to perpetuate the tragic conservatism of "the people without a history", incapable of and uninterested in transforming either their condition or their fate.

Arcand's vision is eloquently encapsulated in this homage to the teaching of his mentor Maurice Séguin:

> The subject matter was humbling: a people of French peasants contriving to survive inconspicuously under the benevolent domination of a British governor and commercial élite. War, revolution or famine would never break the crushing monotony. The same monotony as today. [...] The essence of his [Séguin's] thought was that the French-Canadian nation was too small, too weak ever to aspire to independence, and at the same time too protected, too deeply-rooted to be easily assimilated. It was a people condemned to a fate of perpetual mediocrity, until the demographic weight and the pressure of the American empire would finally relegate it to historical oblivion.[13]

The first scene of *Quebec: Duplessis and After...* opens on empty silence: the hulk of a car lying in the snow, abandoned and lifeless. Similar scenes are soon repeated, intercut with extracts from the Durham Report read and performed by the filmmaker Robin Spry (in a bass voice) in broken French, a whisper in the enveloping silence. Into the boundless melancholy of the Quebec winter landscape and of the graveyards of American consumerism the nasal voice of Duplessis slowly intrudes, in voice-over.

The 1970 election campaign gets underway: pompous speeches in a cascading falsetto of insults are interrupted only by sound reminders of Durham and Duplessis, to which Arcand adds another theme – passages from the *Le petit catéchisme des électeurs (The Voter's Handbook)* read and performed by Gisèle Trépanier. This curious document – the electoral platform of the Union nationale and quite progressive for the 1930s – was the baited hook which Duplessis used to win the 1936 provincial election, only to discard it immediately thereafter. We often hear Arcand's voice asking the question, with the actress providing the onscreen reply:

Voice off: What is meant by marasmus?
Trépanier: By marasmus we mean the phase of languish, of deterioration which precedes death.

In another scene Gisèle Trépanier plays a school teacher quizzing her charges who answer in unison, as if droning the Roman Catholic catechism.

Other innovative uses of sound underscore the high points of the campaign. After the triumph of the pro-worker PQ candidate Robert Burns, a Christmas carol rings out during a playful parade against the backdrop of a restaurant called "Roi de la patate". A Duplessis speech is capped with a Latin motet; the defeat of the Parti québécois candidate Bernard Landry is accompanied by an "Agnus Dei", and the victory of the Liberal Robert Bourassa by a "Dona nobis pacem". Finally, on Durham's last words, "...must not be taken lightly", a resounding "Gloria" rings out.

But Arcand's brilliant *deus ex machina* is his portrait of the charismatic René Lévesque, father of sovereignty-association. The filmmaker introduces him near the end, having showed only the secondary figures until then. Lévesque's arrival comes at the end of a long wait, almost a suspense. The sequence starts with a speech by Duplessis, in full sound and picture. Then, while the speech continues on the soundtrack, Arcand introduces shots of a huge rally, showing Lévesque from behind, in medium shot, gesticulating as he speaks. But the nationalist harangue is still that of Duplessis. The stylistic and historical contradiction creates a shock, a startling distancing not only from the new nationalist catechism and the ostensibly progressive flamboyance of its discourse, but also from the stubborn crease-resistance of its ethnocentric pleats.

This image of René Lévesque carries over into *Comfort and Indifference*. Here he is depicted on the down slope of Referendum defeat and political decline, a sad, faintly ridiculous political icon embodied in the parallel montage of the haughty Elizabeth II passing the Canadian army in review, and Lévesque, the "little prince", invited by French Prime Minister Barre to attend a similar ceremony, hardly able to suppress an ironic chuckle as he reviews the Garde Républicaine. At the end, after the Referendum has been lost, the last image is that of the great Quebec political leader weeping publicly: "Until next time..."

Arcand saves his great moments of irony for the last segment of the film as he presents fast-flowing sequences of the campaign's liveliest moments. Firstly, there is the shouting match over the cost of Quebec independence and/or the preservation of Canadian federalism, which resembles a cascade of figures straight out of a counter-culture comic book. Then, in a grand choral finale, the national anthem "O Canada" is pieced together like a madman's patchwork quilt with measures of music or phrases recorded at different times in different places and sung in all possible keys, stitched together into an ensemble that resembles an ironic, Stockhausen-like "Hymnen" on unity *ad mare usque ad marem*.[14] Emerging triumphant from the crazed mêlée are the 'NON' coalition and Trudeau, promising to renew the Canadian constitution..., and, of course, machiavellian logic: "a clever prince must nourish several enmities against himself in order that, having suppressed them, he may emerge all the grander".[15] The film ends on the sardonic grin of Machiavelli.

Third dialogue

> *Question:* In your feature-length "fictions" of the early 1970s there seems to have been a certain impoverishment, or better, an atrophy in the sound design of your films. Could this be partially due to the difficulty raised by Michel Fano, that a given audio treatment is harder to achieve in a narrative film as compared with, say, animation or experimental films, where the viewer demands clarity and logic in the development of the narrative structure?
> *Arcand:* I do not see any limitation in principle as far as film narrative is concerned. In any event, as I've already mentioned, in my films I draw no distinction between what we call "documentary" and what we call "fiction". I express myself as personally and subjectively in *Quebec* as in *Padovani*, as much in *Comfort* as in *The Decline* or *Love and Human Remains*.

> *Question:* What are the reasons for the audio limitations in your first "fictions"?
> *Arcand:* When you get right down to it, it was a matter of budget. Do not forget that my three feature-length documentaries had the advantage of substantial NFB budgets. We shot over a long period, sometimes more than a year, with sound engineers who recorded and accumulated incredible quantities of ambient or background sound. With my "fictions", it was just the opposite. We could only record within the strict limitations of the shots themselves; there was no time to record wild sound. And in post-production there was not enough money left over for new sound. I no longer had access, back then, to the NFB Sound Library with the exception of the rare clandestine visit. We ended up short of funds for recording the music track, the post-synch and the

mix. For *Padovani* I did the picture/sound editing with Marguerite Duparc; for *Gina* I did it all myself, with very limited means.

I had to wait until *The Decline* (co-produced by the NFB, with excellent voice post-synch), then *Jesus* and *Love and Human Remains* before I could work with top-notch sound crews. On the two last films, I worked with the sound technicians for weeks. Take *Human Remains*; there is a nightmare scene which is a bizarre mixture of music, noise and fantastic sounds like the trumpeting of elephants...

Working title: "The death of Lucie Patriarca"

In the autumn of 1971 Denys Arcand submitted the following to the Conseil québécois pour la diffusion du cinéma:

I have been studying the decadence and the fall of the Roman Empire, a historical period which reminds me of our own. Have you ever considered the fate of the people under Caligula? I see a striking resemblance with our current situation. If I had the opportunity, which is far from certain, I would like to make a film in the manner of Suetonius, on the unspeakable corruption, the folly and the depravity of those who dominate us. The film would be entitled *The Death of Lucie Patriarca*.[16]

The project was to become *Réjeanne Padovani* where, for the first time, Arcand draws a parallel between the historical fall of a great western empire and that of America, as seen from the gates of Montreal.

Despite the modest sound resources at hand, Arcand here carries off one of his greatest tragic inventions, with Gluck's aria "J'ai perdu mon Eurydice". It is first heard during the diegesis, at the dinner party thrown by the mafia chief Padovani for his political friends in a scene which drew praise at Cannes and in Paris, and repeated in the finale, non-diegetic this time, during the ceremonies marking the inauguration of the Ville Marie Expressway. Against a landscape of rain and snow the funereal melody accompanies the assassination of Réjeanne Padovani, who has been cast in a pillar of concrete, while in the background the "accidental" deaths of construction workers are implicit. Ultimately it underscores the decline of the American empire, where Mafia rule, with its tributary politicians and its small time Montreal and Quebec notables, has supplanted the rule of law.

Into this fiction, which rather transparently disguises the political economy of Quebec, stretch deadly fingers of fog like the frigid Atlantic gales which sweep without warning across Acadian Louisbourg, and swirl through *On est au coton* and *Quebec: Duplessis and After*.... Everything takes place within the rigid conventions of classical tragedy: unity of time (the story unfolds in less than 24 hours), unity of place (Montreal), unity of action (death in its inevitability is prefigured in Gluck's aria).

*Gina*, a film much misunderstood at the time, rejected by Arcand's intellectual friends and only rediscovered during the 1980s, marks the first postmodern incursion in the commercial feature-length format of self-referentiality in Quebec cinema. *Gina* signifies the *death* of Quebec cinema, the cinema which arose at the end of the 1950s and was characterized by the documentary style, by the use of black and white, by the creative dynamism of the NFB (Jutra, Groulx, Beauchemin, Brault, McLaren, Bernier, Fortier, Nold, to name only a few). At the same time a more internationally oriented cinema, governed by federal and provincial regulations designed to establish the embryo of a private industry, was beginning to appear in Quebec. This cinema relied less and less on the *cinéma direct* approach in the struggle for a Quebec national cinema.

Seen from this perspective *Gina* is an operatic depiction of the death of an era – and of a cinema. The rape of Gina, the exotic dancer, by a gang of small-time snowmobile hoodlums in a seedy hotel room is both material and allegoric, taking place against the ambient sound of a television set intoning "O Canada" to mark the end of the day's transmission. On a deeper level, death is that of a film on the textile industry halted in the process of shooting by the federalist National Cinema Board bureaucracy, a direct reference to the NFB's censorship of *On est au coton*.[17] Certain scenes of Arcand's earlier film are repeated verbatim, re-enacted by the actors of *Gina* on a small screen, in black and white.

If the filmmaker has embedded his personal micro-history in a commercial colour film, it is certainly as a reminder that he too left the NFB after *Quebec: Duplessis and After*..., that his "fictions" are now filmed in the private sector, that he has set his sights on the domestic and international commercial market, that he must henceforth express himself through the contradictions inherent in what has become a cultural industry. But the reference to the bygone days of the NFB also carries into the present the self-referential manner which Arcand employed in the past – something that tends to be forgotten.

In *On est au coton* we see a security guard quizzing the film crew about their work and checking their authorization to shoot inside the mill (the scene is repeated in *Gina*). In *Quebec* one of the lessons from *Le petit catéchisme* was shot in an NFB editing room. The device of the film within a film was already part of Arcand's method, even before it became part of the narrative structure in *Gina*.

If the film suffers slightly from the modesty of the means available for the soundtrack (the snowmobile massacre scene at the end is not sufficiently distanced from the commercialization of filmed violence it seeks to caricature), it nevertheless embodies its author's inimitable stylistic touch: snippets of wind sound; factory noise; the muffled, choking voices of workers; and several touching moments of counterpoint (a worker speaking in voice-off over the poster of the dancer; a black and white shot of Dolorès the worker cut into Gina's strip-tease number). The finale combines, in a skilful mix, mariachi music at Dorval airport, the sounds of a commercial film shoot, an airplane taking off and, finally, nuptial organ music and bells.

## Montreal: the "Human Remains" trilogy

*Love and Human Remains*, with a scenario by Brad Fraser based on his play *Unidentified Human Remains and the True Nature of Love* (1989), completes Denys Arcand's Montreal triptych: Université de Montréal intellectuals in *The Decline*; the theatre and the media in *Jesus*; and finally, gilded hedonist youth in *Love and Human Remains*.

In just over five years, in a creative renewal which must rank among the most dynamic in the history of Quebec cinema, Arcand has composed a trilogy of tragedies using as his raw material a handful of mutilated, disfigured "human remains", groups which we can no longer identify using the old value systems which once defined Quebec society. We are eerily close to the house of Atreus where, from one work to the next, death strikes at 24-hour intervals. The only difference is that with Arcand families of blood and power are replaced by micro-societies of professors, artists or simply by the insouciant youth of the discos and the amusement arcades. The family, Arcand reminds us, has always been the setting for the greatest tragedies. Could he have been thinking of this savoury snippet of dialogue from Truffaut's *La nuit américaine* (*Day for Night*, 1973)?

– Ah, the cinema, one big happy family...
– So was the house of Atreus!

The triumphant success of *The Decline* springs of course from Arcand's artistic maturity. But from the Handelian overture against the imposing Université de Montréal sports complex, through the short, pizzicato phrases interspersed with the violin and cello legatos which subtly accompany the bodies and erotic fantasies of the characters, to the nocturne which stretches into the finale of the dawn, the film glistens, too, with the concentrated mastery of the NFB and its technical crews.

At the conclusion of these 24 hours of *tragédie en musique* – here dawn is represented by a succession of barely tamed North American landscapes and slides of dawn paintings by Géricault and Caravaggio – the moment of day's first bleak light signals the hour of death. There are no real corpses in *The Decline*, only the ruins of intellectuals, the living dead playing piano with four hands, "living remains" which even a postgraduate autopsy would be hard pressed to identify.

*Jesus of Montreal* takes up the lyrical theme where *Réjeanne Padovani* left off, this time summoning Pergolesi. Two duets from the *Stabat Mater* are incorporated into the exposition: the "Inflammatus et accensus" of the beginning, at the Oratorio where the passion-play is to be staged; then the "Quando corpus morietur" as epilogue, when the two singers are reduced to performing in the subway, the resonant modern-day catacombs, the monumental tomb of the empires of finance where the actor/Jesus has come to die.

But Arcand's mastery of sound and music in *Jesus* is not as complete as in *The Decline*. For example, the finale of the *Stabat Mater* in the subway underlines the real, tragic ending of the film (as indicated in the script), but the ending is prolonged, somewhat artificially, by a reprise of Yves Laferrière's rock theme for the "Big Bang" sequence. In the "Big Bang" and passion-play sequences it is unclear which music belongs to the film in post-synch, and which belongs to the play and thus to the diegesis itself. Neither is identified and both are mixed like conventional film music, in a non-diegetic manner.

There are one or two similar moments in *Love and Human Remains* (a cliché sound crescendo too obviously foreshadowing the rape of the young girl in the pre-title sequence; country music over the western erotic fantasy which should be part of the diegesis). But as a whole the film is carefully structured, with well articulated rock and disco music expressing the hedonistic comings and goings of the gang of youths. Arcand's choice of a quintessentially 1950s ballad, Elvis Presley's "Can't Help Falling In Love With You", in the final third of the film lends particular depth to the living presence of the King, which is viewed as more than an ephemeral fashion: firstly during a concert, diegetically, and then "over" as film music for the finale, as the musical expression and symbol of the *True Nature of Love* aspect of the tragedy in Fraser's play and screenplay.

Last dialogue and arioso

> *Question:* In *Jesus*, the key scene is the "Big Bang" and not the modern-day passion-play, is it not? I am struck by how closely the "Big Bang" follows the planetarium sequence in Ray's *Rebel Without a Cause* (1955). There, just as the astronomer is

explaining how the earth will eventually explode, the flash of the explosion illuminates the group of young people in the audience; the lecture concludes: "At this moment life and history on earth will appear as futile". In dramaturgical terms, Ray places the scene in the first part of the film whence it envelops and pervades the unfolding tragedy.
*Arcand:* True. The "Big Bang" scene is more all-encompassing than the passion-play, and ultimately shapes it. The consciousness of death and emptiness is omnipresent.

*Question:* Yourcenar described this as "entering into death with open eyes". Tragedy becomes a kind of lyrical consciousness of death...
*Arcand:* As the character played by Robert Lepage says right at the beginning: "It's dangerous to stage the Passion".

*Question:* For me this is the theme that ties all your films together – the theme of cosmic tragedy. A vision for our time, if ever there was one.
*Arcand:* Between the "Big Bang" and its finiteness stands the mystery and tragedy of the human being. How can we escape the inevitability of fate? Probably through art; art alone makes it possible for us to touch the mystery, and echo it, for it surpasses our rational capacities. Music, the music of the human voice, best succeeds in expressing the mystery. Seen from this angle, the *tragédie en musique* form is an excellent expressive vehicle.

Like cosmic waves, like resonances which will never be answered or echoed, we cast our music adrift in the universe. But that should not stop us from responding to the mysterious beauty of these waves, from reproducing them. Even though we know it is ephemeral, beauty has a life of its own, it can be heard. If there is anything we have accomplished which ought to be left behind us, it is this. Film must bear witness to it, as far as it is able. Not long ago I had the opportunity of viewing a cutting copy of François Girard's film on Glenn Gould.[18] It shows the supreme expressive capacity of music. In the sequence where NASA launches the Voyager space probe we learn that one of the objects placed aboard the probe is Gould's recording of Bach's *Goldberg Variations*. The music most emblematic of humanity, that which we choose to send to the limits of our universe with no hope that it will ever be intercepted and heard, is Bach as performed by Gould. It is extraordinary, how this gesture lays bare the human mystery in the long evolutionary curve of universal matter, from its birth to its disappearance. I was deeply touched by that sequence.

What drew me to Brad Fraser's play was the curious universe of young people it portrayed, the way the writing was drawn from personal experience with all its abrasive truth. I had never seen anything like it for the screen; there was no hesitation, I wanted to direct it. I had never been shocked quite this way before, and I probably never will be again. I added nothing to Fraser's script; all I did was help Brad solve a few problems related to structure and pacing.

We should have shot the film in Edmonton where the action is set and where Brad grew up, in that desolate city with its boomtown skyscrapers surrounded by poor, squalid suburbs full of idle young people and alcoholic Amerindians... But since it was impossible for us to film in Edmonton we chose Montreal. It would have been unthinkable to use the same settings we did for *Jesus*. I discovered a Montreal unknown to the cinema, in the "lower West End" along the Lachine Canal, from Pointe-Saint-Charles to Ville La Salle. Entire neighbourhoods of poor anglophones, the kind of people who populate the works of Montreal playwright David Fennario.

Brad Fraser has made a rare achievement: he has told the story of young people who can barely articulate, and whose voice can barely be heard when they do manage to speak. Brad gives this dark, desperate world voice through the miracle of his writing. He has produced the words, the sounds and the music of the unsaid, of silence...

Conclusion

There are two kinds of "human remains". Of course, there are the murdered, mutilated girls ("sex is something warm, wet and red"), but they remain in the background. The foreground space is occupied by the snappily-dressed, fashionable young people in their sports cars, reared on the culture of the arcade and the disco. These magnificent young people, so intelligent, so sensitive, yet so empty (with none of the sparkling volubility of the egg-heads and the artistic types), the kind encountered every day in college and university classrooms, are the living dead of hedonist techo-culture, end-of-millenium DOAs. Corroded by an ever-expanding multiplicity of soft political machinery (TV zapping, arcade games, pagers, dance music) they wander day and night – mostly at night – looking for that small great thing, so simple and so complex, called love. Their pathetic short conversations in which "nice car you got, nice apartment, nice dress", in their impenetrable platitude, their clipped phrasing and their communicative silence, mean only: "I want to love, I want to be loved".

In the film's magnificent epilogue, a brief moment of high NFB purity, the actor/waiter David decides to return to the stage, to seek rebirth. In the empty theatre, comforting and luminescent like a freshly created earthly paradise, the fat producer asks if he has anything to say before the audition. "Yes", answers David, "I love you". "What?" "I love you...".[19] Here is all of Arcand compressed into a few seconds of dense critical mass ready to explode: the peace of the stage, of theatre on film, of art. I love you, art and music, the only human cry which still vibrates, awaiting an echo. The sole identification of our remains.

## Notes

[1] The term *tragédie en musique* is used to describe the style of baroque opera created by French composer Jean-Baptiste Lully and librettist Philippe Quinault in the second half of the 17th century.

[2] Voulons-nous franchir la mer?
Où nous entraîne cette passion puissante
qui prime pour nous toute autre passion?
Pourquoi ce vol éperdu dans cette direction,
vers le point où jusqu'à présent
tous les soleils déclinèrent et s'éteignirent?
[translated from the script of *The Westward Road*]

[3] *Toronto Star* 23 December 1972.

[4] "LA MACHINE EST L'INSTRUMENT POLITIQUE LE PLUS EFFICACE". [translated from the script of *On est au coton*]

[5] Dialogues with Denys Arcand were recorded in March and April 1993.

[6] The composer and film sound designer Michel Fano worked on several of Alain Robbe-Grillet's films, as well as with François Bel and Gérard Vienne. He is currently Head of the Sound Department at the Institut de Formation et d'Enseignement pour les Métiers de l'Image et du Son (FEMIS), and president of the Commission Supérieure Technique du Cinéma (CST), both in Paris.

[7] This Quebec filmmaker's films include *Golden Gloves* (1961), *Le Chat dans le sac* [*The Cat in the Bag*, 1964], *Entre tu et vous* (1969), *Au Pays de Zom* [*In Zom's Country*, 1982].

[8] "Courts métrages de l'O.N.F.", *Séquences* 46 (October 1966): 51

[9] "Des hommes audacieux, innocents et cruels qui pensèrent, comme

Machiavel, que les hommes ne peuvent ni ne doivent être fidèles au Prince qui ne peut ni les défendre ni les réprimer".

[10] From Robin Spry's reading of a French translation of Lord Durham's *Report on the Affairs of British North America*, 1839, known as the "Durham Report" [translated from the film script of *Quebec: Duplessis and After...*]. The Report, whose aim was to resolve the crisis in Britain's Canadian colony, contained two principal recommendations: responsible government and union of Upper and Lower Canada. David Mills adds: "Although controversial in its direct influence in the creation of the Province of Canada, the emergence of a party system and the strengthening of local self-government, the Durham Report is generally regarded to have played an important role in the development of Canadian autonomy." (*The Canadian Encyclopedia*, Edmonton: Hurtig Pub., vol. 1: 637-638)

[11] "Il est plus facile de conserver des valeurs que d'en inventer d'autres".

[12] Saint Jean-Baptiste is the patron saint of French Canadians. His feast day, June 24, is celebrated as Quebec's national holiday. But since 1968 the infant Saint Jean-Baptiste and his traditional lamb are no longer a part of the holiday parade.

[13] Denys Arcand, "L'Historien silencieux", in Robert Comeau (ed), *Maurice Séguin, historien du pays québécois* (Montreal: VLB, 1987): 256-257.

[14] Words emblazoned on the Canadian coat of arms: "from sea to sea".

[15] "Un prince habile doit nourrir contre lui quelques inimitiés afin que, les ayant matées, il en sorte grandi". [translated from the film script of *Comfort and Indifference*]

[16] Denys Arcand. *Cinéastes du Québec 8*: 30.

[17] In *Gina* Arcand renames the National Film Board as the National *Cinema* Board.

[18] The film to which Arcand refers is *Thirty-Two Short Films About Glenn Gould* (1993).

[19] The comment refers to an earlier version of *Love and Human Remains* presented at a private showing in April 1993. This ending was later discarded and replaced by the one that can now be seen on general release.

# A cinema of radical incompatibilities: Arcand's early fiction films

*Gene Walz*

Although firmly rooted in Quebec culture and fascinated by Hollywood movie conventions, Denys Arcand found his main inspiration elsewhere when he switched from documentary work at the National Film Board of Canada to fiction filmmaking.[1] European art cinema was his major influence, especially the films of Jean-Luc Godard. The indebtedness to Godard is unmistakable in *La Maudite Galette* [*The Damned Dough*], Arcand's first fiction feature film, released in 1971. His second film, *Réjeanne Padovani* (1973), is less slavishly indebted to Godard and shows a broadening of his range of influences. *Gina* (1975) at first glance seems to be more American, but that is because it is less the work of a faithful student than of a filmmaker with his own emerging voice.

While Arcand was developing as a stylist and rhetorician in these first three films, there are certain constants that seem to constitute the core of his beliefs about society, people, art and cinema. All these point to the fact that Arcand is neither an optimist nor a romantic. His films are so scathingly dark and unreassuring that even to call them political, as several critics have, demands a special qualification, for he does not seem to place much faith in politics or, in fact, in social exchange. The best that can be said is that his first three films are sufficiently sardonic and provocative to urge those who are so inclined to consider collective political action.

The characters in his films, however, are incapable of this positivistic stance. By and large they are stolid, disaffected and (to use a popular term of the time) alienated. Moments of joy, warmth and/or truly communal activity are rare and usually occur near the beginnings of the films. Time and again groups are presented as mere collections of essentially uncommunicative individuals: the four robbers in the pickup truck in *La Maudite Galette*; the basement full of underlings in *Réjeanne Padovani*; and the workers and bar patrons in *Gina*. They are all physically together but emotionally apart. And they appear to be morally, spiritually and intellectually destitute, without the resources to communicate. They are, in a word, incompatible.

These are defining moments in early Arcand films. Individuals are often silent, still, guarded, self-absorbed, enervated and/or protective.

Arcand as a director poses them rather than choreographs them. He also frames and films them to emphasize their detachment not only from each other, but also from the audience. There are few over-the-shoulder shots to connect characters and almost no close-up or subjective shots to generate empathy.

Two consequences of this are worthy of special mention. Firstly, the story-generating occasion for each film involves an "intruder" or "interloper" of some kind "invading" an "alien" space, as if the inability to relate to one another is exacerbated by the arrival of an outsider. The most obvious examples of this are in *Gina*: the eponymous stripper and the Montreal filmmakers venturing into a rural Quebec town. Equally as noteworthy is the return of the unwanted ex-wife in *Réjeanne Padovani*. Ernest, the hired man who boards in his boss's small apartment is *La Maudite Galette*'s near equivalent, but that film proceeds by a series of disruptions occasioned by characters entering into others' spaces. (This is not only a macrocosmic tactic, but also a microcosmic one, since characters often enter scenes or rooms or even shots already inhabited by others.)

The second consequence of Arcand's view of individuals is that his films are invariably studies in the exercise of power. In environments with such minuscule amounts of sympathy or fellow-feeling, simple comradeship or compassion, relationships are necessarily defined by self-interest, manipulation, exploitation, intimidation, violence and other anti-social abuses of power. In Arcand's ontology, the universe is a continuum of conflicting and irreconcilable antagonisms that necessarily and arbitrarily overlap, interpenetrate and disrupt. There are winners and losers, victimizers and victims. The winners drive big cars, are not afraid to use deadly weapons and force, and have sufficient money or position to hire others (thugs, hitmen and pliant women) to do their bidding. Arcand's world is almost unrelentingly Darwinian.

Nor does he seem to have many illusions about art or the cinema. Painting and music are stripped of their transcendental qualities – personal, spiritual or social significance. In *La Maudite Galette* and *Réjeanne Padovani* art-works mock the people who possess them. The pastel ballerinas over the couch in the Soucys' living room in *La Maudite Galette* represent unattainable romanticized ideals, and the crucifix presiding over the murder of Uncle Arthur, in the same film, is a cruel joke. Likewise, the elaborate collection of sterile but showy contemporary art throughout Padovani's suburban mafia mansion does not reflect positively on the man's taste and refinement. And the operas that he claims to revere only recall the chillingly ironic aestheticism of the Nazis listening to Mozart as they presided over the brutality of their concentration camps.

At the end of *Gina* when the documentary filmmaking crew is prevented from finishing their exposé of corrupted capitalism, they quickly and matter-of-factly switch to filming a formulaic police movie. They accept the work, and Arcand presents the change without editorializing. There is no grandiose privileging of one mode of filmmaking over the other. Socially-conscientious documentaries are not better than exploitative fictions. This sober juxtapositioning of one job next to the other reflects Arcand's major cinematic approach to his material.

Ben Shek has discovered in Arcand's films an "habitual binarism"; this is an attractive formulation but one that is too neat and orderly to describe the juxtapositioning that is the director's favourite tactic.[2] Binarism suggests a kind of dialectical approach, balanced and leading to a synthesis. Arcand, at least in his early fiction films, is too much the cynic to settle for this. His films do not resolve, and his juxtaposed units do not build to a satisfying climax or reconcile the opposing forces. This would presume too much about cinema and assign clear values, when Arcand is clearly opposed to these notions. His is a cinema of radical incompatibilities.

Nowhere is this better presented than in the endings of his films. *La Maudite Galette*, *Réjeanne Padovani* and *Gina* do not invoke closure in comfortable ways. Nor are they conventionally ambiguous by balancing options. They introduce new characters, elements and discourses. Revealingly, all three films end with someone beginning a trip. Gina is in an airport heading, presumably (from the mariachi music) for Mexico. Vincent Padovani leaves the freeway-opening ceremony in his Cadillac limo and drives past the destruction of many brownstone buildings, presumably making way for his next freeway, in the company of the wife of a high-ranking government official, presumably his new mistress. At the end of *La Maudite Galette*, Ernest's parents, a surprise addition to the story in the previous sequence, drive through Montreal, presumably on their way to Florida in a new convertible, all financed with Ernest's ill-gotten money. These endings do not resolve the films as much as they deny, in an almost flippant manner, the moral and social significance of what preceded. Life goes on.

In an interview with John Hofsess just after the release of *Réjeanne Padovani*, Arcand revealed what these endings imply. He likes to keep people guessing. "A good film is always pulling the rug out from under people's beliefs and prejudices", he said. "I find it presumptuous to be moralistic, but I like being a jester".[3] Perhaps "jester" is too warm a word to describe Arcand, unless it is used in the same way as it is used to characterize Buñuel or Godard. Arcand is a *provocateur*, perfectly willing to pull the rug out from under people right up until the final frame of his films.

## La Maudite Galette

*La Maudite Galette* is the film of a good pupil. Like Godard's films of the 1960s, it focuses on social transgressions; with its double-cross motif and dispassionate cynicism, it is reminiscent of American crime films of the 1940s, the formative film era for Godard. More particularly, *La Maudite Galette* is indebted to Godard's radical counter-cinema with its stylistic innovations, Brechtian "alienation" effects and collage narratives.

The story (scripted independently by Jacques Benoit) is simple, blunt and unadorned, except for its weird sense of humour. There are no sub-plots, flashbacks, digressions or complexities, and little in the way of conventional depth or dimension. A scrap metal dealer, Roland Soucy (René Caron), pays his hired man Ernest (Marcel Sabourin) and talks to his mistress in his shabby office. He then goes home to a very modest apartment. A genial surprise visit by a rich uncle (J-Léo Gagnon) turns rancorous. Berthe (Luce Guilbeault), Roland's bibulous wife, persuades two sadistic thugs to help them murder the uncle. The four would-be murderers are followed to the rural murder site by Ernest who also boards with the Soucys. He kills everyone but Berthe. Later he wounds her and flees, using the uncle's stolen money to buy a woman and a big car from a gangster in a bar. The gangster sets his thugs after Ernest who escapes to his parents' apartment. Berthe surprises him there, and they kill each other. His parents hide the money from the cops and then use it to begin a Florida holiday in a new car.

While *La Maudite Galette* may appear from this brief synopsis to be clear and straightforward, its rhetoric is quite different. As a film experience, *La Maudite Galette* is like viewing at least three different kinds of film with three different protagonists. It begins as if it were an observational documentary, something in the order of Allan King's *A Married Couple* (1969) in a lower-class setting, with Roland as the centre of the camera's and the narrative's attention (approximately 40 minutes). It then becomes a film noir focused on Berthe's homicidal impulsiveness (approximately 25 minutes), and ends like an absurdist or black comedy with Ernest's activities carrying the narrative line (approximately 30 minutes). As such, it is like Godard's seemingly incoherent or decentralized collage narratives where "the most heterogeneous and permissive of formal principles" apply.[4]

Yet even this tripartite structuration does not provide a complete sense of the film's Godardian strategies. For *La Maudite Galette* zigzags (to use Bart Testa's apt term) much more often in the course of its narration.[5] The title sequence provides a subtle premonition of this. Black title cards with stark red lettering alternate with shots of a grey, industrialized cityscape and then with an unnamed worker mechanically performing crude physical tasks. The eleven live-action shots between the title cards seem to foreground a political discourse about modern urban anomie. These live-action shots clash chromatically with the more melodramatically ominous title cards. The crosscutting never conjoins the two alternating elements; they operate independently and end abruptly and irreconcilably.

Furthermore, the potentially Marxist discourse of the live-action shots interspersed with the title cards is dropped in the following, post-titles scene. In fact, any connection between the titles and this scene appears to be deliberately subverted. The centre of attention (through framing, positioning, movement and dialogue) is now Roland; Ernest, the worker, is present only fleetingly. At first, Roland turns offscreen left and calls him by name (the connection can only be made later); when he pays Ernest his wages, only the worker's hands enter the frame. Ernest is thus present only by his absence. The camera excludes him, neither panning to allow his physical presence entry into the frame, nor cutting to an edited insert to acknowledge him. The narrative in this scene is instead concerned with the anti-romantic relationship between Roland and the woman in his office (and onscreen right) who, it transpires, is his mistress. Sexual politics are the focus here.

*La Maudite Galette* takes a somewhat different direction in the next scene – the longest in the film and the one that has evidently given its few commentators the mistaken impression that the entire film is photographed in long shots and long takes. What earlier were subtle examples of "alienation" effects now become more overt.

The scene takes place in the Soucys' apartment: the kitchen, the living room, the boarder's bedroom and the dining room. Virtually all the shots in this scene are long to medium-long, filmed at a 90° angle to the action, with the camera artlessly framing the characters and reacting to movement by slight (and sometimes slow and "careless") pans and tilts. The dialogue and delivery (and *joual* dialect) appear to be spontaneous and unrehearsed, the blocking minimal: the performers sit and/or stand. The impression is that this is a rather detached and objective observational documentary about domestic or familial interaction.

Two things disrupt this documentary-like scene. While Roland, Berthe and their uncle Arthur eat, drink, laugh and talk around the dining room table at the climax of the scene, four shots of Ernest the boarder are intercut; he is listening at the door of his room to their conversation. The shots are jarringly intrusive. The dining room conversation is photographed in objective long shots to include all three people; the scene here is very brightly lit and arranged for the camera in a distinctive and Godardian "planimetric" style.[6] But the shots from Ernest's bedroom are dark and minimally lit; they are medium to close-up over-the-shoulder shots of Ernest at his slightly-ajar door, and the camera is not perpendicular to the wall but oblique. The crosscutting is therefore visually jarring and, in fact, contradictory since parallel editing and the over-the-shoulder shot are classical Hollywood techniques and at odds with the detached observational-documentary style of the remainder of the scene.

In an analysis of *Tout va bien* (1972) Kristin Thompson describes one of Godard's Brechtian techniques as "contradiction": "the joining of stylistic techniques in a discontinuous manner".[7] The crosscutting between bedroom and dining room certainly demonstrates Arcand's own rudimentary version of this technique. But the second disruption of the primarily documentary format of the scene is a better example. After much joviality, the conversation turns acrimonious. Berthe yells at the uncle and Arcand cuts to a close-up of Berthe seething with rage and glowering almost (but not quite) into the camera lens. The shot is almost primitive in its intensity, which is a startling contrast to the previously detached observations of behaviour. And it is not merely a case of moving from long-shots to a close-up.

This close-up changes *La Maudite Galette* from an exterior portrait to an interior one, from an objective presentation to a subjective one. More importantly, it changes the perspective of the film from Roland to Berthe. Roland, whose entry into shots and placement in the centre of the frame in the dinner episode, and whose initiation of conversations controlled the narrative, is at this point displaced by Berthe. As if to emphasize the transition, the close-up of Berthe is held for an unnecessarily and even uncomfortably long time – much longer than is needed to understand that she is angry and contemplating something. Subsequently she is the character that starts to initiate the narrative activity.

The next major narrative disruption or alienation effect occurs when Berthe and Roland, and their two accomplices, Rosaire and Ti-Bi, journey to the uncle's house. In what looks like an unusually long and continuous take of three minutes and ten seconds (but which is in fact six shots subtly edited together) the camera records the journey through the front windshield of the pick-up. It is a masterpiece of discomfiting self-contradictions.

Firstly, the "travelling shot" seems to be from the position that Berthe occupies in the cab, but no personalized subjectivity is otherwise indicated. Secondly, there is no conversation until the final seconds – indicating a kind of grim purposefulness or resolve on the part of the travellers, yet the journey is accompanied by non-diegetic sound of ironically lyrical Quebec folk music featuring harmonica and violins. Most importantly, the "travelling shot" is presented in what seems to be "real time", but it is photographed in a style straight out of film noir.

Two shafts of light piercing the darkness of a rural highway as a car races through an unfamiliar landscape captured fleetingly in the headlights while the camera records the ride from inside the vehicle is a film noir staple. Robert Siodmak's *The Killers* (1946) and Jacques Tourneur's *Out of the Past* (1947) are notable predecessors of *La Maudite Galette* in this respect.

The robbery-murder scene that follows plays out the film noir patterns more assiduously. Visual stylistics are especially apparent: beams of light piercing the darkness of narrow corridors and sharp corners from hand-held flashlights; gunshot flashes in the dark; silhouettes illuminated by back or side-lighting; singular, garish light sources. But the pathological femme fatale, sadistic brutality and the double-cross plot twists are other obvious film noir markings. This is all rendered eerie by the full shot of the uncle's house which frames the scene. The 19th century Quebec architecture makes it look authentic but oddly out of place, and the lighting gives it more the appearance of a façade than an actual building. The scene is dislocated.

If the journey/murder scene zigs the narrative away from observational documentary into film noir, then what happens after the murder zags the narrative in yet another direction. It moves from film noir to absurdism. The key to this third major section of the film is the inexpressiveness of the now-central character, Ernest, who has displaced Berthe and Roland as protagonist. Because he maintains a deadpan expression throughout and does not talk much, it is impossible to determine Ernest's motives or feelings. His actions are, therefore, increasingly bizarre, inexplicable and absurd.

In that part of an ordinary film in which issues are usually resolved, *La Maudite Galette* insists on raising more questions and not answering them. Why, for instance, does Ernest remove the body of uncle Arthur and toss it off a bridge rather than simply leaving it in the burning house with the other corpses? What exactly is the relationship between Ernest and Berthe? Why does Ernest so openly flaunt the suitcase full of money in the bar when he buys the convertible and the woman? Moreover, how can this transaction happen so fast? Why does the top of the convertible seem to operate automatically when Ernest abandons it? Why does he buy jelly beans for his dour parents? In one sense these unanswered questions are simply a continuation of the Brechtian/ Godardian alienation effects constructed in the first parts of the film. Kristin Thompson's term is "interruption" – "the insertion of material that breaks up a smooth, logical chain of narrative causes and effects".[8]

Yet, in a larger sense they are not just Godardian rhetoric or technique; they underline Arcand's commitment to the irrational, to the contradictoriness of everything. It is surely there in Berthe's shallow and spiteful determination to kill her benefactor, uncle Arthur. It is there in the Hitchcock/Godard-type cameo appearance of Denys Arcand who, together with fellow director Bernard Gosselin, plays a policeman perfunctorily measuring and making notes and completely missing the implications and fruits of the crime. And, of course, it is heavily emphasized in the final shots of the film. Here Ernest's parents respond to the return of their son and the double homicide in their kitchen by hiding "the damned dough" (to clumsily translate the film's title but to capture its culinary slang) in a washing machine, sitting/lying uncommunicatively in their bedroom, and then heading off, presumably, to Florida in a big new car – accompanied by non-diegetic music that disconcertingly recalls the music from the murder-voyage shots. The film ends obliquely and absurdly with a cynical joke and two new protagonists. Crime does not pay in the case of the main perpetrators – the three preceding protagonists, Roland, Berthe and Ernest. But for Ernest's parents crime does pay. The coda of the old couple's journey comically contradicts what comes before.

Arcand's imitation of Godardian techniques reinforces this conclusion. He refuses to arrange or resolve the crosscutting structures in any transcendental way. His camera holds on characters and sets for extended lengths of time yet drains them of metaphysical significance. Even the frequent and dominating planimetric shots, whereby characters are set in front of flat, constraining backdrops, fit in, for they deny ambiguity and a moral/social dimension. What Brian Henderson says about Godard's reversion to a cinema of one plane is equally applicable to Arcand. It "is a demystification, an assault on the bourgeois worldview and self-image".[9] A more succinctly appropriate description of *La Maudite Galette* would be difficult to find.

*Réjeanne Padovani*

At first glance *Réjeanne Padovani* is not at all like its predecessor. Although it also focuses on social transgressions (and, in fact, picks up the gangster-type characters introduced in the third section of *La Maudite Galette*) and is rendered in the same cool, detached manner, Arcand's second fiction film is a decidedly different film experience. It is much less obviously a Godardian film. Noticeably down-played are the resourceful conjunction of cinematic modes (documentary, film noir and black comedy) into a collage narrative and the insistent planimetric composition; *Réjeanne Padovani* is more coherent in structure, and there is more depth or perspective in its design. It is also more subtle in its rhetorical effects. Arcand seems to understand Godard, not just to imitate his tactics. He is looking elsewhere as well for his models.

If the collage narrative and planimetric composition are gone from *Réjeanne Padovani*, Arcand's distinctive reliance on cross-cutting is still very much evident. It is perfectly suited to the upstairs-downstairs story that Arcand and co-scriptwriter Jacques Benoit have crafted.

The film begins at a dinner party celebrating the opening of a new Montreal freeway. Held at the posh suburban estate of the freeway's general contractor, Vincent Padovani (Jean Lajeunesse), the dinner has already begun when a limo delivers the Minister of Public Works, Georges Bouchard (J-Léo Gagnon), the guest of honour who was responsible for the contract. Already in attendance are his secretary, Jean Pierre Caron (Jean Pierre Lefebvre); the Mayor, Jean-Guy Biron (René Caron); a legal advisor, Leon Desaulniers (Roger Lebel) with responsibilities both to Padovani and Bouchard; and their four wives (Thérèse Cadorette, Frédérique Collin, Hélène Loiselle and Margot MacKinnon, respectively). After dinner the women receive pearl necklaces as gifts from Vincent, and later Mrs Desaulniers sings an operatic aria accompanied by a string quartet. Meanwhile, their attendants (chauffeurs, police bodyguards, facilitators, hitmen and pliant women) entertain themselves in the basement. The underlings talk, play shuffle-board, bet on fixed horse races, grumble over inappropriate tie-tack gifts from Vincent, listen in a far-off corner to the aria, and mostly wait to do the bidding of their employers.

The occasion is interrupted by news of the unexpected return to the city of Vincent's ex-wife, Réjeanne (Luce Guilbeault), who has been living in American exile with the son of a leader of a rival Jewish organisation. This news causes Vincent to retreat to his office to brood and set his henchmen into action to deal with the disruption. Two reporters then arrive at the estate and are roughed up by Padovani's men; in the process the reporters inadvertently reveal that radicals have organised a mass demonstration for the grand opening of the freeway.

While the minister's wife is attacking him sexually, Caron is at the same time trying to make a series of telephone calls to smooth over the assault on the reporters and obtain more information on the demonstration. Padovani's men are then dispatched to beat up the demonstration's organisers and ransack their offices. When Réjeanne shows up in the estate's greenhouse to try to appeal directly to her husband – who is being seduced by Caron's wife – she is repeatedly obstructed by her husband's lieutenants and eventually murdered as a fireworks display ends the party. Just prior to the ribbon-cutting ceremony opening the freeway, her body is buried in concrete, becoming part of the roadway that is opening without incident.

Rather than being imposed on the story as in *La Maudite Galette*, the distinctive "Arcandian" alternating or zigzagging structure is more fluid and internal in *Réjeanne Padovani*. Initially, it emphasizes certain obvious contrasts between the polished overlords and their hired help. Upstairs they eat roast beef with all the trimmings and drink fine wines;

downstairs they drink beer and one woman even eats Pablum baby food. Upstairs the wives receive pearl necklaces as gifts; downstairs it is cheap tie-tacks for the men and nothing for the two "hostesses". The upstairs pleasures of foreign travel contrast to the more meagre pleasures of assured overtime and a limo's automatic air-conditioning for the chauffeurs. But increasingly the crosscutting moves beyond these one-dimensional alternatives.

What becomes increasingly apparent in the deployment of the story is that hierarchization and the clarification of distinctions between the characters are not the film's main objectives. The blurring of distinctions foregrounded by the casting of the roles is never fully overcome by the zigzagging structure. The characters, with a few notable exceptions, look, dress and act alike. The Mayor and the minister are quite similar, for instance, and which woman is married to which man is sometimes impossible to determine. Furthermore, the focus slowly turns towards the intermediary characters in the story, the ones who are from both worlds: Dominic, J-Léon and Jean Pierre Caron and his wife. And the way they are all similar in promoting their own agendas and ensuring their own advancement is repeatedly emphasized.

In this regard it is important to note the allusions in *Réjeanne Padovani* to Jean Renoir's classic upstairs/downstairs film *La Règle du jeu* (*The Rules of the Game*, 1939). The references are both obvious and subtle, from the isolated mansion settings, the partner-swapping, the élite entertainment, the concluding homicide, and the insider/outsider overlay onto the upstairs/downstairs base story; to the more covert features such as the greenhouse, the wind-up toy (which Lucky examines in the basement) and the checkerboard symbolism. Both films weave a dense pattern of interrelationships – with Arcand's portraits less varied and even less romantic than Renoir's. Yet both come to surprisingly similar conclusions about the homogeneity, imperturbability and self-perpetuation of their worlds.

Strangely, the similarities between *The Rules of the Game* and *Réjeanne Padovani* also illuminate Arcand's Godardian tactics. The true power and destructiveness of both Renoir's aristocratic élite and Arcand's political-criminal élite are revealed in the moments outside the mansion. In *The Rules of the Game* it is the disturbing rabbit-hunt scene, an unflinching account of casual brutality. For Arcand there are two comparable moments. They indicate just how much more adept he is as a cinematic rhetorician. The Godardian "alienation" effects are more subtle and controlled.

The first occurs when a female journalist shows up with a male photographer at Padovani's door to interview the Minister of Public Works. They are both roughed up by a couple of Padovani's protectors in a scene that is swift and dynamic; there are 26 shots in just over 2 minutes. In the second scene, a group of thugs invades the offices of an action committee opposed to the Mayor and the new freeway. They beat up the young workers and destroy their equipment in a flurry of rapidly edited shots (27 shots in approximately 3 minutes, but with a long shot ending the montage). Henri-Paul Chevrier believes that these quick scenes "recall more the excitations of Hollywood than Brechtian reflexivity", but he fails to see them in their full context.[10] Before these scenes, *Réjeanne Padovani* has been cool and distant in its presentation of action and characters. The abrupt change of pace through camera movement, lighting and editing strategies is surely calculated to achieve the maximum Godardian rhetorical effect.

To fully appreciate just how much Arcand has absorbed the principles of Godard's counter-cinema, however, the dominant cinema of the day must be recalled. *Réjeanne Padovani* was made in the considerable wake of Francis Coppola's blockbuster *The Godfather* (1972). Both films pivot around a powerful, aging underworld figure with considerable influence in both legitimate and criminal spheres, in politics, law enforcement and business, who is threatened by internal and external forces. Arcand, however, has chosen to de-dramatize the action and de-glamorize the characters – a complete reversal of Coppola's approach.

Missing from *Réjeanne Padovani* are the colourful, vital and distinctive supporting characters Coppola used so effectively to enliven his immensely popular film. Arcand's characters are virtually indistinguishable and are rendered in dark greys and cold blues; there is none of Coppola's warm and nostalgic Rembrandian glow in Arcand's film. The characters are also a singularly joyless and self-absorbed lot. This is especially apparent in the calculating and emotionless conduct of Jean Pierre Caron and his wife, whose twin machinations gain prominence in the film's final third. They epitomize the ethic of hypocrisy, betrayal and icy self-aggrandizement at the centre of this world.

Arcand does not subscribe to the romantic gangster mystique; he does flirt with it, however. This is what gives *Réjeanne Padovani* the dimension that *La Maudite Galette* lacks. If the Carons are the least sympathetic and glamorized of the group, Vincent, Réjeanne Padovani and Lucky (Gabriel Arcand), the seemingly sensitive hitman, are, as initially presented, at least potentially sympathetic.

As a repentant wife and prodigal mother returning to her family, Réjeanne is introduced as an intriguing contrast to other characters at the Padovani residence. As a person who is one step ahead of her husband's minions and who is willing to take matters into her own hands, she has even more heroic and empathetic potential. Once she arrives, however, her blatant opportunism and cold-hearted willingness not only to abandon, but also to betray her dying, impotent lover undercut any possibilities for her character.

Arcand's clever reversal of expectations is repeated with Vincent Padovani and with Lucky. Lucky is reading by himself while the other underlings bide their time with less intellectual diversions. He listens longer and more appreciatively than any of them to the aria, and he is called "a quiet one" by one of the "hostesses" who dated him, a handy cliché for indicating sensitivity and depth. Yet he is brutally efficient with a shotgun when executing Réjeanne, and he buries her with reptilian dispassion. Rather than providing a balanced or dimensional character with which to identify, Arcand is clearly interested in setting him up and then undercutting him. The same happens with Vincent Padovani. Initially portrayed as a generous benefactor and loving father who is still suffering from his misplaced love for his ex-wife and is burdened by the responsibilities of his many employees, he eventually turns into a study in self-indulgent lassitude, a kind of Montreal Nazi who can execute, exploit and destroy while listening to opera and collecting modern art. All three portraits (of the two Padovanis and Lucky) ultimately subvert interiority, deny feelings and frustrate identification in a familiar Brechtian/Godardian manner.

Whereas Coppola's film is a romantic family saga hybridized with a dynamic gangster film, *Réjeanne Padovani* is more like a drawing-room play presented in detached documentary style but interspersed with outbursts of violence. A calm, rational and orderly night in the life of a wealthy circle of business associates is interrupted by revealing examples of how they maintain their power and influence. Perhaps a more enlightening analogy would be to Buñuel's film *Le Charme discret de la bourgeoisie* (*The Discreet Charm of the Bourgeoisie*, 1972). Both are concerned with the thin veneer of culture and respectability that covers brutal appetite. *Réjeanne Padovani* is bleaker and more challenging than Buñuel's Surrealist classic because it is without the redeeming playfulness and fanciful wit. Bracing and accusatory, it is alert to local politics, universal issues and international developments in the cinema.

## Gina

Arcand and Godard were moving in opposite directions in the early 1970s. As Godard's career progressed, his films became more confrontational, "difficult" or obscure, and Marxist; those of Arcand did not. The distance between the two filmmakers can be readily measured by juxtaposing Godard's *Tout va bien* (1972) with *Gina* (1975), both of which focus on filmmaking crews going into factories troubled by labour-management discord. Although both deal with issues of money, class, sexuality and nationhood, and both incorporate "documentary" footage into their fictional storylines, Godard's film is the more politically ambitious and cinematically unconventional.[11] Using title cards such as "Today (1)" and direct address lectures to the camera, Godard raises questions about the star system (Yves Montand and Jane Fonda appear in the film), representation (images/word/sound and reality/artifice conflicts) and narrativity (particularly the role of time) which are beyond the range of Arcand's interests or capabilities. This is not to say, however, that *Gina* is straightforward or unproblematic.

In this film Arcand expands on the multi-stranded or polymeric story structure he used so effectively for the upstairs-downstairs contrasts in *Réjeanne Padovani*. This film is an insider-outsider story set in a small, rural Quebec town. After witnessing her bosses abuse another dancer for disobeying orders, Gina (Céline Lomez) obediently takes the train to Louiseville to perform at a local hotel bar. On the train Bob Sauvageau (Claude Blanchard), leader of an unemployed snowmobile gang, brags about the $85 000 government grant he secured for a snowmobile track. At the same time a small filmmaking crew also head for Louiseville to complete a documentary on the textile industry. When these outsiders arrive, tensions between them and the townsfolk immediately surface.

Gina and the film crew become friendly; she helps them as an interpreter for exploited South American immigrant workers, and she teams up with one of them to beat Sauvageau and his sidekick Andy Titel (Jocelyn Bérubé) in an expensive game of pool. Afterwards, she and the brow-beaten wife of the hotel-keeper (Paule Baillargeon) join the filmmakers for a skate on a hockey rink and then up the frozen river to a derelict ship used as a clubhouse by the snowmobilers.

In the course of shooting, the film crew focus their attention on Dolorès (Frédérique Collin), a young factory worker with a vivid memory and a family album of labour-strife photos. After work, Dolorès watches with the filmmakers as Gina performs her act to insults from and to the snowmobilers; later they gang-rape Gina in her room. In response, she telephones her bosses, and they rush into town and beat up the gang aboard their ship. Sauvageau and Andy escape by snowmobile but are chased down and disposed of by Gina. She then calmly heads off for a holiday. Their film cancelled, the filmmakers end up shooting what looks like a big-budget police film. And Dolorès marries her boyfriend.

*Gina* was made during the lengthy and embarrassing interval between the completion of *On est au coton* [*We're Fed Up*, 1970], Arcand's own documentary about the Quebec textile industry, and its grudging release by the National Film Board (1976). The inclusion of at least two exact quotations from that film and the easily recognisable equivalencies of character, setting, approach and dialogue highlight the peculiar autobiographical spin that Arcand gives to one of the hallmarks of Godardian and modernist cinema: self-reflexivity. Although *Gina* uses details from his own filmmaking experience and Denys Arcand's brother Gabriel plays the role of the documentary filmmaker, this is not a self-promoting or romanticized portrait. The film director is not a sensitive artist or visionary on a personal quest; his main gift is for strategic deception – putting on a suit to convince the textile company that he is trustworthy or sneaking a PR man away from the cameras so that his crew can obtain franker interviews. Therefore any modernist criticism of the medium through its maker is subtle and implied rather than direct.

Arcand in *Gina* is also less disruptive and obvious than Godard in his Brechtian techniques. The black and white documentary-like inserts do not blatantly question the "truth" of documentary. Their inclusion in the narrative seems, for the most part, to be "natural"; that is, although the developing, editing and screening processes are never acknowledged, the connections between colour and black-and-white footage have a certain elementary logic. They do not unduly call attention to themselves or undercut themselves.

There is one major exception to this. It shows how uninsistent Arcand is and just how the inserts and crosscutting function in the film. In terms of continuous screen time, almost one fifth of the film takes place in the bar on the night of Gina's performance. Halfway through the scene, once Arcand's typical parallel editing has established the characters' contrasts and antagonisms, Gina and Dolorès meet at a mirror in the women's washroom in a scene that heavy-handedly points out their similarities. During the performance that follows, there is a cut-away from Gina dancing to a clearly out-of-sequence documentary insert of Dolorès talking about her job. She explains: "When you get home from work at night, you're so worn out you don't feel like dancing" and "while you work you must think of something else". The insert does not call into question the use of inserts nor does it foreground the incursion of the director into the diegesis as it likely would in Godard. And it does not merely underline the simple contrasts between the women. For it also emphasizes in the dialogue what has been presented through the images: that the scene is about the subjective, interiorized worlds of a group of isolated individuals. Except for the over-anxious Andy (who heckles Gina) and the seemingly disinterested sound man (who leaves in the middle of the act), no one betrays his or her inner thinking/feeling self through either action, facial expression or verbal language.

The scene is, although declarative in its sexual or parasexual content, really interrogative in its presentation.[12] Precisely what these people are thinking or feeling can only be imagined. What, for instance, must the businessman, whose sexual offer was spurned by Gina, be thinking? Why is Dolorès here and what are her feelings? What is Gina thinking about? In its alternation between three basic shots (Gina dancing alone; Gina seen with the filmmakers and Dolorès in the foreground; and individual or tracking shots of the staring bar patrons), the scene also recalls Hitchcock's playful implication of the cinema-going audience. What are we all thinking?[13]

The increasing sophistication of Arcand's rhetorical tactic evident in this scene is carried over into the subsequent gang-rape scene. Godard's dramatic shock tactic of abrupt, brutal violence is practised almost to perfection here. The scene begins with over 2 minutes devoted to one continuous take of Gina sitting virtually motionless at her mirror; one brief (4-second) cut-away to the sound man reading in bed is included. Then the snowmobilers break into Gina's room, and the scene is a jarring montage of 30 shots in under 2 minutes. The same tactic of calm long-takes followed by jagged montages is used in both the ship-board assault and Gina's vengeful chase.

These latter two scenes, however, seem more like exercises in American genre conventions (the biker film, northern variety). The exaggerated irony or sarcasm of the Canadian national anthem as the televised sound accompaniment to the rape, and the overdetermined metaphors of the helmeted, bulkily-jumpsuited rapists and the surrealistic cargo ship, move the film into the comically eerie realm of self-conscious exaggeration. The black joke of a vengeful woman in white driving the only man who chose not to rape her into the parodic meat-grinder of an oversized snowblower reinforces this. Since virtually all other elements and characters in the film evaporate after the rape scene (until the coda), it is almost as if Gina's generic retribution incorporates all the film's variations on the theme of oppression into one half-serious apotheosis.

The sledgehammer statement of the film's theme (people respect bastards), alongside the sophistication of the parallel editing and European art film techniques, epitomizes the clever mixture of ordinarily incompatible elements which marks the films of Arcand at the end of the first phase of his fiction feature career.

Conclusion

In an odd way *Gina*, *Réjeanne Padovani* and *La Maudite Galette* seem to be responses to an implicit challenge made by Arcand's adopted mentor. Godard, in one of his delightful and characteristic simplifications, once split cinema into two separate modes: "The documentary side is: a man in a particular situation. The spectacle comes when one makes him a gangster or a secret agent".[14] Documentary vs. spectacle. Ordinary people vs. gangsters. Each of Arcand's first fiction features combines these normally incompatible opposites. But they combine other things as well: the straightforward and the parodic; the naïve and the cynical; social commentary and generic escapism; seriousness and, in Bart Testa's phrase, sarcasm.[15] They are films sharpened by anger but calmed by a kind of resignation.

Arcand is not the only Quebec filmmaker to be influenced by Godard.[16] His early cinema is neither as politically revolutionary nor as cinematically radical as Godard's brand of counter-cinema. Yet his early studies of anti-social behaviour, the cynical display of power, and the radical incompatibility of individuals are as thought-provoking in their own unique ways as anything created by Godard.

*Notes*

[1] In the interview reproduced in this volume, Denys Arcand talks about his fascination for Hollywood action movies.

[2] Ben-Z Shek, "A Director's Itinerary: Religion in the Films of Denys Arcand" (First International Conference on French Canada, New Delhi, 13 December 1991), unpublished manuscript: 17.

[3] John Hofsess, *Inner Views: Ten Canadian Film-makers* (Toronto: McGraw-Hill Ryerson Limited, 1975): 149.

[4] Brian Henderson, "Toward a Non-Bourgeois Camera Style", in Bill Nichols (ed), *Movies and Methods* (Berkeley: University of California Press, 1976): 428.

[5] See Bart Testa's essay in this volume.

[6] For a full discussion of the "flatness" of Godard's imagery or his eschewal of composition-in-depth, see Henderson: 431-437.

[7] Kristin Thompson, *Breaking the Glass Armor: Neoformalist Film Analysis* (Princeton, New Jersey: Princeton University Press, 1988): 112.

[8] Ibid.

[9] Henderson: 436.

[10] Henri-Paul Chevrier, "La lucidité et le désespoir", *Copie Zéro* 34-35 (December 1987/March 1988): 35. The scenes "relève plus de l'excitation hollywoodienne que de la réflexion brechtienne".

[11] The black-and-white documentary footage in *Gina* is, of course, actually staged and shot with professional actors to look like documentary.

¹² Parasexuality is "sexuality that is deployed but contained, carefully channelled rather than fully discharged". Peter Bailey, "Parasexuality and Glamour: the Victorian Barmaid as Cultural Prototype", *Gender and History* 2: 2 (summer 1990): 148.

¹³ Elizabeth Janzen, who assisted me in researching this essay, feels that "the long shots with the backs of Gina's audience's heads in the frame remind us that we are always only a secondary audience, voyeurs watching the voyeurs watching Gina". I would like to thank Ms Janzen for her invaluable help on this essay.

¹⁴ Jean-Luc Godard, *Godard on Godard*, edited by Jean Narboni and Tom Milne (New York: The Viking Press, 1968; 1972): 181.

¹⁵ Bart Testa, "Denys Arcand's Sarcasm: A Reading of *Gina*", in Pierre Véronneau, Michael Dorland and Seth Feldman (eds), *Dialogue: Cinéma canadien et québécois/Canadian and Quebec Cinema* (Montreal: Mediatext Publications and la Cinémathèque Québécoise, 1987): 203-222.

¹⁶ Jean Pierre Lefebvre and Claude Jutra, among others, were also influenced by Godard.

# Gender relations in *The Decline of the American Empire*

## Denise Pérusse
TRANSLATED FROM THE FRENCH BY CAROLINE SÉVIGNY

Among the range of female characters imagined and created by Quebec filmmakers during the 1970s, the vast majority occupy secondary roles, and find themselves either in the grip of their inescapable nature, or as the eternal victim.[1] Denys Arcand's images of women are typically hollow and on the margins of history, politics and society. In his films women are, above all, the victims of masculine power. In *Réjeanne Padovani* (1973), for example, Réjeanne is punished for having left her husband and children and, in doing so, for having dared to break the existing social and political order. Likewise, the "proletarian" sisters, Micheline and Manon, in the same film, have no alternative but to surrender their bodies to the holders of political power, while the wives of these men act as sexual "stepping stones" for the social advancement of their husbands. Gina, a character from the film of the same name (1975), is seen as a strong woman; however, she must pay for her strength and sexual autonomy by suffering a gang rape.

With *Le Déclin de l'empire américain* (*The Decline of the American Empire*, 1986), women are no longer the only losers; the upset in male-female relationships touches everyone alike. In this film Arcand approaches the question of male-female relationships in the context of contemporary Quebec society, using union and separation as a paradigm. The story progressively reveals the making, breaking-up and remaking of couples. Putting aside images of women confined to the spaces of private life, he points to the current situation, where the relationships among women, knowledge and space are no longer what they once were. There exists a community of individuals, mostly intellectuals, who question, confront and measure themselves without ever having any real self-knowledge. If culture, work and competence can create a kind of link between the sexes, *The Decline* pointedly reveals the impossibility of real reconciliation. The film demonstrates the dead end in gender relationships, where men and women act according to certain questionable clichés. A strength of the film is the placement of these clichés within the heart of the narrative, rather than making them peripheral issues. This layering of clichés, of déjà vu, creates a bond of cultural recognition between audience and filmmaker and is the central element of what I call the "exchange mechanism", and which, I believe, explains the film's great popular success. As in his previous films, Arcand makes use of various cinematographic techniques to bring the inherent irony to the surface, this time to represent a milieu where knowledge is traded for sex, and sex is the "criteria of authenticity of existence" (Jean Larose).[2]

In *The Decline of the American Empire* the filmmaker takes a lazy and insecure intelligentsia hostage, a sulky élite contemptuous of its own role and duties; in doing so, he forces us to see the film as inextricably linked to the post-Referendum era.[3] *The Decline* is a film about the intellectual vacuity of a society without goals and centred entirely on hedonism. In short, it is a film about both an élite and a society in a state of decline.

The construction of the narrative

The film tells of a group of university lecturers who spend the weekend together at a country chalet on Lake Memphremagog in Quebec. The characters have known each other for a long time and, as a result, are open about discussing their personal and sexual lives. At the beginning of the film we are introduced to four of the intellectuals – three professors of history (Rémy, Pierre and Claude) and a young graduate student (Alain).[4] They are shown preparing a meal in the luxurious country house where they await the arrival of the film's female characters. Simultaneously, the four women are shown working-out at the university sports complex in town. Each of the four women has a more or less stable relationship with one of the male characters: Louise is the wife of one of the professors (Rémy); Danielle studies history and is Pierre's mistress; Dominique teaches history and is head of the department; and Diane is a part-time lecturer in the history department. As we learn in the course of the film, both Dominique and Diane have slept with Rémy, and the former has also had an affair with Pierre.

In the first part of the film, spaces have been cleanly carved out by each sex, a visual metaphor for the gulf separating the two groups. Ironically, it is the men who are in the kitchen while the women pump iron at the sports club. Instead of reproducing at face value the traditional division of sex roles, Arcand has added a twist by reversing them.[5] The film alternates between each group, cutting back and forth to either confirm or contradict what is being shown through the use of flashbacks. Alternately, within their respective groups, the men and women speak of their minor conjugal infidelities, and their romantic and sexual experiences. Confidences about their individual personal lives are shared with other members of their group. The women discuss sex, as do the men.

The two groups of men and women are finally reunited around a dinner table during the second half of the film. Each group has gossiped about the other, and at times delighted in making "catty" remarks; now the groups must face each other. Arcand's highly stylized direction of this meeting leaves no doubt about the real nature of their relationship, although masked by apparent conviviality. The encounter of the two groups is filmed as a kind of western-style showdown. The four men sit on the porch drinking; Rémy (Rémy Girard) rambles on about the secret of happiness.[6] The arrival of the four women in a BMW cuts the conversation short. Then we hear the appropriate music for a western duel. The rhythm accelerates and the camera cuts back and forth between the men and the women as each group advances towards the other. Then, an "empty" frame, quickly invaded by the men and women coming together from each side of the screen. They kiss and embrace; this is a 30-second shot. Cut. The frame reopens with a close-up of the coulibiac (trout dish) pompously presented by Claude (Yves Jacques), the grand chef.

It is in this country haven of tranquillity, around a lavish feast, that the dissolution of the only couple who make a claim to stability, Louise (Dorothée Berryman) and Rémy, will occur. Their relationship for the past fifteen years has been founded on neither truly understanding the other; this misunderstanding has in a sense been the source of equilibrium. The mixing of the two disparate groups, the two sexes, has brought about an imbalance; the couple "is torn away and thrown...in the maelstrom grinder of decline, crumbling, entropy", as Heinz Weinmann argues in his analysis of the film.[7]

The story revolves around two events: the discussion and introduction (to the viewer) of the two groups made alternately, with each confined to its respective space, and the meeting of these groups. The events occur over a period of two days. Scenes referring to anterior events help to explain the characters' current behaviour and situations. These scenes from the past come back to haunt, and are particularly illuminating for the moments when the two groups are shown in parallel situations; they provide precious clues to the intrigues and development of the plot. Moreover, if occasionally the images from the past confirm the remarks of the characters made in the present, they also frequently reveal the contradictions manifest in what the characters say and in what they have done. The various secret love affairs which different characters have shared are revealed first to the viewer. We learn, for instance, that Rémy has slept with Dominique (Dominique Michel) and Diane (Louise Portal), and that Dominique has shared her bed with Pierre (Pierre Curzi) and Rémy. When they become known to Louise during the second half of the film, these intrigues will cause the break-up of the only married couple to have survived.

The opening shots of the film situate the narrative in the field of history and raise the issue that is fundamental to the film, that of decline. The first scene takes place before the film's credits. There is a close-up of a young female Asian student in the university classroom where Rémy teaches history: "Three things are important in history. First of all, numbers, secondly, numbers and thirdly, numbers. This means, for example, that the blacks in South Africa are bound to win some day while North American blacks will probably never make it."[8] In this lesson on demography at the film's beginning, Arcand implicitly raises the question of the decline of Quebec society; or, at the very least, its ability to survive within North America.

Following this scene, Diane interviews Dominique for a cultural programme to be aired on Radio Canada.

> UNIVERSITY CORRIDOR. DAY.
> DIANE: Dominique Saint-Arnaud. You're Chairperson of the History Department and you've just published *Changing Concepts of Happiness*. Can you tell us about it?
> DOMINIQUE: It's my premise that the concept of personal happiness permeates the literature of a nation or civilisation as its influence wanes.
> DIANE: What do you mean by "personal happiness"?
> DOMINIQUE: The expectation of receiving instant gratification in daily life and that this gratification constitutes the normative parameter of existence. [...]
> DOMINIQUE: So I pose the question: is the frantic drive for personal happiness we see in society today linked to the decline of the American empire as we are now experiencing it?[9]

In other words, the decline (of the American empire) to which the film refers, is linked to the search for personal happiness, and the demand for individual rights associated with this search (particularly the right to enjoy pleasure) override collective rights and concerns.

The interview above introduces this thesis which the remainder of the film seeks to demonstrate. Later the filmmaker gives Dominique another opportunity to discuss the signs of decline that she sees everywhere. This decline, says the distinguished professor, has manifested itself through the dissolution of the nuclear family, the liberalization of morals, the access of women to positions of power, the fall in the birth rate, the rejection of moral constraints, and the crisis facing traditional values. The film closes with a kind of epilogue, that acts as a final punctuation mark. We no longer need Dominique, the catalyst of the narrative. Arcand, in a playful mood, punctures this microcosm of a civilisation in decline, revealing the profundity of its decadence. The narrative has returned to its starting point. The day after Dominique's damning revelation of Rémy's infidelities, conversation turns to a colleague's adventure with an Italian woman during an international colloquium and its consequences for the colleague's permanent relationship. Arcand insists on imbuing the story of this "academic on the loose" with a kind of distastefulness in its retelling. The final scene is a *mise en abyme*, a story within a story, which summarizes the last 90 minutes. It recalls once more the stagnation of this group of academics and the circularity of their conversation. The strategic place of this scene in the narrative will be considered further in this essay.

Beyond the conventional structure of plot, the narrative progresses through the repetition of the question of decline that Dominique raises at the start of the film. The demonstration is pitiless, irrevocable and relentless. If we may observe a certain linearity in the construction of the narrative (a beginning and an end, with events occurring in chronological order, and interspersed with flashbacks), it is also accompanied by a discursive element which betrays the filmmaker's point of view. In short, the story advances through the retelling and reinterpretation of events; the attitudes of the characters to these events are determined by gender. Therefore, the initial interpretation of an event is later replaced by another version of the same event. The disparity in interpretations is drawn along gender lines and is an effective way of highlighting the constant potential for confrontation between the masculine and feminine universes. Furthermore, given the knowledge acquired by the viewer about the characters through the flashbacks, their assertions also become questionable. Statements made by the group of men resurface and are reformulated by the women, in a way that makes them distinct from their male counterparts. For example, Louise recounts to the other women her participation in a "wife swap". For her it was a way of fortifying her marriage, whereas Rémy tells the other men that the success of his marriage is essentially due to his dishonesty.[10] Likewise, Louise describes an innocent flirtation with her tennis coach, while Rémy boasts of his visit to a brothel on St Lawrence Street with an African colleague.

The film's montage makes us aware of the discrepancy between what the characters say and how they behave in reality. Time does not flow smoothly, its passage has been blocked. It is as if we are experiencing a precise moment in time but the moment itself has become unreliable. In this context the future dissolves. Through the juxtaposition of these two contrasting universes emerges the filmmaker's point of view, often ironic and occasionally cynical. Through his predilection for showing symmetries, Arcand influences both the way in which situations appear and different characters respond. He does not insist that we share the values conveyed by the different characters in the film. On the contrary, he tears them to shreds. He sets up a situation where viewers must constantly question and assess their feelings about the statements and attitudes of this élite in relation to its own decline.

The layering of clichés

The film works essentially through stacking together a series of short scenes which gives us a sense of each character's space and makes the dialogue of primary importance; as a result action must occupy a secondary position. The extreme simplicity of the diegesis, the meeting of a group of university professors for a meal during the weekend, camouflages a second level of discourse. The way in which the film has been montaged and its dialogue crafted reveals an evident bias.

*The Decline of the American Empire* is about the insular world of academia, a world which is represented as stale. It is a dead milieu, and one's "belonging" to it is communicated through a prescribed, rigid code of one's surroundings, mannerisms, habits and references. Accordingly, they live in Outremont (a stylish part of Montreal); spend their weekends at a country house in the Eastern townships; drive BMWs; cook coulibiac and eat Stilton cheese; drink Pierre Mondavi or imported beer; watch Woody Allen films; read Milan Kundera; make references to painters such as Rembrandt, Georges de la Tour, Géricault and Caravaggio; discuss Karl Marx, R D Laing and the historian Fernand Braudel; quote from the later works of Wittgenstein, Arnold Toynbee, Susan Sontag and Patrick Dupond; and speak of the latest international colloquia under the pretext of erotic-intellectual encounters.

In his documentary-like, almost anthropological treatment of this élite, Arcand has chosen what appear to be virtual stock characters. They serve a synecdochic role, creating a microcosm of the intellectual universe. Arcand's model uses the standard features of this kind of filmmaking and, in doing so, repeats its standard flaws: the dependence upon clichés and stereotypes. However, there is much humour and irony to be found in the caricatures that Arcand has created. The different characters' dialogues are punctuated by plays on words, generalizations and allusions. Moreover, the behaviour of the different characters corresponds to how one would expect them to conduct themselves in certain social situations.

The cast of characters

Arcand's characters tend to have several predictable and stereotypical attributes, and clichés are frequently employed to describe them. Firstly, the women. Louise, the only married woman of the group and mother of two children, is portrayed as the archetypal housewife; in addition, she is faithful, naïve and romantic. Throughout the film we are provided with important clues about the characters' identities; we discover their psychological and social idiosyncrasies, as well as their preoccupations. Significantly, Louise's character is defined mainly through comparisons made between her and the other female characters, with whom she shares neither career nor outlook. The film's montage reveals that Louise's affirmations about the solidity of her marriage are based on delusion. The chronic infidelity of her husband, revealed intentionally by Dominique, puts an end to her illusions and her ignorance. As Jean Larose pertinently stresses:

> She corresponds to the mama Plouffe of our own recent "dark age": a mother who is ignorant, alien to herself and who, in the absence of sex and reason, distills the glue that binds the family. Louise is faithful, idealistic and romantic, in contrast with the cynical "realism" of the others. In this cultivated and sensual milieu, she is doubly beyond her depth. Intellectually, she is not up to scratch; as in the ordinary way of those who learn from reading magazines and watching television, she mistakes the right to have an opinion with the authority of knowledge. In arguing against Dominique's thesis of "decline", she shows her intellectual incompetence by saying: "I am sure there are intelligent people who could prove exactly the opposite..."[11]

Diane is described as a divorced ex-housewife who has to deal with the realities of the job market. After sacrificing her career in order to do a hippie-style "return to the land" trip with her husband and then have a family, she finds herself, upon re-entering the job market, working from contract to contract as a university lecturer. She knows that she can hope for nothing better; this knowledge proves hard to accept, as she is the same age as Rémy and Pierre. She is without job security and must also pick up contracts outside the university to support her children. Diane experiences difficulty coping with the hopelessness of the situation, which mirrors the situation for many university graduates in Quebec; she does not attempt to hide the resentment she feels towards her more affluent colleagues:

> When we were studying, I was every bit as smart as the rest of you. But I fell in love, like a woman is supposed to. So while you were at Berkeley and Pierre at Princeton... I rotted in the country, 'cause Roger was on his nature trip. ... I was

happy. I had two kids. Instead of studying demography I learned how to make jam. Now I have to work as a T.A. at one-fifth your salary and without job security. I'm not covered by the best contract in North America. I can't take a year's sabbatical in Brazil. I have to do radio interviews to send my kids to private school. I'll never have tenure.[12]

Most importantly, Diane's character corresponds to the stereotype of the female masochist. She meets up with a rocker type, with whom she discovers and gives in to her masochistic desires. The idea of women as victims who, despite their protestations, actually enjoy this kind of treatment, is implicit in the portrayal of Diane:

FOOTBALL FIELD. DAY
[DIANE and DOMINIQUE doing exercises]
DIANE: He's never made love to me normally. Always from behind like a man. Before him, I couldn't stand that. The first few times he pulled on my hair like a mane. Then he started spanking me on my ass and thighs. Next it was his leather belt. Then he began tying me to the radiator in more and more degrading positions. I had never come like that. But I have to stop. It's getting dangerous.
DOMINIQUE: You're afraid of him?
DIANE: No. It's me I'm afraid of. I'm the one who always wants to go further. I'm the one in control. I've never felt so powerful. The power of the victim is incredible.[13]

History student Danielle (Geneviève Rioux) supports herself and her studies as an "erotic" masseuse. She met Pierre at the massage parlour where she works, rather than through her connection with the university. Although practically mute, when she does express herself she appears to be the least affected by the decadence that permeates the group. She may be capable of discussing the millennium with ardour as she masturbates her future lover, but she also retains some illusions about love. Illusions which, we may be sure, the group will effectively crush.

Finally, there is Dominique, the most senior member of the group. She has dedicated her working life to a university career. She is the only one of the group to have written a book and, moreover, must submit to the sarcasm of her male colleagues. A hardened single woman, her only sentimental attachments have been to her numerous previous lovers who have left her feeling bitter. Her life revolves around the university, which has also become the place to which she has redirected the unhappiness and anger from her personal life. She complains of this unhappiness and of her emotional inadequacy when she tells her young lover: "If only you knew how much that calm look costs me. Every morning I wake up in a rage. ... Anything, nothing, everything. It takes two cups of coffee to hold me together."[14] Her romantic relationships and her friendships always end in disillusion, animosity and recrimination. When Louise dares to challenge her about her book's conclusions and when Dominique's eminent colleagues prefer to keep quiet rather than defend her, Dominique delivers the final blow with her revelation that she has slept with Pierre and Rémy.

The male characters are scarcely more admirable. Young graduate student Alain (Daniel Brière) represents the next generation; he is shown to be malleable, conformist and full of conservatism. He is young, naïve and even appears to be a little stupid. Like his female counterpart, Danielle, he still harbours certain romantic ideas about love; although, in the climate he finds himself, this will certainly not survive for long. The older members of the group have decided to take him under their wing and take charge of his intellectual and sentimental education. They urge him to complete his doctorate, the necessary passport to a university career. There ends the issue of competence and begins intellectual abdication. It is not a passion for research or a thirst for knowledge that now becomes the impetus for doctoral studies and a career in academia; rather, it is the desire to own an apartment in town and a house in a country. Rémy attempts to enlighten Alain and further his sexual education by using the example of two beetles in the process of mating.

> RÉMY'S COTTAGE. HIS OFFICE. DAY. [Close up to two huge dissimilar insects fastened with pins in a frame on the wall. Zoom out to show Alain and Rémy in front of the frame]
> RÉMY: Two Borneo Heteropteryx. For 100 years, entomologists searched for the male of this one and the female of this one. A major issue in biology. Until one day they found the two of them screwing. He was the male to her.
> ALAIN: It seems impossible. She's a reptile and he's an insect.
> RÉMY: They have one thing in common.
> ALAIN: What?
> RÉMY: Fucking. Think about it. [close up on the frame][15]

This brief lesson in biology constitutes a kind of wildlife metaphor for the relationships between men and women recounted in *The Decline*. "Fucking", to paraphrase Rémy, is the only common denominator that can bind, albeit ephemerally, the most disparate individuals. Alain quickly learns his lesson and will end up in the arms of Dominique, a sexually experienced woman, many years his senior.

Claude, the homosexual in the group, does not escape banalization, ghettoization or being shown as out of touch, any better than his colleagues. The narrative provides him with several attributes that in fact are homosexual clichés: an aesthete, a good cook and a sympathetic listener for disillusioned heterosexuals. He is the most humane of all the male characters. He understands the women better than any of the other men and, as a result, is the recipient of their confidences. However, there is also an element inherent in his homosexuality that appears threatening. We see him pass blood in his urine. He is part of a high-risk group, in terms of AIDS. He is shown walking along the upper pathways of the Mount Royal park, an area in Montreal well-known for homosexual cruising. Claude also admits to his colleagues that he has frequented the saunas of downtown Los Angeles and the most dangerous bars of the St Paul quarter in Hamburg. Homosexuality is associated with death, hence the references to painters such as Géricault and Caravaggio, who painted twilight scenes. This association in turn suggests another, frequently alluded to in the representation of homosexuals in films: that of homosexuality with masochism. The affiliation that exists between the homosexual Claude and the masochistic Diane is not accidental. Significantly, it is Claude that becomes the target for Mario's (Diane's lover) brutal and sadistic sarcasm; Mario (Gabriel Arcand) is the one disturbing and atypical character in this closed circle. In short, this heterosexual vision of homosexuality is revealing in its distribution of stereotypical roles, sexual as much as professional. Male homosexuality in *The Decline* is represented as a marginal lifestyle.

Rémy is a university professor in the history department. Married for the last fifteen years and the father of two children, he is the prototype of the "génération lyrique", the beneficiaries of the Quiet Revolution.[16] He is the embodiment of the eternal Don Juan who deceives his wife and continues to collect ever more "trophies" attesting to his sexual prowess. He has practically "fucked the entire city of Montreal", says Dominique in front of Louise, who up to this moment has been innocently unaware of the extent of her husband's infidelity. For Rémy, women exist above all as sexual partners; however, this does not prevent them from being threatening. We see how sexual relations for Rémy can easily be transformed into a veritable nightmare. His anxiety about female sexuality is evident when he quotes from Masters and Johnson and the Hite Report:

> That's not all. Then you have to make her come. No piece of cake. You have to find her clitoris. My God! ... A delicate undertaking. Like looking for a needle in a haystack. You rack your brains to recall Masters and Johnson, Shere Hite, the

G-spot debate, Germaine Greer, Nancy Friday. Should you use your fingers, tongue or prick? You sneak a look at her. You think to yourself. "She looks like ... I hope she ... I wonder if ..." It's a hell, absolute hell.[17]

Pierre, likewise the inheritor of the benefits created by the Quiet Revolution, has traded in the work ethic for the pursuit of pleasure, mainly in the form of "a piece of ass". He admits candidly to Alain during the afternoon that he no longer dreams of becoming an important historian of the Arnold Toynbee or Fernand Braudel model. "All I have left is sex or love. What's the difference?"[18] Focused exclusively on the moment, he has embraced hedonism and refuses any form of commitment. His love affairs last a maximum of about two years. When Danielle tells him that she would like to have a child by him as a reminder of their relationship after it has ended, Pierre retorts that he has too poor an opinion of himself to want to procreate and that he would make a bad father. As with Dominique, his only emotional ties are within the intellectual community. It is his true family and one for which he is ready to renounce his biological family: "But I do have a family. Here sitting around this table. I feel closer to this family than to my brother, the insurance broker, or my parents who could never figure me out and complain 'cause I don't go to mass. You're my family."[19]

Finally, Mario, a character who is anti-intellectual, brutal and sadistic, is in part a compilation of characters from Arcand's previous films.[20] As stated earlier, his role is that of the stranger; he is an anachronism in the midst of this circle of intimate friends. His speech and rude behaviour isolate him from the others; he is stigmatized by them, excluded and marginalized. The closed world in which the other characters live has made it inevitable that most of their love affairs have occurred within their own group; together, they form a large self-sufficient family. Mario's presence will act as a catalyst for the disintegration of this family. Although he appears only sporadically onscreen, he is significant in that he "personifies the denial of any thought or culture".[21] Through Mario the criticism thrown at intellectuals, and specifically at these intellectuals, is at its most savage. When he finds himself seated at the same table with this group of academics, he takes no pains to hide his contempt for their manners, sophistication and verbosity. Brusquely, he tells them their discussion is sterile and that they seem to prefer talking about sex to actually engaging in it. Placed among this group, Mario proceeds roughly and incautiously.

RÉMY'S DINING ROOM. EVENING.
[MARIO knocks at the door. DIANE lets him in. She comes back with MARIO, bringing him to the table while holding his hand.]
DIANE: Take off your glasses. Mario, you haven't met Dominique, Louise.
LOUISE: Hello Mario.
DIANE: ... and Danielle.
CLAUDE: [gets up] I'll get you a chair.
[CLAUDE comes back with a chair and his place setting. He settles MARIO at a corner of the table, between DIANE and himself.] Would you like some coulibiac?
MARIO: Some what?
CLAUDE: It's a salmon pie, but I used trout instead of salmon.
DIANE: It's good. It's a Russian recipe.
MARIO: I don't like fish.
CLAUDE: Would you like some Stilton cheese?
MARIO: I'm not hungry.
DIANE: But you didn't eat.
CLAUDE: Have some wine at least.
MARIO: Got any beer. [Claude gets up and goes to the kitchen. Embarrassed silence.]
LOUISE: Do you live around here?
MARIO: Talking to me?
LOUISE: Are you from the area?
MARIO: No.

Mario listens to the conversation for a few minutes. The intellectuals are discussing the life expectancy of men and women. Mario is visibly uninterested and in passing rudely says of the beer that Claude has attentively just handed him, "What's with this beer?" (to Claude) "You like this?" Exasperated, Mario interrupts the conversation and tells Diane he is leaving.

MARIO: One more or less. I've had enough of this.
DIANE: We're still eating.
MARIO: This is a drag.
DIANE: We're talking.
LOUISE: Intellectuals love to talk.
MARIO: All you do is talk. All afternoon they went on about sex. I expected an orgy. Instead the big thrill is a fish pie.
DOMINIQUE: What are you suggesting?
MARIO: When I'm horny, I fuck. What d'you say?
DIANE: Mario please.
MARIO: Well, how 'bout it?

DIANE: Mario.
MARIO: I'll be outside.[22]

Mario provides a kind of satirical counterpoint to the discourse of these intellectuals: his presence suggests that where the word reigns, sex recedes. Heinz Weinmann, in a chapter dedicated to *The Decline*, goes further in emphasizing that Mario is the only character that has remained a real Quebecer:

> While the others, "Québécois" as well, are culinary and sexual butterflies, eating coulibiac rather than "tourtière" (traditional meat pie), stilton instead of "Cracker Barrel" or "P'tit Québec" (popular Quebec brand), drinking French wine or Pilsner Urquell in place of a "good Blue", bottled Contrexéville instead of tap water, preferring black BMW over "four-wheel-drive" jeep convertibles, Mario is the "real" Quebecer. He speaks "joual" and is the caricature of the Quebec of the past, "simple", "child-like", straightforward, who says "everything is alright". He is the caricature of a Quebec with a hard on, rather than a Quebec going limp with intellectuals.[23]

The law of clichés in the jungle of replies

While the inclusion of stereotyped characters in *The Decline* directly serves the needs of the filmmaker, the film's dialogue makes a comparable use of clichés, wordplays, generalizations and ironic, even sarcastic, turns of phrase. This use of exaggeration causes a rupture between fiction and narration, reducing the diegetic content to its simplest expression and forcing the spectator to side with the enunciation. The use of certain clichés and stereotypes has the effect of undermining the film's ostensible realistic representation. The film often becomes ironic and approaches subversion in its exposition of clichés through the use of travesty.

This duplicity, this continual balance between what has already been seen and heard, and irony, is evident in the dialogue of the different characters. The clichés used are abundant: "Intellectuals love to talk"; "Life's a compromise"; "That's why age leads to vice"; "The more you screw around, the more you want to"; "In those days, men liked their women big"; "Intellectuals rarely make good parents"; and so on. These hackneyed phrases are proposed by these members of the intelligentsia as universal truths; they are particular to a culture and the expression of a cultural consensus. The group credits the clichés with the globality they suggest; these hollow phrases belong to the extensive repertoire of clichés of a given culture, a particular society. The sense of universality that these clichés are meant to impart is confirmed in the character's use of grammar: the simple present; indefinite place and time ("in those days", "rarely", etc.); and the definite article ("the") used to further broaden the scope of nouns ("the intellectuals", for instance).[24]

The Other, the foreigner, is also one of the favourite targets of empty statements and generalizations from the characters: "With Orientals, I have this feeling. They're giving my money to their sick brother", says Pierre; "French girls for sparkle", says Rémy; "The Jews and Arabs, fragrant of camphor, the Vietnamese with their scent of orange blossoms", he adds; "I prefer African blacks ... In general, Africans are warm. Of course they're polygamous", Diane emphasizes; "I always come back to Italians. They're impossible, but ..." says Dominique; "Such simple souls, they shout 'Mama' when they come", retorts Diane.

Once again, the universal aspect of their quips and their fixed formulas, always directed at others, resurfaces in the film's dialogue through grammatical signs: verb tenses and the use of "like" for introducing fixed formula comparisons. "Universal" formulas are used by the characters to imbue what is actually individual experience with the authority of universality. There is also the connection between the behaviour of the different characters and their correspondences to certain stereotypical social situations, permitting clichés and stereotypes to be revealed in full. For example, when the women talk of the size of a man's penis and its importance, they are the vehicles used to express a widely held belief; in the process, they strengthen this belief through their reaffirmation. Allusions to premature ejaculation, the importance of the penis's size and the obsession that men have about it, surface throughout the women's discussion of these matters as they relax in the club's Jacuzzi. When Dominique describes her encounter with a Sicilian policeman, an enormous man with a ridiculously small penis, the shortcomings of his equipment are exposed and ridiculed without mercy: "A bit dowdy. Portions somewhat stingy. ... Restored mill, but the works are purely decorative. ... Charming garden, but the fountain is dry. ... Impressive manor, but the tower is in ruins."[25]

Also stereotypical is the fact that female homosexuality is treated as a relatively normal occurrence by the women (two of the women admit rather unsensationally to having slept with other women), whereas the men say they would rather "starve" than have homosexual relations (even though one of the men present is homosexual). A horror, among the men, of discothèques and dancing is another stereotype. Finally, when Rémy offers his assessment to his male companions that one must quite simply lie to one's wife – as Pierre recounts how each of his affairs has automatically ended with the unfortunate girl falling in love with him – their bromidic choice of words attests to the banality that underlies masculine prejudices, and divulges a mode of thinking imbued with misogynist elements.

The film's montage, as it suggests the collision of these two different universes, makes us sense the filmmaker's irony. This irony is achieved through the exchange mechanism that operates between the enunciator and the viewer. It does not function primarily within the diegesis; rather, it is concomitant to the cinéaste's perspective on the diegesis – it eludes the characters themselves. Arcand's particular brand of irony partakes in a critical discursive strategy marked by an oblique aggressiveness; "oblique" inasmuch as humour becomes the outlet for this aggressiveness.[26]

In this respect, the final scene of the film is exemplary. We find ourselves in the kitchen of Rémy's chalet the morning after the eventful evening of revelations:

> [DIANE comes and goes from the table to the bar. She sets the table for breakfast. CLAUDE sits at the table; we see RÉMY already sitting, meditating in silence. PIERRE will join them later. Finally, DOMINIQUE will also come in from the kitchen where she is cooking eggs with ALAIN.]
> DIANE: Like when Robert Turmel returned from Venice.
> CLAUDE: I know. I was with him.
> DIANE: So you heard about this hot affair with an Italian.
> CLAUDE: Come on, he spent one night with some specialist of the Pollaiuolos...
> DIANE: His wife said it was more than one night.
> CLAUDE: One night, he told me so.
> DIANE: Anyway, when he got back, he told his wife.
> PIERRE: He didn't tell her!
> DIANE: But I got this from her!
> PIERRE: He should know.
> DIANE: Dominique can settle this....[27]

The conversation continues, each character offering her/his own interpretation of the event. This scene is a kind of synecdoche of the narrative; it has a "reheated" quality, as if we had somehow already heard it. Arcand presents a situation involving cliché on the one hand, and irony on the other. Multiple versions of the same anecdote force the audience to question what has actually happened and, consequently, the spectators distance themselves from the story. There exists a considerable gap between what the characters say and the discourse that the enunciator delivers. The film's use of humour and irony allows some breathing space in what would otherwise be an overwhelmingly cynical comment on the current state of gender relations.

Variations on the theme of decline

*The Decline of the American Empire* is about a representative group of university academics in a state of decline or moral decay; here are intellectuals who no longer accept or respect their standing as the élite of a culture. Underneath this documentary depiction of an élite in decline lies another portrait, that of a Quebec focused wholly on the antagonism between the sexes without a social purpose. The film describes a way of living that revolves around the cult of the individual and the withdrawal of the subject into a private world. The narcissistic characters that populate *The Decline* have pushed the logic of individualism to the furthest possible extreme and brought the logic of happiness to a point of impasse. These narcissists, ranging from 20 to 40 years of age, are the products of a particular social milieu.[28] They live in a state of constant anxiety. Dominique is haunted by her aloneness; Claude lives in fear of contracting AIDS; and so on. All the characters exhibit in their own way the traits generally associated with pathological narcissism: fear of dependence on others; a feeling of inner emptiness; an incredible repressed rage; having pseudo-revelations about oneself; the calculated seduction of others; nervous jokes made at their own expense; and irony used to dismiss uncomfortable thoughts. Freshly liberated from the grip of tradition, these men and women have a liberal attitude towards sex, although the satisfaction they derive in this area is less than complete. Their lack of interest in the future ensues, in part, from their indifference towards the past. They live for the moment and their obsessions are purely personal and immediate. They are connoisseurs of their own decadence, developing their propensity for navel-gazing while at the same time laughing at themselves. However, these nouveaux narcissists look at their reflections not only to admire themselves, but also to search for flaws, signs of weariness and decrepitude. In this context, it is not surprising that these men and women feel themselves to be decaying in both body and spirit. The pathetic scene where Diane speaks of losing her memory is a convincing example: "I'm getting old. I can't read and take notes for five hours straight. My memory's going too. I had to refer to the Kellogg-Briand Pact. I couldn't remember Briand ... only the name of the cereal Kellogg's Corn Flakes!"[29]

Although the discussion of sex reaches a saturation point in this film, it is also concerned with contemporary Quebec society, the bankruptcy of its collective projects and its return to its own strain of conservatism. The narrative gives us an up-front analysis of a generation of intellectuals, in their thirties and forties, who were the beneficiaries of the Quiet Revolution (which transformed Quebec society in the 1960s). They are members of the Quebec lyrical generation, baby boomers who introduced social, political and cultural changes without conclusively bringing them to term. Another legacy of these changes is that women in Quebec have begun to occupy positions in the public, political and social scene that were traditionally taken by men. *The Decline* also provides us with a scathing portrait of the younger generation, a spineless group limited to a narrow pathway in the social space, lacking a future because they do not have a grasp over the present. They are consistently described in negative terms and shown, above all, as malleable. Throughout the film, it is suggested that this generation lacks credibility ("a generation of visual idiots", says Rémy); they carry a conformist, even reactionary, set of values and attitudes. The two characters of the film in their twenties are university students. Their presence serves to highlight the attitudes and actions of their elders. Near silent witnesses of the behaviour and ideas of the others, these younger characters follow in their well-trodden path. Therefore, the emphasis in *The Decline* is on the older members of the group. They are the products of the Quiet Revolution, and have become apolitical and disillusioned. The film offers a detailed portrait of their private lives while avoiding any explicit reference to contemporary politics. However, if specific reference to the Quebec Referendum of 1980 and the high stakes that it involved for Quebecers are excluded, one should not conclude that the film is without political content. The battle of the sexes is fought against a post-Referendum backdrop. Arcand's characters have lost their self-esteem and are basically depressed. Heinz Weinmann has suggested that the characters have been made in the image of Quebec society, a society that is haunted by its own impotence in the Referendum of 1980:

> In the post-Referendum atmosphere, it's not surprising if the film's characters, created in the image of Quebec society, are experiencing depression, or like Louise, have turned to a king of pharmacological prescription for anxiety (valium, librium, mogadon, sorpax), and to calm their nerves, relieve their insomnia, symptoms forewarning a nervous breakdown.[30]

Following his analysis of the Referendum shortly after its defeat in *Le Confort et l'indifférence* (*Comfort and Indifference*, 1981), Arcand has now worked out a kind of psychoanalysis of the more settled post-Referendum situation by having these Université de Montréal professors lie on his couch. From comfort and indifference, they have moved to a state of depression, which is reinforced by their alienation from their community.

Decline of a milieu certainly, decline of Quebec society absolutely, but this film is also about the decline of the family. Most of the characters, with the exception of the couple that has been married for fifteen years, search for sexual satisfaction that can be found outside the conventions of marriage. Sexuality is a value in and of itself; any reference to the future becomes forbidden and no hope for a lasting relationship is offered. The pursuit of sexual gratification becomes a challenge to any form of affectionate engagement. The personal relations experienced by the characters are random, for they do not offer any guarantee of permanence. The different characters live under a new régime of conviviality, where commitment meets with reproof. If Louise and Rémy have managed to survive as a couple for fifteen years, it is due primarily to neither understanding the other. Each character lives in solitude; they know or come to know that their relationships are ephemeral. Their amorous relations continually hang by a thread in this universe where everything must pass through the sieve of ego-gratification. The future is never mentioned, and in this context there can be no question of children. They are practically absent from the film and could not play a major part. The intellectual community has become a substitute for the traditional Quebec family. If the time of the "revanche des berceaux" (revenge of the cradles)[31] is over, the question of the survival of a francophone Quebec in North America remains; it is a question of numbers, to which Arcand alludes at the beginning of the film, using the character of Rémy as an intermediary.

Finally, while *The Decline of the American Empire* seems to focus on the sexual conduct that has been the result of the "liberation" experienced in Quebec during the 1960s and 1970s, it is, above all, a film about the relationship between the sexes; the issue of the family is not considered with the same thoroughness. Most importantly, *The Decline* scrutinizes the dead end of gender relations. In this masquerade where one may swap one's partner within a given milieu, the idea of a relationship necessarily includes an element of confrontation and an over-emphasis on sexual performance – the new weapons in the battle of the sexes.

*Notes*

[1] See the work of Louise Carrière, *Femmes et cinéma québécois* (Montreal: Boréal Express, 1983).

[2] "Critère d'authenticité de l'existence", quoted from Jean Larose, "Savoir et sexe dans *Le déclin de l'empire américain*", in *La Petite Noirceur* (Montreal: Boréal, 1987): 11.

[3] It is worth outlining some of the events that have marked the recent political history of Quebec. In 1976 the Parti québécois was voted into office. The victory of this nationalist party, which has advocated the separation of

Quebec since its foundation in 1968, and the announcement of a Referendum for 1980 on sovereignty-association (a project seeking the political independence of Quebec while maintaining economic ties with English Canada) created a commotion in the country. The nationalist question, which has been part of the political agenda since the Quiet Revolution (see note 16), between 1976 and 1980 covered the entire field of socio-political discourse in Quebec. The Referendum on the constitutional future of Quebec became the arena of an epic battle between the NON camp (composed of federalists and headed by Prime Minister Pierre Elliott Trudeau) and the OUI camp (comprising the nationalists behind the Premier of Quebec and leader of the Parti québécois, René Lévesque). In 1980 Quebec was thus split in two over the national debate. On 20 May 1980 the federalists won the Referendum (NON: 60%; OUI: 40%). Quebec nationalism was plunged into an unprecedented state of depression that would last almost a decade. The 1980s as a whole were characterized by political disillusionment. Collective movements challenging the established order vanished, and were replaced by the cult of the individual and an egocentric ideology.

[4] He is a teacher at the elementary and high school level in Montreal, and also does some marking for Pierre and Rémy.

[5] Is this inversion of roles part of the logic or the thesis of the film? Any departure from tradition may be interpreted as an indication of decadence.

[6] According to Rémy, he needs four women to be happy, just as the Koran prescribes it: a faithful spouse like Louise; a famous writer, say Susan Sontag; an Olympic high jumper; and a super dirty girl (a real sex maniac).

[7] "est emporté...dans le maestrum broyeur du déclin, de l'effritement, de l'entropie", Heinz Weinmann, "*Le déclin de l'empire américain*: fin du party", *Cinéma de l'imaginaire québécois* (Montreal: l'Hexagone, 1990): 148.

[8] See original French version of this passage in Denys Arcand, *Le Déclin de l'empire américain* (Montreal: Boréal, 1986): 11.

[9] For original French version, see Arcand: 12-14.

[10] Both Rémy and Louise enjoy making these confessions which ultimately, however, actually conceal more than they reveal. The pseudo-avowal of Louise about her participation in exchanging partners shows that she has lied even to herself. Louise justifies her presence at the party by her motives. Following her revelation is Rémy's denial to the other men of ever having participated in any such exchange. The film's editing brings out the delusions which allow the individual members of the couple to maintain their relationship.

[11] Translated from the French: "Elle correspond, dans nos années de petite noirceur, à ce que représentait, naguère maman Plouffe: la mère ignorante, aliénée et totoñne qui, dans le sommeil du sexe et de la raison, distille la colle qui fait tenir la famille. Louise est fidèle, idéaliste et romantique, en contraste avec le "réalisme" cynique des autres. Dans ce milieu cultivé et jouisseur, elle

est doublement dépassée. Sur le plan intellectuel, elle ne fait pas le poids; à la manière ordinaire de ceux qui s'intruisent dans les magazines et devant la télévision, elle confond dans la discussion le droit à l'opinion avec l'autorité du savoir. Contre la thèse de Dominique sur le "déclin", elle a cet argument qui n'est jamais qu'un aveu d'incompétence intellectuelle: "Je suis sûre qu'il y a des savants qui pourraient prouver exactement le contraire..."" (Larose: 10).

[12] For original French version, see Arcand: 113-114.

[13] For original French version, see Arcand: 31-32.

[14] For original French version, see Arcand: 160.

[15] For original French version, see Arcand: 94-95.

[16] The expression "génération lyrique" is borrowed from François Ricard, *La Génération lyrique* (Montreal: Boréal, 1992). The Quiet Revolution (or "Révolution tranquille") was a period of political and social reforms conducted in the early 1960s by Jean Lesage's Liberal government. These reforms, which were an attempt to catch up with the rest of Canada and North America, had a profound impact on all the institutions of Quebec. The aim was to accelerate the process of modernization initiated soon after World War II, but which had been idle for fifteen years under the conservative Union nationale government of Maurice Duplessis. The period starting in 1960, with the election of Lesage's provincial Liberal party, saw the utter rejection of the alienating past and the beginning of an unprecedented rush towards modernization. The Quiet Revolution witnessed the emergence of new intellectual and political élites, together with rejuvenated trade unions (consisting, essentially, of baby boomers), who undertook the foundation of the modern State of Quebec. Many of those who embarked on this project in the 1960s, such as Jacques Parizeau, are still active today.

[17] For original French version, see Arcand: 93.

[18] For original French version, see Arcand: 62.

[19] For original French version, see Arcand: 118.

[20] It is comical that this anti-intellectual is the only one to make explicit reference to the current state of Quebec, which he does in offering Diane a book written by one of Quebec's most nationalist historians, Michel Brunet: *Notre passé, le présent et nous* (Montreal: Fides, 1976). The title that appears on the cover of the book in the film is *Notre passé présent et nous*.

[21] Mario "incarne la négation de toute pensée et de toute culture". (Larose: 14).

[22] For original French version, see Arcand: 119-126.

[23] Translated from the French: "Alors que les autres, "Québécois" pourtant

aussi, papillonnent culinairement et sexuellement dans le monde en mangeant du coulibiac à la place de la tourtière, du stilton au lieu du cheddar Kraft "Cracker Barrel" et du "P'tit Québec", en buvant du vin français ou de la Pilsner Urquell à la place d'une Bleu "bonne rare", du Contrexéville en maxi-bouteilles à la place de l'eau de la "champlure", en conduisant une BMW noire au lieu de "chauffer" une jeep à quatre roues tractrices décapotable, Mario est le gars "d'icitte", qui parle "joual", caricature d'un Québec d'antan "simple", "enfantin", qui va droit au but, qui agit parce "y n'a pas de problèmes". Caricature d'un Québec "bandant" plutôt qu'en "débandade" comme celui de ces huit intellectuels." (Weinmann: 168).

[24] On the subject of clichés, see the work of Anne Herchberg-Pierrot, "Problématiques du cliché", *Poétique* 43 (September 1980): 334-345.

[25] For original French version, see Arcand: 102-103.

[26] See GROUPE $\mu$, "Ironique et iconique", *Poétique* 36 (November 1978): 442.

[27] For original French version, see Arcand: 167-168.

[28] The expression "narcissists" is borrowed from Christopher Lasch, *The Culture of Narcissism: American Life in an Age of Diminishing Expectations* (New York: W W Norton, 1978).

[29] For original French version, see Arcand: 114-115.

[30] Translated from the French: "Dans ce contexte postréférendaire, il n'est pas étonnant que les personnages du film, à l'image de la collectivité à laquelle ils appartiennent, ont connu leur "dépression", comme Louise...ou ont tout simplement eu recours à la pharmacopée anxiolytique (valiums, libriums, mogadons, sorpax), pour calmer leurs angoisses, combattre leurs insomnies, symptômes avant-coureurs des dépressions." (Weinmann: 146).

[31] Until the 1940s, the birth rate in French Canada was significantly higher than in English Canada, which resulted in an increase of Quebec's demographic weight in the country as a whole. At the time, certain French-Canadian nationalists were projecting that, thanks to this "revenge of the cradles", francophones would eventually form the majority in Canada. Unfortunately for them, the babyboom phenomenon in North America boosted the birth rate in the English-speaking provinces, and in 1951 the anglophone population was growing at the same pace as its francophone counterpart.

# Arcand's double-twist allegory: *Jesus of Montreal*

Bart Testa

I. Synopsis: a Jesus in Montreal

Moments after his performance in a stage adaptation of Dostoyevsky's *The Brothers Karamazov*, actor Pascal Berger (Cédric Noël) greets a friend, Daniel Coulombe (Lothaire Bluteau), who mentions that he is about to play Jesus. Daniel is also an actor, and a dramaturge of great, though quiet, brilliance and integrity. He has been contracted to revise a Passion pageant by a priest, Father Leclerc (Gilles Pelletier), for a Montreal church. Daniel assembles a troupe of four actors, drawing them away from pointedly unartistic pursuits, such as dubbing porno films and posing for perfume commercials. He researches the life of Jesus intently and produces a wholly new text, transforming the play from stale piety to a magically powerful, but decidedly modern version reflecting current historical scholarship on Jesus. After a very successful opening night in which he himself plays Jesus, Daniel is offered connections that could make him a celebrity. On the other hand, however, the clerics in charge disapprove of the unorthodox production and demand heavy revisions. Leclerc finally orders the show to be cancelled. However, the members of the troupe defiantly perform their original play; during a scuffle with security guards, the cross is toppled with Daniel/Jesus on it and he is hurt. At first the injury seems slight, but as he and the two women of the troupe wander about Montreal, its seriousness becomes apparent and Daniel collapses in the metro. Soon afterwards, he is diagnosed in hospital as being brain-dead. An alert doctor asks if he may remove Daniel's organs, and the film follows these to two patients, a man whose life is saved by Daniel's 30-year-old heart, and an Italian-speaking woman whose vision is restored with his transplanted eyes.

The city of Montreal which surrounds the hero, and which he must traverse on several occasions, is a place where art is travestied, degraded and bruised by commercial culture. In this commercial city there is, effectively, no art, only mass-media products and vulgar celebrity. Much of the action of *Jésus de Montréal* (*Jesus of Montreal*, 1989) concerns the hero calling disciples out of this commercial city and back to art: the project of mounting an authentic theatre piece. The play is both redemptive as art for these actors and a Passion of Christ.

Rhymes between the process of creating authentic theatre and the Christian salvation drama initiate the film into allegory.

## II. An unlikely allegorist

For Denys Arcand to film any Christological allegory is initially puzzling. As Ben Shek details in a recent paper on the director, Arcand has persistently subjected religion, and Catholicism in particular, to mockery and derision in many previous films, documentary and fiction alike.[1] Indeed, the dominant tenor of his filmmaking is political, its tone also rather famously sarcastic and cynical. These factors suggest Arcand is among the least likely directors to make a religious work. Nevertheless, Shek observes that the title of *Jesus of Montreal* is characteristic of the director's "habitual binarism".[2] The essence of Shek's term is this: Jesus/Montreal – the meanings the names carry into the film are antinomic, and the director sustains opposition of the person and the city throughout.

Very near the end of the film, just before his fatal collapse, Daniel makes a delirious last speech. It is a collage of paraphrased apocalyptic sayings voiced to the indifferent, mystified patrons waiting for the metro, prefaced with a variant on the famous pericope "not a stone will remain upon a stone" in which Jesus prophecies the fate of Jerusalem. Daniel says: "Big buildings like this, the big projects, they will all be destroyed...one day". Beside a giant advertising poster featuring a close-up of Pascal Berger's face, having become the visage of "L'homme sauvage", the poster boy for a line of men's cosmetics, the body of Daniel's speech climaxes with a warning against false saviours. The poster provides an apt juxtaposition.

In his preface to his published script Arcand speaks of the paradoxes and doubling, contradictions which he says gave rise to the film.[3] In the light of the "end of history" Arcand attempts in his previous film, *Le Déclin de l'empire américain* (*The Decline of the American Empire*, 1986), with which *Jesus of Montreal* forms a diptych of sorts, the director's resort to biblical eschatological allegory, so glaring in this apocalyptic speech, begins to seem less puzzling, for in both films the very ground seems to tremble beneath the characters.

There are, however, temptations that we should avoid. It is naïve, for example, to think that the film asks the questions, "What if Christ came back to the modern metropolis?" or "What would it mean to retell a life of Christ in Montreal?" Such questions are probably the wrong ones, even if posed in relation to hypothetical allegorical films, and some actual ones, such as *Parable* (Fred A Niles, 1964), that could plausibly answer with sentimental Christian humanism. They are simply misdirected at *Jesus of Montreal*.

Nevertheless, there are some strong and seductive impressions that lead in this direction. These arise especially from the performative tone of the film, so different in its warmth from Arcand's usual harsh treatment of characters. Daniel Coulombe's virtues are indeed rather Christ-like. His asceticism, ease with children, and absoluteness are deftly combined with moral tolerance. The affair the self-proclaimed "bad priest" Leclerc has with Constance Lazure (Johanne Marie-Tremblay), one of the troupe's members, prompts no criticism from Daniel. Nor does he lash out at the cleric's cowardice, hypocrisy and final betrayal, despite great provocation. In contrast, his unwavering certainty as an artist, then his anger and violence aroused by the contempt shown to actors at an advertising audition, and his forthright self-awareness under psychiatric interrogation all mark his character with strength as well as sweetness. Together, the things which Arcand lets Daniel reveal of himself, as well as the enigma of the things he withholds, conform to sophisticated stereotypes of Jesus. Moreover, Lothaire Bluteau's performance as Daniel brings these virtues to the screen with quiet conviction rarely seen in Arcand's films. Daniel's precedents are few – the occasional privileged portraits in the filmmaker's documentaries and their fictive epigone, the textile worker Dolorès of *Gina* (1974). However, taken simply as impressions arising from acting and characterization, Daniel's virtues are themselves of no determining significance, as Bluteau's sadly replicate performance in Bruce Beresford's *Black Robe* (1991) illustrates. Daniel only assumes Christological weight and value through the film's narrative allegorization.

III. Ellipsis, narration and structure

Arcand develops *Jesus of Montreal* as an allegory through the narrative articulations of the film, in a manner at once distributive and structural, momentary and fine-grained. As is his tendency, Arcand does not narrate this film in a classical-style continuum but in a rather elliptical fashion. Although Arcand is not a particularly innovative or subtle stylist, he is assured and self-aware in this respect. Analysis of this allegorical film must therefore begin with consideration of the director's elliptical stylistics.

In the classical style, exemplified by, but not exclusive to Hollywood cinema, filmic narration strictly maintains the pretence that narrative structure arises and is resolved immanently. Narrative theorists sometimes explain this by situating classical style on the side of *histoire* (or "story") where the narrative seems "to tell itself", rather than *discours* ("discourse"), where enunciation is marked and so operates at some remove from the diegesis of the work.[4] If we understand ellipsis to be any break in spatio-temporal continuity, it follows that we do not usually take ellipsis to be a feature of the classical style, which tends to be a famously seamless or even invisible narrative system. Nevertheless, it is obvious that classical filmmaking must also to some degree be elliptical. Any shift from one space and time to another – that is, any shot change whatsoever – marks an ellipsis. Such a shift also presents a threat to the diegetic continuum and, therefore, to the pretence of diegetic immanence. In the classical style, such a threat is regulated by a narrational system that operates both within and across scenes, usually by motivating all space-time shifts to strictly narrative exigencies, such as characters' gestures and dialogue, looks and, more widely, movements from one scene of action to another. Classical films maintain the immanent diegetic ground for all such shifts, however complicated, by this kind of narrational motivation. Even special cases, such as chases or parallel narration, which do give rise to spatial disjunctions, prove negotiable by syntagmatic figures of temporal simultaneity and are habitually mastered by closure of all such shot series.[5]

Ellipticality, therefore, is not a concept that distinguishes between kinds of filmmaking, but should be considered a concept of degree or deployment. Although he is not an assertive formal innovator, and could hardly be said to have founded a different cinematic form, Arcand relies on ellipsis to assume a more directly structural function than it plays in conventional narration. In fact, ellipsis provides a key to understanding his stylistics. If we allow that *histoire* and *discours* are also concepts of degree, and do not represent strictly different kinds of narration, Arcand is simultaneously a formally conventional narrative filmmaker and a rather more discursive one than the classical style of narration customarily implies.[6]

Although he has often been mistakenly associated with *cinéma direct*, a documentary style that, in the terms we have been using, sought to radicalize diegetic immanence and ground meaning in immediate and pure *histoire*, Arcand often complicates the diegesis. For example, in *On est au coton* [*We're Fed Up*, 1970] he uses a double diegesis – the distant past and the near-past – and he mediates these by voice-overs, at times even by the intervention of a lecturer, and through strong cross-cutting, which structures his film around *discours* to generate comparisons and contrasts.

Important aspects of his documentary style of fashioning narration recur in Arcand's fiction films. In *Gina* and *The Decline*, for example, the narrative arenas are apparently singular; at the level of the "story" space-time is generally unified.[7] However, the use of contrastively twinned syntagmas – and sometimes elongated alternating syntagmas, or cross-cutting – shuffles narration between two markedly disjoined facets of the diegesis, and sets them in contrastive relationships. This type of mild fracture of the diegesis occurs so often that we might well take it as emblematic of the director's developed style, and the stylistic key to interpreting his films. In *Gina* the twinned structure counterpoints the making of a film within the film – it is a documentary-in-process on textile workers – with the narrative of stripper Gina's visit to Louiseville, a small industrial town in Quebec. The resulting twinned narrational structure is sustained (although sometimes slowed, sometimes quickened), for the whole film.[8]

The celebrated first extended segment of *The Decline* uses a similar twinned structure through alternating montage. Here the male professors cook and talk at the chalet while the women talk and work-out at the gym. While this cutting pattern is not sustained for the whole film, the opening alternation firmly establishes *The Decline*'s interpretive protocols. The pattern also recurs sufficiently often later in the film to justify saying that alternation organises the whole text and that this structural feature provides a key to its interpretation.

In *Gina* diegetic fracture is demarcated along twinned class lines, and the film's theme arises through contrasts between them; in *The Decline* the demarcation moves along gender divisions. The ellipses between scenes and the cross-cutting which creates an open series that shuttles between them exceed mere configuring of temporal simultaneity, or other diegetic negotiations found in classical film narration. They open a site from which Arcand projects discursive formations upon his narratives. Indeed, his consistent use of alternating syntagmatic figures both widen and accent ellipsis in order to engender staggered or "zigzag" structures of narration. Such structures promote counterpoint and juxtaposition, thematic effects that the director supports on the soundtrack with similarly assertive cross-fades, ironic dialogue matches and music.

As a preliminary summary, there are two general consequences of Arcand's developed style that might be mentioned here. The first is a partial diffusion of the classical style's linear narrative enchainment in favour of what can be termed a diagrammatic narrativity, often assuming a zigzag shape between an emphatically twinned or faceted diegesis. Its purpose is not directly to rupture classical narration, but to loosen and twist it in order to open discursive sites. The second effect of the style is to situate the narrational operator, and consequently the viewer's reception, in an interpretive position at some critical remove from the diegesis. My slightly idiosyncratic choice of the term "narrational operator" rather than the more familiar "narrator" is intended to emphasize that narration in Arcand's films is not a matter of another literal voice – as voice-overs are in documentaries – but a matter of his endistanced deployment of ellipses in the process of a somewhat emphatically discursive procedure of signification.

IV. Daniel's circle and the commercial city

In *Gina* and *The Decline of the American Empire* the features of the director's stylistics I have been outlining can readily be disclosed in quite straightforward formal terms, for they are largely a matter of Arcand's contrastive syntagmatic arrangements and sound-image counterpoints. In *Jesus of Montreal*, however, Arcand does not use alternating syntagmas or other montage figures nearly so often to build up parallel blocks of contrasting material. Although there are instances, such as the cross-cutting between the contradictory theatre critics reporting on Daniel's triumphant performance, these are occasional comical exceptions to the style of the film. Instead, the director freights the film with a semantic significance, derived from the Christ story; much of the narration now shuffles the viewer back and forth between the film's diegesis and another, already counterpointing story, the life of Jesus, which serves as the verticalized paradigm. This mode of the discursive double, in which the film's story invokes correspondences with the paradigm story, is the obvious and conventional way that *Jesus of Montreal* is to be seen as an allegory. However, I want to postpone discussing the film's allegorical system of correspondences until something further has been said of its style. In fact, the initial obviousness and conventionality of the film's allegorization proves more complex than it appears.

Arcand's alternative to his customary reliance on cross-cutting and other montage-based tactics in *Jesus of Montreal* is, in formal terms, a direct concatenation of scenes. But this should not be taken to mean that Arcand has resorted to the classical style's linearity. On the contrary, ellipsis remains a conspicuous feature of style in this film as well. Relying strictly on straight cuts, Arcand in places shears off episodes, prunes away preparations to succeeding scenes, and generally opens gaps between scenes; in other places he distends shots and whole scenes beyond their conventional narrative function. These strategies again generate a zigzag structure, and juxtaposition is again a persistent strategy. But it occurs laterally, through the rhythms Arcand uses both to accent the succession of scenes and to articulate their internal dynamics.

For example, Arcand cuts directly from a complex series of shots depicting a conversation between Daniel and his freshly recruited actor René (Robert Lepage) to a single tracking long take showing a nearly naked woman undulating dreamily past a fountain. Only the vaguest hint in the previous sequence prepares us to identify this overdesigned *mise en scène*. The woman's image, exotically different from the shots preceding it, is so slow and eroticised that it temporarily eclipses the narrative connection to what came before. Here Arcand's contrasts – the rhythms and iconic tones of the two scenes are sharply distinct – produce disjunction between the two scenes. The viewer is left momentarily at sea in terms of narrative sense, and Arcand stretches that moment by holding the track for some time. The contrasts between the scenes also express sharp connotative differences: between a creative group dialogue that is forming in Daniel's artistic troupe and the spectacle of commercial eroticism; between a fluid exchange of the characters' dialogue and their images and this fetishized, silent spectacle. The woman is Mireille (Catherine Wilkening), the actress René mentioned, adding, "She may not be the type you are looking for". This dialogue set-up could be said to mediate the two scenes narratively – we do cut to her – but the gulf between René's remark and this sexy vision, which is not identified as Mireille for a long while, forces a strong connotative juxtaposition on us, before we grasp the denotation, for it is well in excess of the normal narrative purpose of the transition.

This transition might be merely confusing and satiric, except that it is an episode in a long repetitive segment where Daniel draws his four actors from their compromised jobs. The segment provides ample opportunity for Arcand to develop a system of contrasts between Daniel's project (which is shown as intimate scenes of summons and developing comradeship) and the fixed, elongated tableaux characteristic of the media-work of the commercial city. In fact, despite the narrative linearity, tied together by Daniel's round of visits assembling his actors, ellipses – by which I mean a refusal to seam the difference between types of scenes – generate a structure no less diagrammatic and contrastive than found in other Arcand films. As another example, Arcand cuts directly from a warm, intimate conversation between Daniel and Constance to a porno dubbing session, which he distends into an comic tour de force for Rémy Girard (Martin) when he is ordered to do the voices of two men "going at it" on the screen.

In the first half of the film, before the passion-play has been performed, such systematic juxtapositions between Daniel's circle and the media industry dominate the film. Executing transitions elliptically between these two types of scene, and then extending the latter media-industry scenes (such as the dubbing sessions and the perfume commercial) well beyond their immediate narrative purpose into vulgar and absurd tableaux, Arcand postpones the forward movement of the film sufficiently to regularize juxtaposition as a binary structure generating its own significance: precisely, Jesus/Montreal. On one hand there is Daniel and his troupe of artists; on the other, the surrounding commercial city of media exploitation. Although after the brief triumph of the passion-play, the tone and themes of *Jesus of Montreal* change – the film darkens and its meaning twists – this contrastive system of structured episodes does not.

Arcand's style, what I have generalized as his diagrammatic narrativity, operates in *Jesus of Montreal* not only through elliptical succession. As the examples offered suggest, it is also important to see how Arcand uses ellipsis within scenes – entering them late or leaving them early, distending them before delivery of their narrative point or shortening them into suggestive icons. The internal dynamics of his scene-articulation, which in this film are unusually controlled, provide another principal register through which episodes, images and dialogue take on thematic weight in *Jesus of Montreal*. Particularly true are the crucial instances where we are led by such accentuated rhythmic effects to discern repetitions, to draw comparisons and to interpret sections of the film as thematically – and intertextually – intertwined, even when they are narratively distant from each other.

Two examples can clarify Arcand's purpose and prepare us to address the film as an allegorical whole. These examples are Pascal Berger's three brief appearances and the two scenes where Father Leclerc defends his compromised priesthood. As noted above, the film opens with a stage performance. It is so abrupt a start that we seem to have entered into the film without preliminary on a close-up of banknotes being lifted from a bible. When the next shot assumes a more theatrical distance and angle, we soon realise that we are watching a play within the film. In fact, it is the climax of a heavily revised scene of the third confrontation with Smerdiakov (played by Pascal) from Part 4, Book 11, Chapter 8 of *The Brothers Karamazov*. Differently from the original, Arcand's version concludes with Smerdiakov delivering an anguished speech against suicides while he prepares to hang himself.

Then, after the curtain falls, while Pascal is being applauded, Arcand cuts to a close-up of the advertising executive Denise Quintal (Monique Miller) in the audience telling her companion, "I want his head". She actually means she wants his face for her "L'homme sauvage" campaign, but in the terms the film will quickly develop, Pascal's sell-out of his art to the commercial media will trope literally on Quintal's predatory expression. Her success will "mean his head", Pascal's artistic death. The stage-play passage is slow and ponderous with overwrought drama. Quintal's passage is swift and nervous with brittle cleverness. Even within scenes, from the outset, Arcand doubles the film's tenor rhythmically as well as textually.

Much later, Pascal attends the première of Daniel's passion-play. After the performance, in the midst of a busy scene – an exact comic repetition of the post-curtain *Karamazov* party, complete with choppy one-liners and cartoonish minor characters, such as the drama critic

Garibaldi – Pascal becomes distraught, tears himself from the group and flees the scene. In fact, he duplicates, though swiftly now, the tone of his previous stage acting. The next time we see his face, it is as the "head-shot" in the metro poster for Quintal's campaign that looms over Daniel's last speech.

The carefully reworked Dostoyevsky scene broadcasts several suggestions. Firstly, Smerdiakov's irreligious despair and the murderous anguish of the modern world it expresses will be answered by Daniel's biblical passion-play. And yet, these dire themes are enfolded by Dostoyevsky's novel in a profoundly religious, indeed allegorical fiction, already a modern equivalent of the Passion. Secondly, the climax of the hanging cannot help but suggest Judas, the betrayer of Christ. Not only is Smerdiakov himself complicatedly a modern Judas-figure, but in Arcand's bowdlerization he is also, like Judas, a despairing suicide. When the distraught Pascal flees after seeing the passion-play – which has no Judas of its own – he, in effect, supplements its dramatis personae, out of the frame of the pageant's performance. In the presence of Daniel's theatre art, Pascal's sell-out of his own art to Quintal sends him into Judas-like despairing flight. In his last appearance, as "L'homme sauvage", he has hanged himself on the subway wall, the staring icon of artistic betrayal and suicide.

Typical of the film's host of minor characters, Pascal's moments in *Jesus of Montreal* are brief and so minor and so widely spaced that one might scarcely recall who he is across the whole film. However, if we attend to the way Arcand fashions his film's constellation of allusions and self-references, using near-duplicate scenes and especially rhythmic repetitions in his direction and cutting, even in this minor case we see what it means for Pascal to move from volcanically passionate Dostoyevskian theatre to frozen advertising icon: he becomes a "Judas" to art. There is more, however. After his *Karamazov*, in the scene where he is being adulated, Pascal turns from the risibly effusive Garibaldi – who is just then declaring him "the greatest actor of your generation" – to Daniel and declares, "Excuse me, but there is a good actor". It is the very first time Arcand shows us Daniel, and Pascal directly identifies his character/talent as greater than his own. Promptly, Daniel says he is going to play Jesus, announcing this name first to us, before his own, and then adds, "I came to get inspiration".

This is a mutual recognition scene, a common expository device in film scriptwriting. However, when reading *Jesus of Montreal* as a Christological allegory, the scene, placed near the very start, can be seen to correspond to the episode of mutual recognition between Jesus and John the Baptist that in the Gospels prefaces Christ's ministry. Even the inane Garibaldi's "this generation", which recalls the prophets' use of the expression, suggests this. Moreover, Quintal's play on Pascal's "head" can be interpreted retroactively, for the Baptist lost his head as Herod's payment for Salomé's dance. And while Denise Quintal is no Salomé, she does correspond to Salomé's legendary mother, who plotted her daughter's dance and the deal that cost the Baptist his life. As an advertising agent she later auditions dancers for the lewd delight and profit of those instantly recognisable kings of Canadian commerce, beer company executives. (The equivalences here are exemplary of what critics call Arcand's sarcasm.) Pascal's last appearance in the film, his head served up on a platter, is the garish advertising poster, confirming Quintal has got what she said she wanted of him.

Although analysing this example has drawn us towards interpretation of *Jesus of Montreal* as a system of allegorical correspondences, my purpose at this point is only to suggest its tactical elaboration. The example is intended to indicate that Pascal's slippages, and obviously conflations of identity as well, are pointedly a matter of textual roles assigned and revised – constellated from outside the diegesis, as *discours* which the viewer grasps and extends across the film's episodes and images – rather than developed within the immanent diegesis. None of this is a matter of Pascal's character psychology, for he is barely possessed of personality. Typical of all the characters in *Jesus of Montreal*, Pascal does not know the allusive names pasted on him, or the significance of the allegorical gestures Arcand has him make as the text's Judas or John. These are a function of the shifting positions the director Arcand assigns him – assigns everyone – in the unfolding diagrammatic narrative of the film.

Our second example is Father Leclerc. The *Karamazov* play also intersects with Leclerc's speeches, although at a considerable remove. The words Arcand assigns Pascal/Smerdiakov are not entirely those Dostoyevsky gave him; some of the speech paraphrases the discourse on the Grand Inquisitor. As a narrative agent, Leclerc is true to his name ("the cleric"). He speaks for the priests and acts like their conspiring biblical equivalents, as Daniel's nemesis and *provocateur* of his Passion. But Leclerc's two apologies for his priesthood depart strikingly from his narrative agency, for here he speaks of himself.

When Daniel arrives at Constance's loft, he interrupts her tryst with Leclerc in the upper bedroom. The priest sheepishly emerges and then launches into a long explanation – starting "I'm not a very good priest" – of how he became a cleric to escape poverty, how he travelled and grew to love the theatre. Finally, he confesses, he remains a priest because he stills fears poverty, and refuses to surrender the comfort of the rectory to take up Constance's offer to "move in here". With a series of fixing close-ups and pinioning pans, Arcand's camera follows Leclerc, who is anxious to escape but driven to explain himself. Leclerc is unmistakeably pathetic, a coward and a lecher, the fornicating cleric caught out, reduced to fingering the necktie he has yet to put back on (a sign of his falsehood).

Nothing about Leclerc's character changes. However, his second apologetic speech, although again made to Daniel and Constance, and strongly marked as rhyming with the scene in the loft, comes off differently. Now he is in his church, wearing his Roman collar; his movements and gestures visually draw the sanctuary into his words, and Arcand's camera centres on him. He attacks Daniel for "undermining the lives of those around you". He defends the Church and his own ruined priesthood. At least, he says, he performs the role the institution has been given to perform: to comfort the sick, the poor and the miserable. "Even a bad priest is still a priest", he insists. Leclerc is still pathetic and a coward; he gains no personal stature in the film. But this apology is no longer just a defence of his comforts, and that is something Daniel and Constance, significantly, fail to distinguish between his two speeches. His evocation of the people who desperately need his compromised priesthood is stirring, and something Leclerc says will even be proved to be true. He says to Daniel, "I don't know if you are familiar with our hospitals, but if you're looking for a bit of comfort, you're much better off coming here." These are prophetic words, for Daniel will soon die from neglect at one of those hospitals, abandoned among the broken and sick.

The text Arcand gives Leclerc to speak is a humiliated rendition of Dostoyevsky's arrogant discourse of the Grand Inquisitor. This famous passage is perhaps the greatest (if also the most darkly ironic) text in modern literature justifying the ways the Church disburdens people of their freedom and their suffering alike, and all really in accord with their deepest human desires. Closing a circle opened by Pascal's despairing speech on stage, Leclerc goes to the core of the issue when he contrasts the Church's work comforting the poor and sick with modernity's bromides – psychoanalysis, pop culture, modern medicine and, emphatically, the historiographical truth that Daniel has woven so artfully into his updated passion-play. Even when it mystifies, when its priests are cowards and fornicators and censors of truth, Leclerc says, the Church knows and answers to human misery and despair. Modern nostrums, including Daniel's art, can make no reply to this suffering. The effect of Leclerc's speech is deeply ambiguous, not least because it acts as a prolepsis. *Jesus of Montreal* soon opens to the nightmare of the suffering city, the site of Daniel's own passion.

V. Allegorization and correspondences

Although I have already commented several times on taking the film as a Christological allegory, sought to describe Arcand's film style and diagrammatic narrative method in *Jesus of Montreal,* and have engaged in some interpretation in order to do so, discussion of the film's allegory as a whole has been postponed. It will now be addressed more directly.

By allegory is meant a story or other representation that rests upon a previous text, itself a story or a doctrine, that the allegory repeats under disguise, like a coded symbolism, or through a system of displacements. Allegorical repetition is never exactly that, for allegory always also interprets in order to represent its predecessor, and so raises questions of interpretation and comprehension.[9] One of the key questions lies in the difference between the previous text and the allegory which acts as its supplement. In effect, when the original appears again "under" the allegory, it appears as a paradigm or vertical structure. One interprets not the allegory itself directly, but effectively one interprets *through* its sequence to that structure. Such features of allegories prompt Craig Owens to the following summary formulation:

> Allegory concerns itself ... with the projection – either spatial or temporal or both – of structure as sequence; the result, however, is not dynamic, but static, ritualistic, repetitive. It is thus the epitome of counter-narrative, for it arrests narrative in place, substituting a principle of syntagmatic disjunction for one of diegetic combination. In this way allegory superinduces a vertical or paradigmatic reading of correspondences upon a horizontal or syntagmatic chain of events.[10]

The biblical life of Christ is tripartite: the Infancy portion runs from the Annunciation to the meeting with John the Baptist and Jesus's baptism, the preface of the ministry. It should be noted, however, that The Gospel According to Mark, the earliest of the Gospels to be composed, has no Infancy.[11] Although the four canonical Gospels differ in their inclusion and distribution of specific episodes, aside from this exception of Mark, they conform in the larger structural units. The ministry opens with the calling of the apostles, develops with Jesus's preaching and miracles (which climax with the raising of Lazarus) and concludes just before the Psalm Sunday entry into Jerusalem. The Passion begins with the announcement of the failure of the ministry in Jerusalem and concludes with the Crucifixion and Resurrection.

Segmenting the first long section of Arcand's film, when Daniel recruits his actors and the passion-play is prepared, leads us to see it as a set of correspondences to, and a structure of episodes homologous with, the ministry of Jesus. Arcand is highly programmatic about this, pointedly recalling episodes in the life of Christ and staging equivalent episodes here. Mapping Daniel's story on the Gospels, Arcand prefaces the ministry, as discussed above when we looked at the encounter with Pascal, with an equivalent of the encounter with the Baptist. Daniel's past remains mysterious, his biography suitably undefined and, partly because of this, his presence is a little enigmatic. (This is Mark's theme of the so-called "Messianic secret".) Interspaced between the calling of his disciples – the equivalent in the film is the long section discussed above where Daniel recruits his actors – Daniel's parallel to Christ's "fulfilling the Scriptures" is doing his historical research, consulting a theologian and working in a library. In the scriptures Jesus's calling of the Apostles is abrupt and steadily serial, while his acquisition of female disciples is leisurely and occasional. Arcand combines both scriptural episodes – his equivalent is Daniel summoning the actors out of their inartistic jobs. Mireille is Mary Magdalene, while Constance Lazure is obviously the sister of Lazarus. However, Constance is also, in an ironic turn, "the woman caught in adultery" with Leclerc (in the Gospels priests preside over the stoning of the woman, which is interrupted by Jesus). Such conflations and doublings of character-codes are common in allegories. In addition, just as in those places where the Gospels indicate Jesus had women disciples, Daniel's scenes with Mireille and Constance are warmer and more domestic than his relationships with the two male actors Martin and René. However, it must be added that these relationships, while modernized, are not in the slightest sense erotic.

In the scriptures, Jesus's long cycle of miracles and preaching makes up much of the ministry. These are radically encapsulated in the first performance of Daniel's passion-play. The Gospel climax of Jesus's miracles is the raising of Lazarus, and the performance not only represents this miracle inside its text but, as a whole, Daniel's passion-play also resurrects the dead Lazarus of a church pageant into compelling modern religious drama. This claimed correspondence requires some explanation.

Daniel's play is the long and complex centrepiece of *Jesus of Montreal*. It is also the most beautifully crafted and compellingly performed passage in the whole of Arcand's filmmaking. Yet, although it constitutes an indulgence in aesthetic pleasure extraordinary for this obdurately didactic filmmaker, the teaching force of the pageant is still very pronounced. The play is objectively Daniel's occasion to demonstrate the redemptive power of art, as opposed to the vulgar seductions of commercial media culture. However, the aesthetics of that demonstration are Brechtian. The play is a theatrical "montage" deploying abrupt shifts in modes that triangulate emotionally charged speeches – like the Gospels, these are taken from the *ipsissima verba* (the "very words") of Jesus – spectacle (e.g. the Crucifixion) and interruptive scholarly expositions. The latter are drawn from historiographical research, but as Daniel has rewritten this research (as a Brechtian might), and as they are in collision with the speeches and the spectacle, these expositions powerfully refresh the Passion drama. Indeed, Daniel restores the passion-play by injecting it with history and, while the knowability of the so-called "historical Jesus" is repeatedly questioned, Christ's historico-political significance is only thereby augmented.

It may initially seem perverse to suggest that in *Jesus of Montreal*'s allegory the performed passion-play is the summation of Jesus's miracles. However, this is, first of all, an instance of what Angus Fletcher sees as metonymic displacement in allegory.[12] The part that stands for the whole here is a theatre piece that condenses a whole integral life, a life in art, which Arcand contrasts with media exploitation in the commercial city. Daniel's redemptive power, felt and openly discussed by his actor-disciples (and very explicitly by Mireille), is his daemon as actor and dramaturge. It places him, in a sense, between heaven and earth, or in the terms the film deploys, between the purity of art and the all-too-human consumption and decadence of the commercial city.[13] Daniel's power is to draw those who follow him out of that commercial city and into his ministry. Thus, the play manifests the efficacy of Daniel's daemonic power by raising up both actors dead to their art and a dead religious artifact back to artistic life.

Secondly, the potential for rebirth of Christian symbolism through historical knowledge, figured under the sign of a redemptive recollection which art offers, is extended beyond the troupe to the chosen but lost people who attend the play – potentially everyone – and who are moved by it. We should extend this further. The political redemptive power of historical memory potentially to restore public morality and social justice has been the crucial, and constantly repeated leitmotif of Arcand's filmmaking since his very first documentaries and certainly since *On est au coton*. In this respect, it is important to recognise that the corrosive bitterness veiled so poorly in the comedy of *The Decline* is everywhere in the film bleakly associated with the abandonment of political engagement among the emblematic group of professors who are, in fact, historians. *The Decline* actually opens with one of them pronouncing the "end of history" in a glib paraphrase of Jean-François Lyotard's pronouncement of the finish of the *grands récits* (usually translated as "master narratives") of the West in his *The Postmodern Condition*.[14]

Daniel's resurrection of one of those historical *récits*, indeed a primal one, the Passion story, through the insemination of modern biblical historiography into its ecclesiasticized corpse should be taken – very much against what Arcand shows to have happened in *The*

*Decline* – as nothing less than a miracle.[15] Even when Arcand sharply qualifies Daniel's accomplishment, suggesting that art is not sufficient, the central pathos of this aesthetic/didactic miracle of recovered religico-historical memory in Daniel's theatre piece remains. Indeed, we might remember that the Gospels themselves imply that when the culminating miracle of the ministry, the raising of Lazarus, fails to convert the people, the Passion, although eternally fated, becomes necessary. And yet, in the Gospels Christ's own Resurrection is adumbrated by this miracle over death.

Arcand's allegorization of the scriptural "failure of the ministry" is complicated by three intersecting tracks of narration. The first is the false coterie of admirers, the media critics who, in one of the few, but very sarcastic, cross-cutting segments of the film, offer competing versions of who Daniel is, and precisely miss the point by starting to turn him into a celebrity. They correspond to the Scribes and Pharisees who question Jesus about who he is, and the confusion of the people in the Gospels on this matter spells his failure. In *Jesus of Montreal*, however, such confusion is contained and restricted to comedy.

The second is Daniel's "driving the money-changers from the temple", his violent outburst at a television commercial audition. Having accompanied Mireille, who returns for a try-out at her old job in need of money, Daniel watches her being abused by Quintal who demands that she strip for "the clients", the representatives of the brewery. In a rage, Daniel destroys equipment, the clients flee, and then he whips Quintal in the face with a cable. The episode resolves the false religion (media world)/true religion (theatre) opposition of the film in the form of a violent confrontation – in which Daniel actually destroys the absurd media-world tableau – as well as making the last appearance of Pascal's head, shot as the visual correlative of a beheading, that much more forceful.

The episode also leads to a court appearance, in which the film's director himself appears as a rather avuncular Pilate figure who turns Daniel over to a psychiatrist. After questioning him, she is disarmed and pronounces him sane. This narrative track is also mainly comedic and inconsequential. The intervention of the law is suspended (a point to which we will return). The court scene leads to a meeting with the media lawyer Richard Cardinal (Yves Jacques). Here Arcand interpolates an earlier episode of the Gospel in which Satan tempts Jesus in a "high place" and offers him dominion over the earth. On their way to lunch at the top of a skyscraper, the glib, charming Cardinal offers Daniel the modern commercial city's equivalents to a deal with the devil – media fame, a book contract, talk-show appearances, good lunches.

In the Gospels the priests conspiring against Jesus view his violence in driving out the money-changers from the temple as the final outrage, a point Daniel's play also makes. Arcand is not alone in seizing on this episode, one in which Jesus's show of violence provokes political anxiety. It also serves as climactic event and point of transition into the Passion in Pier Paolo Pasolini's *Il Vangelo secondo Matteo* (*The Gospel According to St Matthew*, 1964) and Martin Scorsese's *The Last Temptation of Christ* (1989). If the affair of the audition is, however, narratively less consequential in *Jesus of Montreal*, it closely precedes Leclerc's strong speech and his closure of the passion-play – the "plotting priests" structurally correspond once again – which precipitate the catastrophe of its defiant, final performance.

Following directly after Leclerc's final speech, discussed above, this last performance is only presented in a short excerpt, at the point of the Crucifixion. A fight with the security guards reduces it to a shambles – in fact, what was so moving earlier is revisited as a farce – the cross falls over and Daniel is carted into an ambulance. Here the film plunges into Daniel's allegorical *via crucis*: the segments set in the Catholic hospital, out onto the night streets and subway of Montreal, and then finally his death at the Jewish hospital.

At this point, when the last performance breaks up, *Jesus of Montreal* changes, and its allegory of the Passion bursts the microcosmic artistic world in which Daniel had played out the ministry. As Leclerc unwittingly predicted, Daniel enters the realm of contemporary history. Here the allegory of *Jesus of Montreal* assumes its double-twist and forces questions of comprehension and interpretation on us that reach beyond the direct allegorical correspondences we have been pursuing. Together with other critics, Shek observes, Daniel "plays Jesus *within* the pageant but also *without*".[16] This recognition of the doubling in the film's allegory is crucial but to reduce it to a kind of *mise en abyme* begs the question: what happens at the threshold between Daniel's theatre and what lies outside it?[17]

For Arcand's allegorical premise is not, as remarked above, a literal "what if Jesus came back", nor its popular disguised equivalent in recent films such as John Carpenter's *Starman* (1984). Nor is it a modernization of Jesus, like the films made by Pasolini or Scorsese. Comprehension of *Jesus of Montreal* requires that we understand that the film is much closer to classic devotional allegories such as *Imitatio Christi* (*The Imitation of Christ*) of Thomas à Kempis. In such works, the events of Christ's life are written as a series of episodes that form a narrative template on which a devotee maps his or her life story, thus becoming a protagonist who, by travelling the same road, achieves salvation. In theological terms, the structure of grace in the spiritual life is projected as a biographical sequence. The devotee does not become another Christ but an imitator and, having become "Christ-like", is redeemed. Outside the devotional literature, there have been many fictional "imitations" constructed on this model.[18] In cinema, the *locus classicus* for such an imitational premise is Carl Theodore Dreyer's *La Passion de Jeanne d'Arc* (*The Passion of Joan of Arc*, 1928). Roberto Rossellini, Federico Fellini, Ingmar Bergman and Robert Bresson, among others, have made "imitations" of this kind, and in European art film the structure provided a favoured mode for modern spiritual biography.

*Jesus of Montreal* is a very critical variant of such a spiritual biography. Arcand does cast Daniel under an *imitatio Christi*, as we have seen, according to the narrative programme of the ministry. The miracle is a work of art in the city where there is no other art, but only commercial media. His play, or rather his absolute dedication to it, makes him a Christological imitator, but in artistic, not spiritual terms. Although the fact that the play is a depiction of Christ's Passion lends those artistic terms greater moral force than if, say, Daniel were mounting a play by Racine, Arcand executes a crucial displacement in the allegory away from the religious towards the artistic. The moral force of the play derives from its opposition with the vulgar exhibitionism of the media productions, against which Daniel and his troupe are repeatedly juxtaposed. The play's Passion is the film's miracle of art, and this Passion in art is allegorized as the climax of the ministry and decidedly not of Christ's Passion.

VI. The double-twist

In order to continue, we must now baldly restate an assumption endemic to critical writing on Arcand: that his core concerns are always political. Arcand has no other metaphysic and is certainly not (not even ambivalently) a religious artist. Nor, more importantly, is he confident in the political efficacy of art.[19] Interpretation of *Jesus of Montreal* must lead to Arcand's politics, to see how this film's double-twist allegory turns on the political. But how does Arcand figure politics? In his documentaries he does so by situating issues historically. In his fiction films Arcand creates a microcosm, and in this sense he has long been an allegorical artist.

*The Decline of the American Empire* again provides a vivid example. It is a film ostensibly about the end of politics; its companion piece is the documentary *Le Confort et l'indifférence* (*Comfort and Indifference*, 1981). In *The Decline* the characters' own condition equals the postmodern "end of history", which spells the end of the great political themes and "narratives" (*récits*). Such an end, too, is political, for history cannot end (Arcand is neither Daniel Bell nor Francis Fukuyama).[20] Of course, it may be objected that in this film Arcand only shows us a small group of professors at a cottage, making and consuming a meal, discussing the past and their petty betrayals. But the professors' state is really exemplary of the end of the political capability of Quebec intellectuals.  The film is not as particular or individual as it might suggest, for this group represents ideological leadership, the conscience, of a powerful political ethos.[21]  The characters form a microcosm (while *Comfort and Indifference* depicts a wider social dispersal).  That they have despaired of political commitment, surrendered to consumerism and now distract themselves with sex and food, academic intrigues and endless cynical repartee, is an end of sorts.  Yet inscribed within *The Decline* lies the emergent triumphant other, supposedly a non-politics, which we may call sexual politics or personalism.  About these Arcand is hardly sanguine.

*Jesus of Montreal* begins in a similar non-political personalist microcosm, that of art, and seems to set up its basic oppositions within an aesthetic politics: the consumerism and sexual exploitation of the media-world and the intense artistic integrity and sexual equality of the Jesus-like Daniel and his followers.  The two films are, on such a reading, congruent as well as successive.  The microcosm is the theatre troupe of *Jesus* encircled by the much larger media-bound, commercial city of *Montreal*, in the opposition Shek astutely observes.  But both are really enfolded by one microcosmic orbit – true and false aesthetics.  When Arcand juxtaposes the two in the zigzag narrative structure discussed above, he is inscribing difference, but within a determinate circumference.  In relation to *The Decline*, Daniel's miracle of resurrecting the passion-play by injecting it with history, as I argued above, has a powerful intertextual significance as well, for Daniel effectively reverses, through the art of theatre, the end of history and politics.  Yet that reversal is itself circumscribed by aestheticism – art informed by history and politics.  We must take Arcand's own powerful rendering of Daniel's passion-play segment as self-ironizing to some degree, since the director returns to it twice again in excerpt, both times undercutting its original power with farce.[22]

In Arcand's Christological allegory, Daniel's passion, like Christ's Passion (which begins with his entry to Jerusalem on Psalm Sunday), breaks the microcosmic circle.  Here we need to understand that there are two cities in *Jesus of Montreal*.  In this sense Arcand's double allegory twists itself on the intertext of Augustine's *The City of God* as well as the Gospels.  There is not only the commercial city that Daniel traverses for the first sections of the film, but also the suffering city which he traverses following his injury.  After the cross has been toppled, an ambulance arrives; it is cinematically a remarkable intrusion, when it pulls into the space of the play, breaking the aesthetic spell over the film.  Instead of Pilate's rough centurions, Daniel's attendants are two proletarian but conscientious ambulance drivers.  Then, suddenly and with gruesome force, Arcand thrusts his hero among the broken and bleeding bodies stacked along a hospital corridor. When he seems temporarily to recover, Daniel, Mireille and Constance wander into the night streets, descending into the metro (coded as an inversion of the *via dolorosa* up to Calvary), where the patrons appear as somnambulists. It is here that Daniel delivers his collage of apocalyptic sayings, his very dark, penultimate performance.

Reading back into the film, we note that the two cities antinomy in *Jesus of Montreal* is wider than one might have previously noticed. The commercial city is where bodies are for sale; in the suffering city, bodies are in pain. Daniel's passion-play takes as its central theatrical spectacle the body in pain, the Crucifixion, notably stripped in his text of its classical theological explanation and vividly refitted with historical details of the cruelty of ancient times. It is precisely here at this point in the play, revisited twice as farce, that the passage from the microcosm of Daniel's art to the suffering city occurs, and where Arcand's allegory of the Passion begins. The spectacle of Daniel's theatrical play-passion is answered, finally, by a singularly unspectacular, even ambiguous death of the film's artist-Jesus. Daniel succumbs to internal bleeding, his death is "brain death", an ironic inversion of body-soul dualism, for his body remains technically alive.

Finally, there is the Resurrection. In Daniel's modernized, heavily historicized passion-play, Christ's Resurrection is represented with maximum ambiguity and ambivalence. However, it does conclude with a stranger appearing and offering the bread of the Eucharist to the abandoned Apostles. Arcand's Jesus/Daniel is also resurrected, and just as ambiguously, when his body parts are taken from his body to be used for transplants, in a long but swift montage sequence. Here the ambiguity of the post-Resurrection Eucharist Daniel unwittingly offers is twisted back, to a life-saving and vision-restoring literalism.

When he breaks the microcosmic circles of the theatre troupe and commercial city, Arcand ensures that *Jesus of Montreal* opens very unambiguously towards politics. Indeed, the suffering city was never absent from the film, only recessive. Daniel encounters Constance for the first time in a soup kitchen serving men who are not merely poor, but broken. Later, in the packed courtroom, the other prisoners look the same, and the judge is, like Pilate, a civilised man hopelessly assigned the task of administering justice in the face of abject stupidities, barbarity and madness. Therefore the suspension of the law in Daniel's story mentioned above also suggests its impotence generally in the decline of justice's social rule. Arcand does not place a sufficiently strong accent on these episodes and, until the end, he seems unsure of what tone to take with them.[23] At the première of the passion-play, for example, a Haitian woman mistakes Daniel for the real Jesus, which has the effect of momentarily breaking theatrical absorption. But how to read the intrusion beyond this formal function remains uncertain. It is not perhaps until Leclerc's speech that her simple desire gains an explanation. While the bad priest is the least likely source of political awareness, he actually predicts the social nightmare of *Jesus of Montreal*.

That nightmare is the hospital. This is specific to Canadian culture perhaps, but the collapse of socialized medical care is a palpable, real-life nightmare symbol of the collapse of politics rooted in humane reason and human charity. It is also the symbol of the material consequence of the triumph of the commercial city in obscuring and becoming indifferent to suffering. Leclerc speaks falsely of virtually everything because of his cowardice but not of the real failure of modernity. And if he is too smug, in his pathetic way, about the need to respond to human suffering, the need he announces is no less true. The francophone hospital that neglects Daniel to the point of killing him is called Saint-Marc, named for the Gospel Arcand says inspired the film, the first station in Daniel's passion. The second, the metro, is his Calvary and one in which Arcand inscribes the apocalyptic collage, at which point we may realise the significance of the name Daniel as not only a "type" of Jesus that Christians have historically discerned in the Hebrew scriptures – Daniel in the lion's den – but also Judaism's crucial post-exilic eschatological prophet. The third station is the anglophone Jewish Hospital, efficient and empty, the site of death. Daniel's final posthumous image, in cruciform on an operating table, about to be dismembered and, in a literalist and ironically "materialist" sense, resurrected.

*Jesus of Montreal* completes the structure of its Christological allegory but, at the same time, breaks the ranks of its "paradigmatic reading of correspondences" by shifting its horizon from that of art to politics when the film passes beyond allegorizing the ministry to allegorizing the Passion. The language of "shifts", however, suggests a process smoother than the forceful disjunctions-in-succession that Arcand affects everywhere in the film, but especially at the crucial moment when its allegorical discourse twists in a new, political direction. Indeed, it is through his control of these disjunctions that *Jesus of Montreal* manages to become a wholly remarkable Christological allegory that doubles itself to become Arcand's most powerful and elaborate discourse on art and on politics.

*Notes*

[1] Ben-Z Shek, "A Director's Itinerary: Religion in the Films of Denys Arcand" (First International Conference on French Canada, New Delhi, 13 December 1991), unpublished manuscript, 19 pp.

[2] Ibid: 17.

[3] Denys Arcand, "*Jésus de Montréal*", trans. Matt Cohen, *Best Canadian Screenplays*, eds. Douglas Bowie and Tom Shoebridge (Kingston: Quarry Press, 1992): 339-340. The original French script, with the same preface by Arcand, was published by Boréal in 1989. Quotations of the film's dialogue in this essay are taken from Cohen's translation.

[4] These categories *histoire* and *discours* were originally devised by linguist Emile Benveniste and developed by narrative theorist Gérard Genette. They have since been deployed in many studies of filmic narration. For example, see Brian Henderson, "Tense, Mood, and Voice in Film (Notes after Genette)", *Film Quarterly* 36: 4 (summer 1983): 4-16; also see Seymour Chatman, *Story and Discourse: Narrative Structure in Fiction and Film* (Ithaca: Cornell University Press, 1978).

[5] See Christian Metz, *Film Language* (New York: Oxford University Press, 1974) for the now-standard taxonomy of such syntagmatic figures, his *"grand syntagmatique"*.

[6] See David Bordwell, *Narration in the Fiction Film* (Madison: University of Wisconsin Press, 1985): 22-26, for criticism of the strict delineation of the story/discourse difference.

[7] I am not here referring to the use of flashbacks in *The Decline*. In fact, this brief discussion entirely brackets these, although obviously they further complicate the diegesis of that film.

[8] See my analysis of the film in these terms, "Denys Arcand's Sarcasm: a Reading of *Gina*", in Pierre Véronneau, Michael Dorland and Seth Feldman (eds), *Dialogue: Cinéma canadien et québécois/Canadian and Quebec Cinema* (Montreal: Mediatext Publications and la Cinémathèque québécoise, 1987): 203-222.

[9] See Angus Fletcher, *Allegory: The Theory of a Symbolic Mode* (Ithaca: Cornell University Press, 1964): 73-84.

[10] Craig Owens, in Scott Bryson, et al. (eds), *Beyond Recognition: Representation, Power, and Culture* (Berkeley: University of California Press, 1992): 57. The text was originally published in *October* 12 (spring 1980): 67-86.

[11] Arcand cites Mark as the scriptural source for the film. See his preface, *Best Canadian Screenplays*: 339. He does not, however, mention any specific consequences of this choice for the film.

[12] See Fletcher: 87-113, on allegorical synecdoche, the isolated emblem and the twinned strategies he terms "kosmos" and "ornament", from which I have drawn some of the argument here. Note especially 101-105, his discussion of Eisenstein's montage.

[13] See Fletcher: 38-39. Fletcher writes: "The hero [of an allegory] is either a personified abstraction or a representative type...in either case what is felt as a narrowed iconographic meaning is known to us the readers through the hero's characteristic way of acting, which is severely limited in variety. We must return to the allegorical hero's behaviour for our answer. We find that he conforms to the type of behaviour manifested by many people who are thought (however unscientifically) to be possessed by a daemon." Fletcher continues, arguing that the "daemonic possession" in question is wider, as well as much older, than the common sense of "demonic possession" (i.e. by Satan). In allegories, the daemonic signifies the hero's possession of a single emblematic trait or capability – a virtue or vice, strength or meaning – that effectively determines characterization as a restricted singularity. Further, this determination signifies "the real lack of freedom in all these stories"(64) and "he does not choose to do this or that....His choices, if they can properly be so called, are made for him by his daemon".(67) In this sense, "He will act part way between the human and divine spheres, touching on both".(68) The allegorical hero is a liminal character, existing at the threshold between what we usually think of as characterization and abstraction. Fletcher remarks that Romanticism especially is attracted to such liminal figures.

[14] See Jean-François Lyotard, *The Postmodern Condition: a Report on Knowledge*, trans. Geoff Bennington and Brian Maussumi (Minneapolis: University of Minnesota Press, 1979). Lyotard's "report" was commissioned by the Conseil des Universités of the Government of Quebec. The book's fame and influence have spread far beyond these origins, however.

[15] A somewhat similar thematic economy exists in the relation between the repressed *On est au coton* and *Gina*. In the latter film Arcand's film-being-made-within-the-film is very like that of his textile documentary, and it is halted. The fictional director (played by Gabriel Arcand, the real filmmaker's brother) goes on, at the end, to make a fiction film that seems a little like *Gina*. Although Arcand treats the substitution of a fiction film (a trope for art) for a documentary (history) with ironic scepticism in *Gina*, the artist's vocation remains for him a political necessity.

[16] Shek: 17. Emphasis in original.

[17] See Martin Lefebvre, "The Scriptures Through Postmodern Strategies: Challenging History", *Canadian Journal of Political and Social Theory* 14/1-2 & 3 (1990): 225-227. In an essay that is mainly concerned with showing how three recent religious films question the validity of using scriptures as history, Lefebvre takes the view that Daniel's passion-play is a double, or "discursive referent...in a strange *mise-en-abyme* for the rest of the story".

[18] For a survey of such works since the 19th century, see Theodore Ziolkowski, *Fictional Transfigurations of Jesus* (Princeton: Princeton University Press, 1972). The works which the critic selects, however, tend strongly towards the ironic.

[19] See Judy Wright and Debbie Magidson, "Making Films for Your Own People, an Interview with Denys Arcand", in Seth Feldman and Joyce Nelson

(eds), *Canadian Film Reader* (Toronto: Peter Martin Associates, 1977): 231. Arcand customarily contrasts political realities and cultural discourses, as he does in this discussion, refusing the conflation of them typical of the Griersonian tradition of Canadian film culture. He is, then, deeply suspicious of the power of art to affect social change and, although a political filmmaker, he is very modest about the political significance of cultural productions, especially his own.

[20] See Francis Fukuyama, *The End of History and the Last Man* (New York: Avon Books, 1992). Although published several years after *The Decline* was made, Fukuyama's book represents a very successful popularization of the "end" of history and politics. Daniel Bell's *The Coming of Post-Industrial Society* (New York: Basic Books, 1973) is its best known "neo-conservative" precursor.

[21] In French translatable as both "conscience" and "consciousness", an ambiguity of undeniable significance, particularly in francophone Marxist-Hegelian political discourse.

[22] The second excerpt occurs the night after Daniel has wrecked the beer commercial audition. The scene consists of two sections, the first and serious one shows Daniel delivering Jesus's speech against "the priests", which was not heard the first time the pageant was performed. Here it is spoken face-to-face to Leclerc and his superiors attending the play. The second section is not actually of a piece with the play's performance but is a comic scene during which two policemen arrest Daniel for his violent outburst, lifting him gently right off the cross, after the audience has moved to the next "station" in the pageant. The third excerpt is quickly interrupted by the mêlée with the security guards in which the cross is toppled.

[23] However, there is some indication in the published script that greater focus might have been planned at some point. For example, Arcand excised a scene that would have perhaps fixed the meaning better, an episode in which the penniless Daniel goes to a pizzeria and successfully begs for "five pizzas, all dressed". The owner's blunt speech about being an immigrant and how hard he works might have threatened the charmed aesthetic circle around Daniel. Perhaps too soon. What limited charm this episode's correspondence to the Christ's miracle of the "bread and fishes" might have provided would probably not have compensated for the potential it possesses in puncturing Daniel's Christological inflation.

# No big picture: Arcand and his US critics

*Peter Wilkins*

Undoubtedly the Americans have had more to do with the slow development of Canadian cinema than any other force. How, therefore, has this giant neighbour reacted to the emergence of international successes from Quebec? This essay is an attempt to reveal the ways in which US critics have constructed Denys Arcand's *Le Déclin de l'empire américain* (*The Decline of the American Empire*, 1986) and *Jésus de Montréal* (*Jesus of Montreal*, 1989), the only films by the director to have triggered a sizeable response in the United States. The reviews cited are representative of positions taken with respect to the issues of the films, rather than a complete collection. I have tried to create a dialogue among the reviews, rather than simply to list them. The only condition limiting my choice is that the reviews had to be published in the US press. The reviews range from short daily newspaper articles to longer commentaries in film magazines. None of them could properly be described as "academic"; even those from film journals are still in the realm of popular journalism.

In examining the reviews I wanted to discover what US critics responded to in the films, and especially whether they discussed them in relation to Canadian or Quebec culture or abstracted them from any cultural location. I wanted to see how these critics dealt with issues such as Quebec's relationship to Canada and Canada's relationship to the United States. Canada is accustomed to the saturation of its cinemas, television sets and newsstands with US product. To see films such as Arcand's achieving success in the United States (as well as the world at large) was a chance to observe, however briefly, a reversal in the flow of culture.

Indeed, the American response to the films may have had an impact on how anglophone Canadians responded to them, simply because anglophone Canada is so enmeshed in the US media network. Arcand makes this point in an interview with Robert Sklar: "This is the drama of English Canada: they read American magazines and then they read about this guy from Quebec – he must be good if the Americans are saying this about him, we should go out and see his films. I'm kidding but there's a kernel of truth there, I'm sure."[1] This "kernel of truth" is problematic for Canadian culture; French-Canadian films, in order to acquire appropriate media credentials, have to travel a circuit through the United States to reach anglophone Canada.

In this essay the theme I develop most is that of the two films' cultural or national placement. I argue that the US critics' fundamental misunderstanding is their failure to grasp Arcand's questioning of the cultural positioning of both Quebec and Canada with respect to the United States and "Western" culture in general. I suggest that Arcand's perspective in this questioning is particularly postmodern in its neutrality that allows no simple decoding of irony or allegory. Of course, the issue of cultural positioning is itself postmodern in the sense that nationality and nationalism become problematic in an era of cultural globalization and flattening, traits typically associated with our "postmodern condition". I also suggest that the cultural positioning of Quebec and Canada is especially at risk in the postmodern sphere, because Quebec has always been vulnerable to assimilation by English Canada, and the latter, in turn, by the United States. The US critics' failure to see these important issues in Arcand's films is symptomatic of their belonging to the dominant cultural power in this scenario, which tends to be blind to its effects upon the less powerful and less stable cultures that neighbour it.

While *The Decline* provides the most immediate and provocative context for a discussion of cultural positioning, thanks to its problematic title, *Jesus of Montreal* also participates in the issue by playing the Jesus "of Montreal" against the more universal conception of Jesus as the saviour of mankind. The film's concern with images, representation and the media deepens the relationship between cultural positioning and postmodernity which Arcand sets up in *The Decline*. Just as the US critics do not grasp the issue of Quebec and Canada's relationship to the United States in *The Decline*, they fail to see the problems which the media produce for cultural specificity and universality in *Jesus of Montreal*. The result is a body of responses which, in its perplexity over Arcand's work, draws attention to the difficulty generated by the filmmaker's perspective.

*The Decline of the American Empire*

"[T]he quintessential Canadian situation is people sitting on a couch and talking. It's no use looking for big action, there's none. The country is empty. There's no big friction." (Denys Arcand)[2] Thus, in describing the situation of *The Decline of the American Empire*, Arcand states that the film is particularly Canadian. He also embraces the whole country – not just Quebec – in a tacit belief in a "Canadian situation", if not a Canadian identity, which crosses ethnic and linguistic boundaries. Ironically, however, if relaxed talk is the "quintessential" Canadian situation, it is neither particularly defining nor exclusive. In typical Canadian fashion, the quintessential dissolves into invisibility. Most things which define the "Canadian" are only "visible" to Canadians themselves, who share the secrets of their national mystery. Canada is especially invisible as a cultural entity to the United States, whose pervasive culture tends either to blot out or absorb the "Canadian".

The phenomenon of invisibilization is pervasive throughout the realm of Canadian cultural production, especially anglophone Canadian production. Canadian television personalities, especially news anchors and comics, so frequently move to the United States to become absorbed by US culture that it is possible to speak of a "media drain". Americans can easily ignore the fact that people such as John Candy, Peter Jennings, Robert MacNeil and Mike Meyers are Canadian. Indeed, *Wayne's World* (1992), which Meyers wrote with suburban Toronto in mind, was transplanted to Chicago without many people noticing. Anglophone Canadian film directors, such as David Cronenberg and Norman Jewison, have achieved great success, but not by making what one could call "Canadian" films; they are Canadians making American films.

Arcand, however, makes films in Canada, sponsored partly by the National Film Board and Telefilm Canada. He is also a French-Canadian working in French (until recently with *Love and Human Remains*, 1993), and therefore hardly likely to be co-opted for US culture in the same way as anglophones have. If anything, his work will be integrated into Franco-European culture.[3] Indeed, Arcand identifies his work with French-speaking Europe as much as with Canada. He was surprised by *The Decline*'s North American popularity because he anticipated a primarily European audience: "This was an accident, more or less. It was made to be seen only in Montreal, then play maybe a month in Paris, and be sold to French, Swiss and Belgian television."[4] Clearly Arcand expected the film to bypass not only American audiences, but also English-Canadian ones, making the film an exposition of the "Canadian situation" for European export. Instead, *The Decline* became a sensational success in North America as one of the most popular Canadian films ever for Canadian and American audiences. Consequently, Arcand's status as a "Canadian" director and the "visibility" of Canadian elements in *The Decline* became issues to US reviewers, as the critics argue whether or not the film has a "Canadian sensibility".

The title, *The Decline of the American Empire*, suggests a grand socio-political scope, echoing titles such as Gibbon's *The Decline and Fall of the Roman Empire* and Spengler's *Untergang des Abendlandes* (*Decline of the West*). Hence, the US reviewers are surprised that *The Decline* is an intimate film in which eight people (three history professors, an art history professor, a lecturer, a graduate student, an undergraduate and one of the professor's wives) discuss their sex lives, mostly in disaffected, alienated terms. The characters' relationship to the discipline of history is the only link between the private realm of sex and the public realm of imperial politics.

Dominique, the head of the university history department, posits the film's grandiose backdrop of American decline. In the film's first exchange of dialogue in an interview with Diane, a lecturer and part-time reporter for CBC, Dominique describes the theory of her latest book. She claims that whenever the members of an imperial power give themselves over to personal happiness rather than to the good of the community, the empire is in decline; Dominique argues that this is currently the case with the United States. She makes no bones about the fact that Canada is a part of the "American empire" albeit on "the outskirts" – a fact which may soften the experience of decline.

The characters are also discussing Dominique's theory towards the end of the film when she makes her quasi-apocalyptic revelation that she has slept with Rémy and Pierre, two of the other historians. She reveals this in front of Rémy's naïve wife who, although she believes he has had a few flings, has no idea that he has slept with Dominique, not to mention a great many others from Montreal's female population. The fact that this revelation, which sets up the conclusion of the film, is made in the context of Dominique's theory means that the notion of American imperial decline brackets the film's presentation of the characters' talk of sex. It suggests a juxtaposition, if not a conflation, of public and private realms.

The relationship between Dominique's theory and the interaction among the characters is the primary ambiguity of *The Decline*. It is especially ambiguous to the US reviewers, who have difficulty seeing how this group of French-Canadian academics participates in the American empire. The title alone is sufficient to provoke discussion, as Robert Sklar of *Cineaste* magazine states: "Who, of whatever ideological persuasion, would not be drawn to a film which promised so portentous a theme?"[5] While the title may work as a marketing strategy, as Sklar hints, it also serves as the site of a kind of ideological boundary dispute over where Canada stops and the United States begins in the ideascape of this film.

John Simon, writing for the conservative *National Review*, suggests that Arcand is fraudulently exploiting the United States in using the premise of an American empire. He thinks the title reflects the film's pretentiousness: "it must pretend, to convince itself of its own importance, to pertain to an 'American empire', which presumably includes the US and Canada, though not the Eskimos".[6] Simon accuses Arcand of a Canadian opportunism in presuming that this provincial, parochial story has any bearing on America. Arcand is not criticising the empire, according to Simon, but attempting to benefit from it as a means of universalizing his otherwise limited story.

Others, such as Stanley Kauffmann in *The New Republic*, view the term "empire" more benignly, but still in a way which emphasizes the idea of universality. Kauffmann's complaint is that the title is misleading: "*The Decline of the American Empire*, topical though it sounds, is really an imprecise title. It ought to be at least *The Decline of the North American Empire*, since it is set in Canada; better, it ought to borrow Spengler's *The Decline of the West*."[7]

Kauffmann's confusion over the title of *The Decline* is symptomatic of the fact that Americans do not see themselves as having any imperial control over Canada. Kauffmann sees Canada as broadly equal to the United States in "imperial" status, able to combine with the US to produce a "North American Empire". He equates the term "empire" with geographical space and a presumed cultural sameness, rather than political power. When he states that the film ought to be called "The Decline of the West", Kauffmann suggests that the film has no bearing on the specific relationship between Canada and the United States, but is rather applicable to the whole of Western society. Unconsciously, Kauffmann has broadened the boundaries of the American empire; for him, decline in the United States is decline everywhere in the western hemisphere.

George Williams of the *Sacramento Bee* also suggests that the imperial relation between Canada and the United States is associative rather than hierarchical: "By 'empire,' Arcand means the United States and its Canadian neighbours who are closely tuned to the US lifestyle and profit from its wars".[8] Canada's association with the United States brings "profit", not oppression. Nevertheless, Williams's phrase "tuned to the US lifestyle", with its communications metaphor, perfectly defines, whether intentionally or not, the imperial relations between the United States and Canada. For US imperialism with respect to Canada is media and information imperialism. Because physical and cultural traffic crosses the Canadian border with ease, Americans tend to see Canada as less a foreign country than a parallel or complementary one. Canada is not quite the United States, but neither is it Mexico.

However, Canadians, particularly artists and intellectuals who feel the threat of encroaching US culture, see the relationship as more antagonistic, for the same reasons that Americans see it as benign. For example, Margaret Atwood complains that the United States exerts imperial control over Canada: "The fact is that the United States is an empire and Canada is to it as Gaul was to Rome".[9] Atwood then claims that Americans do not recognise their imperialism with respect to Canada: "[I]ndividual Americans seem not to know that the United States is an imperial power and is behaving like one. They don't want to admit that empires dominate, invade and subjugate – and live on the proceeds – or if they do admit it, they believe in their divine right to do so."[10] Thus, where Americans such as Kauffmann and Williams see a bond of complementarity, if not equality, Canadians such as Atwood perceive one of subjugation. Hence "The Decline of the American Empire" would not be a tragedy but the fulfilment of a Canadian fantasy, even if it took Canada down with it.

While Atwood's sentiments are stronger than anything in *The Decline*, the film does include references to cultural traffic from south of the border. The housewife Louise's reference to Rémy's obsession with getting his Sunday edition of *The New York Times* serves as an example of the nature of Canada's not only voluntary, but also enthusiastic, subscription to US cultural imperialism. The fact that Rémy and Pierre acquired their PhDs from Berkeley and Princeton respectively illustrates that the "empire" covers intellectual pursuits as well as entertainment. These examples show Canadians "buying into" American culture, ensuring their own cultural colonization. They would seem to support Williams's claim of Canadians profiting from the American empire. However, the relationships of consumption to which Arcand alludes are more complex. For American imperialism over Canada – as far as those such as Margaret Atwood see it – puts the United States in the position of culture pushers exploiting the Canadian market. Even though in *The Decline* the level of feeling on this issue does not in any way approximate that of Atwood, her attitude is a common one in Canada and the film plays upon it. I refer to it to show how the ramifications of the term "American empire" are potentially different for Canadians and Americans.

The relationship between *The Decline*'s content and the American empire raises the issue of the film's status as "Canadian". For the US critics there is no middle ground on this issue: *The Decline* is either immediately identifiable as "Canadian" or it is not Canadian at all. John Simon takes the former view in order to disparage Arcand's parochialism: "*Le Déclin de l'empire américain* is very much a Canadian, indeed French Canadian, film in content and sensibility". According to Simon, this sensibility is related to the "heavy curse" which hangs over Canadian filmmaking. Canada can produce good documentaries and cartoons, but not features: "neither from French nor from English Canada, has there come a single outstanding feature film....not one solitary Canadian master work".[11] Simon considers a "master work" one which combines box-office success with aesthetic credibility: "parochial art house favorites" of which Canada has produced a few, "though not on an international scale", do not qualify. Arcand and Canada tend to produce "provincial" films which speak to local, but not universal issues.

Simon argues that Canada's lack of filmmaking strength stems from the country's national make-up: "Canada is a tragic country, saddled with three separate but equal inferiority complexes: toward France, toward England, and especially toward the United States".[12] The inferiority complex towards the United States, more equal than the other two, is the crux of Simon's complaint about the status of *The Decline*. It is as if *The Decline* is attempting to break out of this inferiority in the pretension of its title, but failing to do so. Arcand's use of ideas, particularly those about history, also defines the film's Canadian sensibility: "such truths are too trite to pass for ideas anywhere except in a Canadian movie".[13] Simon considers *The Decline* to be a charlatan film; it pretends to universality but cannot escape its provinciality or parochialism. Although we may not agree with Simon's criticism, it does define the uneasy place of *The Decline* with respect to universality and particularity, not to mention nationality. The film locates itself between its Quebec/Canada setting and some kind of universal human condition.

Whereas Simon sees *The Decline* as a particularly Canadian film trying to disguise this fact, Lawrence DeVine of the *Detroit Free Press* and J Hoberman of the *Village Voice* both think it has no Canadian traits. DeVine writes: "You may look for a Canadian sensibility at work here, but you won't find it".[14] Unlike Simon, however, DeVine does not say what a Canadian sensibility might be. Hoberman is more detailed, arguing that *The Decline* is "so denatured it might have been produced anywhere".[15] According to him, the film has no historical or political connection to where it was produced: "What's most remarkable about this gang is that neither they nor Arcand...have an iota of historical consciousness of themselves as Quebecois, Canadian, or the products of a strongly Catholic and highly puritanical society". Indeed, Hoberman curiously identifies *The Decline* with US politics in the 1980s; it is "social satire for the age of Reagan – toothless and grinning". It is as if *The Decline*'s lack of political-historical reference allows the "American empire" to absorb it.

Hoberman is correct in that *The Decline* makes virtually no reference to Canadian or Quebec politics – for example, to Quebec's position with respect to the rest of Canada. In the discussions of social decay, no one talks about any relation between it and the state of separatist, nationalist feeling in Quebec. All historical references are to other parts of the world. While it is unfair to demand that a film from Quebec must address the issues that dominate Quebec politics, it seems odd that Arcand would make his characters historians and have them avoid all mention of the history that most pertains to them. It also raises the question of how overt a film has to be in terms of political or historical reference in order to identify itself as belonging to a particular culture.

Robert Sklar in *Cineaste* argues that Arcand may have contrived this absence to make an overt political statement. Sklar's interpretation returns *The Decline* to a particular cultural frame by arguing that the lack of reference to Quebec politics "is surely a deliberate omission on Arcand's part". This omission draws attention to the failures of the Quebec separatist movement which have cast it into the category of forgotten "loser" which both Rémy and Diane mention in separate classroom shots in the film but without referring to Quebec. History, they say, only remembers the victors. Arcand's aim, according to Sklar, is to provide a "fundamental insight into the two Quebecs, of the hedonistic present with its historical amnesia, and of the repressed, unrepresented, but not yet reconciled past".[16] This comment gives *The Decline* an intriguing quasi-psychoanalytical twist; it evokes the "political unconscious" of Quebec.

Elliott Stein, writing in *Film Comment*, agrees with Sklar: "These aging academics are surely disillusioned survivors of the Quebec separatist movement... Their silence on the matter speaks volumes on its failure – and theirs".[17] Stein suggests that the characters were once political activists who have given in to middle-class, middle-age complacency. Sklar's and Stein's readings are questionable because they convert an absence into a presence allegorically; there is no way of verifying their claims from structural elements within the film. The absence of politics may be more ironic than allegorical.

Whether Arcand is being ironic or straightforward is the crux of the criticism of *The Decline*. The problem extends beyond the realm of geopolitics into that of sexual politics. The reviews of *The Decline* examined so far may give the mistaken impression that they are completely concerned with the film's geopolitical positioning. In fact, most US critics discuss it as either a sex farce or a satire on sexual mores of the 1980s, without much considering its cultural or political context. This is not surprising given that the film is devoted almost entirely to the characters' discussion of their sex lives. For the older male characters Rémy and Pierre, sex appears to be the only thing separating them from utter disappointment. Pierre says that once he knew he was not going to be a great historian, sex was the only thing left to him. Hence the question of Arcand's irony in terms of sex revolves around whether or not the film is criticising the characters for their banal single-mindedness.

Arcand's stance in *The Decline* is remarkably neutral. He presents his characters without overt judgment or condemnation. Pauline Kael of *The New Yorker* is one of the few critics to allow the film this quality: "Nobody is being judged – not even the American Empire is being judged. It's a very unassuming picture".[18] It is as if after making politically charged documentaries Arcand had decided to direct a pseudo-documentary in which he shoots domestic drama as if it were

*Denys Arcand*

*Réjeanne Padovani*

*On est au coton*

*Love and Human Remains*

*Seul ou avec d'autres*

*Le Confort et l'indifférence*

*Québec: Duplessis et après*

*Le Déclin de l'empire américain*

*Le Déclin de l'empire américain*

*Jésus de Montréal*

*Jésus de Montréal*

*Jésus de Montréal*

*Jésus de Montréal*

*Gina*

an episode of a nature programme on television. The film produces an uncomfortable oscillation between involvement and distance, as Vincent Canby suggests: "It's like finding yourself at a dinner party where you're the only stranger among intimate friends".[19] *The Decline* thus puts the critic in a difficult position because it offers neither judgments, nor heroes or villains for the reviewer to evaluate; the film simply presents the characters' frank discussion of sex.

Those who like the film find the talk of sex lively and witty; those who dislike it find it banal. Canby writes: "not since Alain Tanner's *Jonah Who Will Be 25 in the Year 2000* has there been a comedy that so entertainingly and successfully expresses itself through intelligent characters defined entirely in their talk". George Williams of the *Sacramento Bee* describes Arcand as a "north-of-the-border Woody Allen" for his "witty and intelligent and very funny" script.[20] For these critics the film's wit is an end in itself even though they might feel ambivalent about its sexual content. Jami Bernard of the *New York Post* writes: "*Decline of the American Empire* is really quite good, but you'll hate yourself in the morning".[21]

Ironically, the critics who dislike the film because the talk is banal may have a more accurate sense of what the film is trying to achieve than those who celebrate it purely because of its wit. J Hoberman writes: "for a sex farce, *Decline* is oddly punitive", incapable of offering any jouissance: "all we ever see are grotesque scenes of Rémy frantically pulling up his trousers and hotfooting it home from some torrid matinee".[22] David Denby of *New York* magazine writes: "[Arcand] has reduced a group of intelligent men and women to a single set of preoccupations...and then teases them for being obsessed with fornication".[23] Arcand treats the characters unfairly, according to Denby: "the itch never lets up, but anyone who scratches it is bound to make an idiot of himself. *Decline* is a rigged game posing as satire". Both Hoberman and Denby criticise Arcand for not having sufficient sympathy, and for treating his characters too ruthlessly. However, it is hard not to think that these reviewers are criticising the film for succeeding with its point. There is no pleasure here, no dignity or happiness in this realm of sexuality, only varying degrees of intensity and anxiety. If these characters represent the quest of the individual for happiness, according to Dominique's theory, they certainly are not achieving any. Nevertheless, the US critics want some form of redemption, if not a happy ending.

One way of finding this redemption is to project it onto *The Decline* in a way that flattens the film's ambiguity. In some cases, this reduction to some positive moral leads to a dismissal of the film. For example, Dave Kehr of the *Chicago Tribune* declares that the film is "haunted by a complacency" because Arcand supposedly embraces conventional morality at the end.[24] For Kehr, Louise is the film's moral centre and broadly its hero: "It's Louise who bears the brunt of the evening's truth-telling session, and Louise who, in the inevitable cold light of dawn, must make the leap of faith necessary to redeem her marriage and – by metaphorical extension – the human race". In his desire to identify a centre and some kind of figurative representativeness, Kehr projects his own moral sense onto the film and then criticises Arcand for it. His claim is dubious because it is just as easy to identify Louise as a naïve dupe as it is as a hero.

In another attempt to locate a thematic centre in *The Decline*, Joseph Gelmis of *Newsday* writes: "It's a movie about women who are, most of them, sexually freer than they used to be, but are no happier and no more fulfilled than their male peers or the men in their lives".[25] This statement may be true but it converts one aspect of the film into the whole story; like Kehr's reading of Louise, Gelmis's reading can easily be turned on its head. Other reviewers such as Jami Bernard in the *New York Post* just as easily criticise the film as misogynist: "If you haven't gotten enough of sexual politics and fear and loathing of women from recent movies like *The Men's Club*, then you can have your fill here".[26]

Reviews which limit their comments to the film's sexual content and to gender politics do not find much material for discussion. Critics notice such things as the fact that the male characters are preparing the dinner while the women are working out and treat the situation as either a subtle or heavy-handed role reversal. Denby writes: "This role reversal...is intended to demonstrate that Arcand is no square when it comes to showing behaviour allegedly natural to each sex", while others such as Kauffmann call the "reversal" a "nice touch".[27] Of course, suggesting that this situation is in fact a "reversal" says more about the critics than the film, which gives no hint that it is reversing anything. Only Kael reads the set-up in a way that departs from the simple logic of inversion. For her, the women are working out because they "need to keep in shape in order to appeal to men".[28]

Claude, the gay character, and Diane, who is involved in a sado-masochistic affair, attract a lot of attention but mostly for their deviance value. They are "different" so they are easy to discuss. Few critics, however, consider the way in which Diane's boyfriend intrudes upon the dinner as an outsider. He is not exactly working-class, but he certainly comes from a different world than the others. His brief appearance at the dinner when he criticises the imported beer and says that when he is "horny" he "fucks", produces the most discomfort for the characters until Dominique lets drop her bombshell of a revelation. While not qualifying as a class critique, it at least shatters the insularity of the group, illustrating that they are not representative of society as a whole, only a particular aspect of it.

This non-representativeness is crucial to the way in which Dominique's theory relates to the situation of the characters; the climax of the film, which critics tend to ignore, best illustrates this relationship. Dominique's revelation may be the key to how the characters' sex lives intersect with history. She reveals that she has slept with Rémy only after Louise, Rémy's wife, has disagreed with her theory. Louise believes happiness is possible, not only for her, but also for society at large; Dominique is simply being cynical. Almost immediately Dominique reveals she has slept with Rémy, using her life and the lives of those around her to exemplify, even prove her theory and to shatter Louise's sense of "personal happiness". The pettiness of this gesture, combined with its effectiveness, suggests that Dominique is theorizing her own friends and acquaintances as if they were representative of society at large, when in fact they merely represent themselves. In contrast to the decline of the American empire, which is supposed to be a long, drawn-out process, Dominique's revelation introduces an immediate shock to the group's veneer of camaraderie. There are now no illusions about how the group interacts. The relationship between Dominique's theory of cultural decline and the cataclysm she introduces into the group is contrapuntal, rather than mirroring. This group does not "represent" the decline of the American empire, it merely intersects with it in an oblique way. While it would take another essay to articulate this intersection, we could argue that the US critics might have been less confused by both the geopolitics and sexual politics of the film if they had thought about them in a more integrated way.

*Jesus of Montreal*

From *The Decline* to *Jesus of Montreal*, Arcand shifts from one broadly controversial subject, sex, to another, religion. In the film Daniel, an actor, finds himself becoming increasingly Christ-like as he performs in a passion-play. While *Jesus of Montreal* does not produce the same kind of opportunity to discuss the way Americans respond to Canada that *The Decline* does – thanks to its provocative title – the film nevertheless invites questions of cultural framing. This Jesus is specifically located in Montreal, immediately creating a tension between Christ's supposed universality as the saviour of humanity and the particularity of a city in Canada. The US critics avoid the question of this particularity, which is curious since the location of *The Decline* was such an issue. The US critics treat the Jesus story as always already universal.

Nevertheless, a few reviewers criticise Arcand for having a provincial or parochial outlook in *Jesus of Montreal*, as if he were not making the film sufficiently universal. David Ansen of *Newsweek*, for example, writes that the film at times "strikes a provincial moralistic tone".[29] David Denby of *New York* argues that Arcand mistakenly confuses the problems of Montreal with those of the world; he needs to "escape the nurturing atmosphere of Montreal, whose provincial embrace – cozy and 'sophisticated' – may include corruptions he's not aware of".[30] Neither Ansen nor Denby considers that the particularity "of Montreal" in the title might intentionally limit the scope of the film, playing against "Jesus of Nazareth".

Some critics find the film to be limited in its religious specificity, if not its setting. For example, Howie Movshovitz of the *Denver Post* suggests that the film might be more appealing to Catholics, especially Jesuits, than to non-Catholics: "When I first saw *Jesus* in Cannes a year ago, people from Catholic countries appreciated the picture more than others".[31] Vincent Canby, who, after singing the praises of *The Decline*, disliked *Jesus of Montreal*, makes a similar remark: "The theology may seem less muddled in Roman Catholic French Canada than it does on the French Riviera, the land of topless hedonism".[32] In any event, whether the limitations in the scope of *Jesus of Montreal* are simply religious or overdetermined by a number of cultural factors, they show that ideas of cultural positioning and boundaries are just as problematic to *Jesus of Montreal* as to *The Decline*. The fact that the US critics tend to decry the "parochial" or "provincial" elements of the film indicates a demand for universality which Arcand is not willing to supply.

A natural reference point for the reviews of *Jesus of Montreal* is the controversy surrounding Martin Scorsese's *The Last Temptation of Christ* (1988), which preceded Arcand's film. *The Last Temptation*, of course, is about "the" Jesus Christ, and thus his story has more claims to universality. Scorsese's film was protested against all over the United States for what Christians felt was blasphemous manipulation. Apparently, *Jesus of Montreal* had difficulty securing a US distribution deal, despite winning the Prix du Jury Œcuménique/Ecumenical Jury's Award at Cannes, because of nervousness about similar repercussions. When it was released in the United States, the film had none of the scandal and problems with audiences that *The Last Temptation* had, partly because the film was not as hyped by the media, but also probably because it did not have the same pretensions to universality.

The thematic link between the films nevertheless invited critical comparison. Indeed, David Kronke of the *Dallas Times Herald* writes that the film "mirrors the crucifixion of Martin Scorsese by religious leaders for his film *The Last Temptation of Christ*".[33] That Arcand found himself in the company of one of the most celebrated American directors certainly did not hurt his reputation, especially when his film fared the better in most comparisons. For example, Tom O'Brien of

*Film Quarterly* argues that *Jesus of Montreal* succeeds where *The Last Temptation* did not because "it doesn't posture as much, as heavily – or as neurotically".[34]

Most critics feel that Arcand's treatment of religion is sympathetic if not entirely original or fulfilling. James M Wall, discussing the film in an editorial on the Montreal International Film Festival in *Christian Century*, wholeheartedly approves of *Jesus of Montreal*. Bemoaning the difficulties the film had securing US distribution, Wall writes: "It would be too bad if US audiences were deprived of seeing a Jesus film as it should be made, one relevant to a contemporary audience but authentic to the original story".[35] Wall calls the film "the best film dealing with the Jesus story since Pier Paolo Pasolini's *The Gospel According to St Matthew*". Given that Wall is writing for a Christian magazine, his positive response suggests that *Jesus of Montreal* is not a film like *The Last Temptation of Christ*, set to give rise to controversy. This is a film that some Christians at least can identify with.

However, not everyone agrees with Wall. Some accuse Arcand of trivializing the Christ stories, while an anonymous review in the *New York Tribune* finds *Jesus of Montreal* offensive: "the film...exposes Arcand's insufferable pandering to the trendy left's feeble attempts to comprehend and dismiss Jesus Christ, whose teachings continue to topple empires and change lives". This review says Arcand's popularity (including all the awards he has won for *The Decline* and *Jesus of Montreal*) is symptomatic of the moral ills of the film industry: it "demonstrate[s] the impoverished state of the film community. The ideological decision to be anti-Christ and pro-humanist has overcome good taste".[36] This reviewer feeds the film into the American cultural debate over "secular humanism". The language is that of the Christian right which often criticises Hollywood and the media in general for promoting a liberal humanist agenda and disparaging traditional Christian morality. Clearly, the *Tribune* reviewer has slotted *Jesus of Montreal* into a particular position in the cultural debate without considering the elements of the film which criticise the very things which the American Christian right objects to, namely the media's forsaking any kind of morality in favour of sensation.

Perhaps a more crucial subject than the appeal of Daniel as Christ figure to various religious sensibilities is the way in which Arcand subjects the Gospels to a kind of postmodern milieu in *Jesus of Montreal*; the supposedly "foundational" story of Christ is superimposed upon a media-saturated world of ephemeral images. Arcand employs the postmodernist techniques of pastiche and stylistic heterogeneity in restructuring the film. He says that he wanted to make a film of "ripping contrasts" which would combine elements of absurdist comedy with those of serious drama and all intermediate stages.[37] Obviously, such a strategy potentially plays havoc with the coherence and unity of the film. Those critics who demand such things are unhappy with *Jesus of Montreal*. Howie Movshovitz argues that the film tries to do too many things: "At one moment, it's a direct retelling of the life of Christ in modern dress, and the next it's an angry piece about discrimination against French-speaking Canadians in a predominantly French city".[38] Maria Garcia of *Films in Review* writes: "The plot...is an excuse for the presentation of a pastiche of facts, myths and half-truths. Like a research paper, it has no central vision".[39] Garcia clearly expects a kind of novelistic "realism" from the film, for she also criticises the film for its "mistrust of emotion, of the power of the cinema, and its ability to draw us into a character's internal struggles".[40] Steve Murray of the *Atlanta Journal* says that the film is "all over the map".[41] It is tempting to play the reviewers' demand for universality, which I discussed earlier, against this criticism of stylistic heterogeneity, for it illuminates the fundamental crisis which *Jesus of Montreal* evokes: how can the film be both culturally specific in one sense and "all over the map" in another? The answer may be that postmodern techniques allow Arcand to have it both ways.

Several reviewers see *Jesus of Montreal* more as having a split personality; they complain that Arcand wants to be parodic on one hand, while sincere on the other. These critics seem to hope that *Jesus of Montreal* will be what the *New York Tribune* review says it is: a "humanist" critique of religion. David Kronke complains that *Jesus of Montreal* becomes "literal and pedantic" by the time it ends.[42] Caryn James of *The New York Times* agrees, saying that the film balances satire and seriousness for the first hour, "before it gives in to leaden, self-conscious Christ imagery".[43] Marcia Pally of the *Boston Herald* finds virtually the same pattern: Arcand begins as "a deliciously sarcastic humanist" who eventually "falls into the trap of self-righteousness".[44] Perhaps this is the aspect of *Jesus of Montreal* that is most surprising. It leads the viewer into believing that it is going to be one thing, but it ends up being something else. Given the tone of *The Decline*, we might expect Arcand to deny us any kind of affirmation. But *Jesus of Montreal* is in many ways the inversion of *The Decline*'s relentless bleakness, in that it at least inquires into the possibility of affirmation, if not faith. The film's serious moments perform the same kind of task as its humorous moments in this inquiry, but from a different perspective; they question the apparent chasm between the desire for some kind of "value" or faith and the seemingly valueless postmodern sphere.

As with *The Decline* the central point of critical confusion is the purpose of Arcand's set-up; even more than with the reviews for *The Decline*, we see the critics attempting to recuperate a unifying meaning from the film in a response to Arcand's heterogeneous strategy. The parallels between Daniel's experience and the Gospels especially invite allegorical interpretation, but such interpretation tends to shuttle back and forth between the Bible and the film, leaving the purpose of the repetition unclear. Most allegorizing critics judge the film in terms of whether it is a good or bad retelling of the Gospel, as if that were the film's point.

Whether Arcand is clever or heavy-handed depends on the receptiveness of the critic to Arcand's project. Those who see an isomorphic correspondence between the film's elements and the Gospels are more likely to disparage the use to which Arcand puts the Bible; those who see more play between the film and the biblical referents are more likely to approve of his manipulation. The scenes most often referred to as biblical parallels are Daniel's acquisition of the actors (the gathering of disciples); his trashing of a television studio (driving the money-changers from the temple); and the donation of Daniel's organs to others after his death (the Eucharist). Howie Movshovitz of the *Denver Post* says that the obviousness of these parallels "hits you like a hammer, and it's hard to take it seriously", while Caryn James of *The New York Times* writes that the Resurrection scene is "beyond belief".[45]

A more frequent but just as reductive method of fixing a meaning to *Jesus of Montreal* other than simple allegorization is to treat it as a social critique. The critics who judge the film on these terms are often dissatisfied, partly because they treat society as a generalizable term, once again not specific to place. James Verniere of the *Boston Herald* writes that *Jesus of Montreal* "beats that tired old nag – the loss of values in the modern world".[46] Richard Freedman, of the *Star Ledger* (Newark, New Jersey) complains of the "shopworn" themes that the film employs in order to illustrate the banality and superficiality of modern civilisation.[47] According to Freedman, not only is the premise of *Jesus of Montreal* shopworn, but also its critique of society is frivolous, since it focuses on the media rather than on serious social issues: "Surely the subject of capital punishment would be more likely to engage the moral attention of a modern Jesus than the subject of beer commercials, which, to judge from *Jesus of Montreal*, you would think were the most serious blight on modern civilization". Freedman forgets that the film is set in Canada where capital punishment is not practised; for a Jesus "of Montreal" this issue would not be relevant. Freedman's "universalizing" tendency is, in fact, a confusion of the problems of the United States for those of the world. Nevertheless, we accept Freedman's point: this Jesus is less concerned with "real politics" than with the politics of representation. It is debatable whether or not these politics are as important as those which involve "capital punishment".

Critics such as Roger Ebert of the *Chicago Sun Times* and Tom Jacobs of the *Los Angeles Daily News* like the way Arcand criticises the modern world, but still from a universalizing perspective. Ebert writes that the film is "an original and uncompromising attempt to explore what really might happen, if the spirit of Jesus were to walk among *us* in these timid and materialistic times" [my emphasis].[48] Jacobs says that while Arcand can be accused of using the film as "a personal pulpit", it is "always to decry the shallowness of *our* popular culture rather than to make fun of religion" [my emphasis].[49] Whether or not the reviewers who evaluate the film as a social critique do justice to the specificity of the film, they grasp the fact that the relationship between popular culture and religion in the film is one which plays the sincerity of one against the ephemerality of the other. The question becomes whether or not the religious images can avoid dissolving into the media ephemera.

We might ask what Arcand means by making the passion-play into a popular culture phenomenon itself. Jami Bernard of the *New York Post* claims that popular culture is the butt of Arcand's satire: "If Jesus were alive today, Arcand says, there would be a pitched battle for the book rights, and the TV critics would give his life 8 1/2 out of 10. Thumbs up!"[50] Christ is simply absorbed as one more media event. Even David Denby, who dislikes the film, grants Arcand this one success: "he gets at the way modern media society turns every event, no matter how seriously intended, into sensation".[51] Daniel's agony is that he cannot get his audiences to see beyond the idea that the play is a media event, a show. Arcand's media consciousness in *Jesus of Montreal* gives the film a postmodern aspect. While Arcand is hardly a Baudrillard-influenced postmodernist, his treatment of a medium which cannot escape its own simulations and overloads itself with spectacle so as to produce a kind of flatness shows that *Jesus of Montreal* participates in postmodernism's pre-eminent theme: media saturation.[52]

The film's emphasis on media, especially acting in its various forms, leads some critics to find central meaning in the film's self-reflexivity, an aestheticizing counter to interpretations of the film as social critique. The conceit of the film, that of an actor playing Christ becoming Christ-like, invites an allegorical relationship between "the theatre" and the Christ story as *Jesus of Montreal*'s primary theme. David Denby of *New York* is the most forceful exponent of this connection. According to Denby, the film is about actors and the difficulties they have retaining their integrity. The film's weakness is its presumption of the general importance of the actor's plight: "the conception of the movie is smug from the beginning. Some of us may not care to have our souls saved by actors."[53] Denby identifies Arcand with 1960s theatre radicals:

"theatre revolutionaries of twenty years ago – hectoring actor-prophets who wanted to provoke but had nothing of interest to say". If Arcand's purpose were truly what Denby suggests, he would be converting a universal story into a very particular one indeed. There would be a huge imbalance between the sides of the allegorical equation. If *Jesus of Montreal* were a stage-play and not a film, Denby's criticism might apply, but the medium of film objectifies and displaces that of the stage play.

It is worth considering this displacement, for Arcand himself is staging a passion-play of sorts by setting up the play within the film. The medium of film is not just a means of demonstrating the plot; it is also an intermediary between the world of acting on the stage and the commercial world of television advertising. One might argue that the world of modern film production is closer to television advertising than it is to stage-acting and that Arcand recognises the complicity of filmmaking in the media wilderness that his film exposes. It may even be possible to suggest that Arcand is staging his own popularity in this film. While not exactly Christ-like, Arcand has been touted as the saviour and resurrection of Canadian cinema. For Denby to ignore the status of film in his criticism of Arcand's treatment of the theatre and acting is a critical blindness which reduces *Jesus of Montreal* to a simple equation.

Few critics share Denby's absolutist reading of *Jesus of Montreal* as a theatrical allegory, but the role that theatre plays in the film captures several critics' interest. For example, Roger Ebert, while disagreeing with Denby about the merits of the film, also thinks that "in a sense, *Jesus of Montreal* is a movie about the theatre, not about religion".[54] Ebert is not forthcoming on why precisely this is so, but one suspects that he thinks Arcand is doing what Denby thinks he is, only with a higher opinion of it. The *San Francisco Examiner*'s Barbara Shulgasser, under the headline "Another actor who thinks he's divine", questions the rebirth of Jesus as an actor: "The real Jesus was supposed to have been self-effacing. Whoever heard of an actor without ego?"[55] It is curious that no critic suggests that Arcand might be viewing the original Jesus as an actor of sorts growing into a role, and that the temptation by Satan is a test and ultimately a resolution of the question of role-playing.

Malcolm L Johnson of the *Hartford Courant* writes that the theatre itself is "a metaphor for community and belief".[56] The actors "through the powers of the theatre, come to believe deeply in the play and in their leader". In contrast to Denby, Johnson does not see the theatre as the terminus of the film's figurative play; rather, it is an intermediary between Christ and the possibility of community in a modern context. In this reading, placing Christ in a theatrical context is a means of displacing the specific religious content of his story and replacing it with a secular story of community. While this secularization of the film denatures any of its religious content, it raises the issue of the relationship between the small group, in this case the actors, and the larger society, which is also a prominent idea in *The Decline*. As with *The Decline*, the question for *Jesus of Montreal* is the representative status of the group. Are the actors a synecdoche for "society" or a displaced deviation from society? Johnson, while not satisfying this question, at least raises the issue of community, which most of the US critics avoid. Ultimately, the key to understanding Arcand's work in both *The Decline of the American Empire* and *Jesus of Montreal* may be finding out which community his films refer to: a non-specific "human" community, as most of the US critics suggest, or some community more particular and more subtly defined.

Conclusion

The positions taken in the US reviews of Arcand's films indicate that perspective is the most problematic feature of his films. Arcand's perspective is thoroughly ambivalent, though not exactly indeterminate. He sets out interpretive paths which the viewer may or may not follow, depending upon what kind of film he or she wants to construct: farce, melodrama or satire. Multiple perspectives are more apparent in *Jesus of Montreal* than in *The Decline of the American Empire* where the ambivalence is broadly binary, oscillating between ironic critique and simple, "documentary"-style presentation of banality. However, *Jesus of Montreal* is, as Arcand says, a film of "ripping contrasts", demanding that the viewer perceive what is going on from several different angles. It is no wonder these films cause the critics such problems when they are always taking the ground of judgment out from under the audience's feet.

This ambivalence, which I hesitate to call irony, defines Arcand as a postmodernist filmmaker. Fredric Jameson has argued that in postmodernity, aesthetic productions lose their critical perspective in a kind of depthless sphere which flattens all irony.[57] In Arcand's films irony does not disappear, it just becomes harder to perceive and judge because of oscillations in the perspective. We are used to thinking of irony as a literary trope, as a means of "saying one thing while meaning another". In this definition a stable pole of meaning corresponds to the deceptive ironic signifier; we expect the deception to fall away to reveal the truth. In Arcand's filmic irony, however, the perspective renders everything at once "flat" and unstable; no clues will correct the irony for us and make us feel sure that we are perceiving the message in the right way. The US film reviewers want stability, to the point of projecting stable themes on the film in order to grasp it. Recalling Dave Kehr's criticism of *The Decline of the American Empire* for supposedly relying on Louise as the moral backbone of the film will serve as a case in point.

While it is tempting to state that the US reviewers are somehow at fault for their projections, such criticism would be unfair. It is the reviewer's task to determine the film in some sense, to package it for the prospective audience. However, some films are more packageable than others; they fit into genres, make moral statements, depict characters as heroes and villains, and are thus capable of being judged in the terms they establish for themselves. Most American films, produced by the Hollywood machine, are formulaic constructions aimed at pushing specific affective buttons in members of the audience. US reviewers, even though they often decry the formulas Hollywood produces, demand those same formulas from Arcand; however unstable a film may start out as being, ultimately it has to reaffirm some kind of stability. Arcand, however, refuses to restore the balance. He produces possible identifications of themes, characters and points of view, only to resist them.

In terms of national culture, Arcand's perspectival ambivalence resists incorporation into the American sphere of cultural influence, simply by not fitting into the categories that sphere sets up. *The Decline of the American Empire* and *Jesus of Montreal* assert their visibility by refusing consumption. They establish a precarious balance between the local and the placeless, depthless postmodern realm. The locations "on the outskirts of the empire", specifically "Montreal", persist in the more general subjects of sex and religion. The relationship between the particular and the general testifies to the postmodern anxiety of the dissolution of all particulars. For Canadians, this means the threat of disappearing into the United States. Arcand, I think, produces a "quintessentially Canadian" means of playing upon the line that separates the visibility of a culture from its disappearance. The problem for Anglo-Canadians is that it is harder to play upon the slight differences which separate them from the Americans than it is for the Quebecer Arcand.

In an essay on globalization, the anthropologist Arjun Appaduri tries to diminish the idea that globalization is the same thing as Americanization:

> [I]t is worth noticing that for the people of Irian Jaya, Indonesianization may be more worrisome than Americanization, as Japanization may be for Koreans, Indianization for Sri Lankans....for polities of smaller scale, there is always a fear of cultural absorption by polities of larger scale, especially those that are nearby.[58]

For Canadians, however, the United States is the proximate large scale polity, placing them in a kind of double jeopardy as far as the globalization/absorption threat is concerned. The Quebecers are in an even more precarious position, threatened as they are by cultural absorption by English Canada as well as by the United States. With the permeation of English Canada by US media, this double threat to Quebec may become a difference in degree rather than in kind.

We could say that the resistance Arcand's films exert against "capture" by the US reviewers, even as they achieve a certain popularity, defines their cultural position as unassimilable in their own small "quintessentially Canadian" way. I mean this simply as an effect of the films rather than their intention. Their ambivalence is perhaps a model for/of Canadian ambivalence – a means to gain recognition from the cultural power to the south, without dissolving into that culture. There may be "no big friction" in the Canadian situation but there are sufficient persistent ambiguities to prevent wholesale assimilation. Ironically, it may only be through identification with Arcand's Quebec that English Canada can effect the same resistance.

*Notes*

[1] Robert Sklar, "Of Warm and Sunny Tragedies: An Interview with Denys Arcand", *Cineaste* 18: 1 (1990): 14.

[2] Robert Sklar, "Decline of the American Empire: An interview with Denys Arcand", *Cineaste* 15: 2 (1987): 50.

[3] The dynamic of the relationship between Quebec culture and French culture is too complex an issue to discuss here. It is certainly different from the cultural relationship between Canada and the United States. My point here is simply to point out the different networks English-Canadian and French-Canadian cultural products enter into.

[4] Ted Mahar, "*The Decline of the American Empire* surpasses ambitions", (Portland, Oregon) *The Oregonian* 5 January 1987 (located in Review of the Arts [Microform], Film and Television, 1987, 74: F7, fiche).

[5] Robert Sklar, "*Decline of the American Empire*" (Review), *Cineaste* 15: 2 (1987): 47.

[6] John Simon, "Worst Declension", *National Review* 39 (30 January 1987): 61.

[7] Stanley Kauffmann, "Long Twilights", *The New Republic* 195 (8 December 1986): 28.

[8] George Williams, "Intimate tale reflects larger *Decline*", *Sacramento Bee* 13 March 1987 (located in Review of the Arts [Microform], Film and Television,

1987, 117: F8 fiche).

[9] Margaret Atwood, "Canadians: What Do They Want?", in Henry Knepler and Myrna Knepler (eds), *Crossing Cultures* (New York: Macmillan, 1991): 330.

[10] Ibid: 332.

[11] Simon: 61.

[12] Ibid.

[13] Ibid: 63.

[14] Lawrence DeVine, "Talk kills all the action in Montreal", *Detroit Free Press* 23 January 1987 (located in Review of the Arts [Microform], Film and Television, 1987, 74: F14 fiche).

[15] J Hoberman, "Talk Dirty To Me", *Village Voice* 25 November 1986: 57.

[16] Sklar, "*Decline*" (Review): 47.

[17] Elliott Stein, (Review) *Film Comment* 22 (December 1986): 51.

[18] Pauline Kael, "The Current Cinema", *The New Yorker* 62 (15 December 1986): 87.

[19] Vincent Canby, "*Decline*, a Comedy By French-Canadians", *The New York Times* 27 September 1986: 11.

[20] Williams, see note 8.

[21] Jami Bernard, "Sex on the half-shell", *New York Post* 29 September 1986 (located in Review of the Arts [Microform], Film and Television, 1986, 29: D5 fiche).

[22] Hoberman: 57.

[23] David Denby, "Bull Session", *New York* 19 (24 November 1986): 80.

[24] Dave Kehr, "*Empire* a limited spectacle", *Chicago Tribune* 26 November 1986 (located in Review of the Arts [Microform], Film and Television, 1986, 63: G13 fiche).

[25] Joseph Gelmis, "Ironic Conversations on the West's Decline", (Long Island, New York) *Newsday* 27 September 1986 (located in Review of the Arts [Microform], Film and Television, 1986, 29: D4 fiche).

[26] Bernard, see note 21.

[27] Denby: 80; Kauffmann: 28.

28 Kael: 85.

29 David Ansen, "*Jesus of Montreal*", *Newsweek* 12 March 1990: 87.

30 David Denby, "An Actor Died for Your Sins", *New York* 23 (4 June 1990): 76.

31 Howie Movshovitz, "*Jesus* heavy-handed yet touching", *Denver Post* 13 July 1990 (located in Review of the Arts [Microform], Film and Television, 1990, 90: C14 fiche).

32 Vincent Canby, "Critic's Notebook: Old Favorites Are No More At Cannes", *The New York Times* 18 May 1989: C23.

33 David Kronke, "*Jesus* faithful as allegory and satire", *Dallas Times Herald* 28 September 1990 (located in Review of the Arts [Microform], Film and Television, 1990, 122: D11 fiche).

34 Tom O'Brien, "*Jesus of Montreal*", *Film Quarterly* 44: 1 (1990): 49.

35 James M Wall, "Jesus and Others at Montreal Festival", *Christian Century* 106 (27 September 1989): 836.

36 Anonymous, "*Jesus of Montreal*: The City of Nazareth Ought to Sue!", *New York Tribune* 28 May 1990 (located in Review of the Arts [Microform], Film and Television, 1990, 67: F1 fiche).

37 O'Brien: 48.

38 Movshovitz: see note 31.

39 Maria Garcia, "*Jesus of Montreal*", *Films in Review* 41 (October 1990): 491.

40 Ibid: 492.

41 Steve Murray, "*Jesus*: Satire wholly lacking in savvy", (Atlanta) *Journal* 24 August 1990 (located in Review of the Arts [Microform], Film and Television, 1990, 112: G12 fiche).

42 Kronke: see note 33.

43 Caryn James, "A Modern Passion Play in Montreal", *The New York Times* 25 May 1990, C11.

44 Marcia Pally, "*Jesus* screened in controversy at Cannes", *Boston Herald* 19 May 1989 (located in Review of the Arts [Microform], Film and Television, 1989, 60: C10 fiche).

45 Movshovitz: see note 31; James: see note 43.

46 James Verniere, "Lack of passion casts *Jesus* as mediocre", *Boston Herald* 8 June 1990 (located in Review of the Arts [Microform], Film and Television,

1990, 81: B2 fiche).

[47] Richard Freedman, "Passion play gives rise to *Jesus of Montreal*", (Newark, New Jersey) *Star Ledger* 2 June 1990 (located in Review of the Arts [Microform], Film and Television, 1990, 81: B3 fiche).

[48] Roger Ebert, "Passionate, angry *Montreal* resurrects spirit of Jesus", *Chicago Sun Times* 18 July 1990 (located in Review of the Arts [Microform], Film and Television, 1990, 100: D9 fiche).

[49] Tom Jacobs, "*Jesus of Montreal* blessed with spirituality, humour", (Los Angeles) *Daily News* 1 June 1990 (located in Review of the Arts [Microform], Film and Television, 1990, 81: B1 fiche).

[50] Jami Bernard, "Fantastical Method to This Messiah", *New York Post* 25 May 1990 (located in Review of the Arts [Microform], Film and Television, 1990, 81: B4 fiche).

[51] Denby (1990): 76.

[52] See, for example, Jean Baudrillard, *The Ecstasy of Communication*, translated by Bernard and Caroline Schutze, edited by Sylvère Lotringer. Foreign Agents Series (New York: Semiotext[e], 1988).

[53] Denby (1990): 76.

[54] Ebert: see note 48.

[55] Barbara Shulgasser, "Another actor who thinks he's divine", *San Francisco Examiner* 3 August 1990 (located in Review of the Arts [Microform], Film and Television, 1990, 100: D6 fiche).

[56] Malcolm L Johnson, "Questioning, daring *Jesus* is divine work", *Hartford Courant* 17 August 1990 (located in Review of the Arts [Microform], Film and Television, 1990, 100: D8 fiche).

[57] See, for example, Fredric Jameson's "Postmodernism and Consumer Society", in E Ann Kaplan (ed), *Postmodernism and its Discontents: Theories, Practices* (New York: Verso, 1988): 13-29.

[58] Arjun Appaduri, "Disjuncture and Difference in the Global Cultural Economy", *Public Culture* 2: 2 (spring 1990): 5.

# "I only know where I come from, not where I am going": a conversation with Denys Arcand

*André Loiselle*

Interview conducted in Toronto, April 1993; translated from the French and edited by André Loiselle. Translation approved by Denys Arcand.

**André Loiselle**: *You made your first film* A l'Est d'Eaton *[East of Eaton's, 1959] when you were only 18 years old; a few years later, when you were a student in the department of history at the Université de Montréal, you made your first feature film* Seul ou avec d'autres *[Alone or with Others, 1962]. What stimulated you to make films at such an early age? Did you grow up in a family of film buffs who encouraged you to pursue a career in the film industry?*

**Denys Arcand:** No, not at all! My father was a sailor and he had no interest at all in the cinema. As a matter of fact, he scorned the cinema because, for him, the movies were a form of entertainment for the poor. He remembered the 1930s, when the victims of the depression would try to forget their misery by going to the movies. For him, the cinema always remained associated with this image of an escapist diversion for the lower classes. The only performing art my father enjoyed was opera. That was noble and sophisticated enough for him. Actually, he passed on to me his love for opera. Like him, I have a passion for opera. And it shows in some of my films, such as *Réjeanne Padovani* and *Jésus de Montréal* [*Jesus of Montreal*], which are very operatic... But beyond that, my parents did not foster my interest in cinema. Nobody at home cared about the movies, except me.

My own fascination with films started only when, as a college student, I became exposed to other influences. Back then, I would spend all my spare time in cinemas. But in the 1950s in Canada it was absolutely impossible to become a professional filmmaker. The only place where anyone could make films was the National Film Board [NFB] and, of course, there were virtually no openings there. Becoming a cinéaste was a hopeless dream, in my view anyway, so I was satisfied with being an avid cinéphile. In fact, what really interested me, in practical terms, was the theatre. There was a theatre workshop at the Université de Montréal in which I was very active, and it is actually through this workshop that I became involved in *Seul ou avec d'autres*

Some of my fellow students had decided to make a film on life at the university. They had elected to make the film in the *cinéma direct* fashion, which meant that there would be no screenplay, and the whole thing would be improvised. Moreover, one of the initiators of this project, Denis Héroux, who has since become a successful film producer, had convinced the NFB to help the students with the production by lending them the services of Michel Brault. Brault had virtually invented *cinéma direct* and had just returned from France where he had shot Jean Rouch's *cinéma direct* classic, *Chronique d'un été [Chronicle of a Summer,* 1961]. Denis knew that I was working on improvisation in the theatre workshop and so he asked me if I could work as an acting coach on the production, giving themes to the actors from which they could improvise before the camera. And that is how I became involved in film production, as an "actor's director".

*Shortly after the production of* Seul ou avec d'autres, *you were hired by the NFB to make* Champlain *[1964]. The first few films that you made for the NFB* – Champlain, Les Montréalistes *[*Ville-Marie, *1965]*, La Route de l'Ouest *[*The Westward Road, *1965] – all deal with the early history of Canada. Is it because you were employed by the NFB as a historian, or were you personally interested in historical projects?*

I got a job at the NFB for the sole reason that I was a historian, and they appointed me to those historical projects. It was in 1962, the Centennial of the Confederation was only five years away, and the NFB had been requested by the Federal Government to make documentaries on the history of Canada for schools, to give students a sense of our past. Initially I had just applied for a summer job at the NFB because I thought it would be fun to make films. At first they were not interested in hiring anyone. However, when I told them that I had a degree in history, they decided to hire me to do the background research and write a screenplay for a forthcoming project on Champlain. Originally, I was not supposed to direct the film. But there was no one else at the NFB willing to work on boring school documentaries; that is the kind of production that does not interest anyone. So, in desperation they retained my services to direct *Champlain*. I had no experience at all. For *Seul ou avec d'autres* I had worked exclusively with actors; I had not dealt with any of the technical aspects of filmmaking. But the NFB had been ordered by the Government to make films on the history of Canada, and I was the only person they could find. So, over the next few years I made three half-hour films as part of this series of historical documentaries. And that is how I learned... or began to learn how to make films.

The good thing about this programme was that nobody cared. I was working on small films, with virtually no budget, for the school networks, completely in the margin of the regular NFB production. So I could experiment as much as I wanted to. I tried everything: I made some animation, I shot in museums, I shot on location. It was a fascinating way for me to learn the ropes. Unfortunately, I always ran into trouble with censorship at the post-production level. Because of my unusual way of thinking, each of the films contained some elements of information that shocked the directors of production. They wanted colourless and odourless films that would simply repeat the official version of history found in textbooks. But I always offered non-conformist interpretations challenging accepted notions about our history. For instance, in the first film, I suggest that Champlain was attracted to very young girls and, of course, no one wants to be told that the founder of Quebec City was a pedophile. So they were always on my case, asking me to cut scenes or change some of my comments. It became very aggravating for both sides, so they decided to cancel the programme after the third film. In the meantime, however, I had become a permanent employee of the NFB, so I got to work on other films, although the initial programme was discontinued in 1965.

*Did you start working on more personal projects at that time?*

No. I never initiated any personal projects over that period. You see, my academic background exerted a profound influence on me. My professors used to tell my fellow students and myself: "you will be allowed to have ideas when you undertake your doctorate. Before that, content yourself with learning". I always thought there was some value in this principle. It is important to learn your craft before trying to be innovative.  So, throughout the first few years at the NFB, I just concentrated on becoming familiar with the tools of the trade. I felt it was too early for me to embark on my own projects. Nowadays young people follow a completely different path. They are only 18-years-old and they make their own films, projecting their own style, conveying their own personal message. When I was young I did not have any message to convey, I did not have anything to say. I would only wait to be commissioned by producers to work on a project and I always tried to do my best on each job. Unfortunately, "my best" was not always appreciated by the authorities.  That is one of the many contradictions that have shaped my career.

*In those early years were you under the influence of certain filmmakers or movements? Were you trying to emulate Godard or Truffaut?*

No. I was not trying to emulate anyone. My primary influence came from my elders at the NFB – Claude Jutra, Michel Brault, Gilles Groulx. But I never attempted to imitate them. They were all about ten years older than me, they had a lot more experience, so talking with them about the theory and practice of cinema, as well as other subjects such as music and literature, was very enriching and it probably influenced me. But it was an indirect influence. For instance, I learned more from Claude Jutra the person, than from Jutra the cinéaste. He was very intelligent, extremely well-read, he had an amazing knowledge of film history. So he would talk to me about books, movies and so forth, and I would just absorb everything like an amoeba. But it did not have a discernible impact on my films.

Similarly, I was absorbing all the international trends, because I was seeing 8 or 9 films a week. I even used to go to New York with friends to see films that did not make it to Montreal; we would watch 4 or 5 films over a weekend. Everything from the French New Wave, to the later films of the old American directors who were active making films in the early 1960s: John Ford, Howard Hawks. And, of course, it was the apogee of Japanese cinema and the Italians were also producing their best films at the time. For me, 1955 to 1965 represents the golden age of world cinema. There was virtually one absolute masterpiece every year. Kurosawa, Buñuel, Antonioni and Bergman were all at the peak of their careers. I consider myself very lucky to have started my career at a time of such effervescence and renewal in cinema. All these influences made an indelible impression on me. But again, there was not one figure that inspired my work directly. Except, perhaps, Buñuel. It might sound pretentious of me to say this, but I always felt very close to Buñuel's universe. His films captivate me. From the first image to the closing credits, a Buñuel film sends me into raptures. Although I do not think you can find any obvious similarity between my films and those of Buñuel, there is something in his work that touches me deeply.

*If nothing else, you and Buñuel certainly have one point in common: you both had films banned by censors. I am referring to* On est au coton *(We're Fed Up, 1970], the documentary on textile workers which you shot between 1968 and 1970, but which NFB Commissioner, Sydney Newman, literally banned until 1976. What is the story behind* On est au coton? *Was it yet another commissioned project that went wrong, like the historical documentaries?*

On est au coton is different from the historical documentaries in many respects. After the series on New France was cancelled, I remained at the NFB for another couple of years, with a salary but without any important project to work on. The only significant thing I did in that period was writing the screenplay for Michel Brault's *Entre la mer et l'eau douce* [*Drifting Downstream*, 1967]. That was my first experience working on a fictional text. However, the NFB, which was supposed to produce the film, turned down the screenplay, so Michel shot it with the support of an independent production company [Pierre

Patry's Coopératio]. Shortly after that I left the NFB and founded a private company, with Michel Brault and others, called Cinéastes Associés. That lasted only a year or two and nothing came out of it. So I returned to the NFB, but this time I felt ready to embark on my own projects. The first personal film I made was *On est au coton*.

I came up with the idea of making *On est au coton* because at the time Marxist ideology was predominant among the members of my generation. What had struck me about Marxism was its focus on the proletarian struggle and, back then, I had no idea what the working class was all about. I had been raised in a rural area, surrounded by farmers and sailors, like my father. I had never set foot in a factory. If I wanted to talk about Marx's doctrine with other intellectuals, it seemed essential to know the working class at first hand. And since in the 1960s the most important industry in Quebec was textile, I decided to submit to the NFB a documentary project on the working conditions in textile mills; the proposal was accepted.

One of the first things I learned about the industry was that textile mills are private establishments controlled by people who do not like having would-be Marxist filmmakers nosing around their property. I had to negotiate some arrangements with the representatives of Dominion Textile requiring me to show them all the footage before completing the film. Of course, they were appalled by what they saw, because the film depicted with great honesty the terrible plight of the workers. Among other things, I had used an interview with the president of Dominion Textile, Edward King, to contrast the position of the French-speaking workers in relation to the English-speaking workers. King had himself begun at the bottom of the ladder, in the mill, at the same time as a francophone worker profiled in the film. But while the French Canadian remained on the floor, King had made it all the way to the top, not through machiavellian scheming or anything dishonest, but simply because he was an anglophone. This segment was not insulting at all for King, but it showed the difference between francophones and anglophones in the industry, and that was not acceptable to them. So Dominion Textile put pressure on the Federal Government which in turn advised the NFB to can the film.

Ironically, the censorship of the film actually helped my career because it caused quite a turmoil in the community. The mistake that Dominion Textile and the NFB made was to allow the film to be shot in the first place. For censorship to be effective, it must be imposed before the film is shot, otherwise, once the film exists, even if it is not released, it can still be distributed illegally. And this was even easier for *On est au coton* because video equipment had recently become available. This facilitated the copying process and the circulation of the film in the parallel networks of cinémathèques and university cine-clubs.

Unfortunately, the film did not reach the public it was addressing, namely the workers themselves who did not have access to these underground networks. But among the so-called "intelligentsia" everyone saw my cause-célèbre documentary. And for the first time in my life I had a "reputation". Before *On est au coton* I had made only a handful of obscure documentaries that only very few critics and odd cinéphiles had heard of. It is only from 1970, with the *On est au coton* controversy, that I became known to a broader audience.

*In your feature film* Gina *[1975] you look back at the events surrounding the shooting of* On est au coton. *In some scenes we see the filmmaker, played by your brother Gabriel, having to lie to the director of the textile mill about his intentions and having to interview workers in secret in order to obtain honest responses. How close is that to your actual experience? Did you have to lie and hide to get the film done?*

All the time. Otherwise, it was impossible to shoot anything of any interest. This is one of the most unpleasant aspects of the documentary; the constant necessity to lie, to hide, to pretend that you are not doing what you are doing. All the documentaries in which I have been involved have been made in this situation of antagonism. Whether you are dealing with company managers or politicians, as I did in later films, it is always the same story. They do not want the truth to be told, so they refuse to cooperate and they try to stop you from doing an honest job. They will even call the police to kick you out of their property. There is a scene in *On est au coton* showing a policeman asking me a thousand questions about the film, requesting written authorizations and all that. It is extremely difficult to work in such conditions, and that is why after ten years I gave it all up.

*This explains why you decided to work on a fiction film* La Maudite Galette *[The Damned Dough] in 1971.*

It is part of the explanation. But there were other reasons as well. Firstly, fiction filmmaking interested me. Ever since I had worked on the screenplay for *Drifting Downstream* I had been thinking about directing a feature film. But even by 1970 I did not feel an urgent need to jump into fiction. Right after *On est au coton* I actually started shooting another documentary, *Québec: Duplessis et après...* [*Quebec: Duplessis and After...*, 1972], on the 1970 provincial election. But again I ran into trouble with the censors. The NFB commissioner asked me to remove a couple of scenes and change the title of the film [from "Duplessis est encore en vie" to "Québec: Duplessis et après..."]. It was not as drastic as with *On est au coton* but still it irritated me. After *Quebec: Duplessis and After...* the only topic that interested me for a documentary was the terrorist activities of the Front de Libération du

Québec [FLQ] and the 1970 October Crisis. But, of course, no one would ever let me make a film on a subject as controversial as terrorism. My reputation, coupled with the political climate, which had never been worse, made this venture absolutely impossible to realise. So I found myself without a project to work on. And it was at that time that Jean Pierre Lefebvre, a filmmaker who also had his small production company, offered me the chance to work on a feature film. Therefore I moved from documentary to fiction because the former was leading me nowhere and there was an opportunity for the latter.

*You once said that "*La Maudite Galette *is an obvious example of someone who knows nothing about dramatic cinema but who insists, nevertheless, on asserting his ignorance".[1] This is probably why the film often leaves the audience somewhat perplexed. What were you trying to say in this film?*

I do not think I was actually trying to "say" anything. I think that the fiction film is like a novel and, keeping this literary parallel, I would suggest that a documentary is like an essay – that is, a rational reflection on reality. The fiction film, however, like the novel, is a re-creation of reality through a displacement similar to what we experience in dreams. So I believe that in a fiction film the filmmaker is not trying to say anything specific. There are no "messages" in fiction films, at least not in mine. *La Maudite Galette* is nothing but a vague conception of misery in Quebec.

When I was shooting *On est au coton*, and even *Quebec: Duplessis and After...*, I was exposed to people who lived in extreme poverty, grappling with problems of acculturation, plagued with physical and mental illnesses. The intensity of their distress captured my imagination and I tried to give form to these images of misery in my first fiction film. But I knew very little about the language of narrative cinema at that time. I had never been on the set of a fiction film before. So *La Maudite Galette* became a shapeless expression of my outrage, shot in the strangest style. I did not know how to edit a scene, how to develop the cinematic discourse, hence the endless sequence-shots that make up the film. Since I did not know anything, I had decided to resort to the most primitive rudiments of the language: fixed shots, always from the same position in relation to the action. There are two ways of making a first feature. Either you put everything in the first film and refine your style as you gain experience – most young cinéastes nowadays adopt this approach – or you start with nothing and increase the level of complexity from film to film. I chose the latter. The progression is obvious when you view my films chronologically. *Réjeanne Padovani* is already more sophisticated technically than *La Maudite Galette*. There are close-ups, tracking shots, a more creative use of sound.

Similarly, *Gina* is more elaborate in terms of movement and narrative structure than *Réjeanne Padovani*. And, of course, films such as *Le Déclin de l'empire américain* [*The Decline of the American Empire*] and *Jesus of Montreal* are a lot more complex than the earlier features.

*The most bewildering scene in* La Maudite Galette *is the one showing Roland, Berthe and her two brothers in a pick-up truck, driving towards uncle Arthur's house. The scene presents images of small Quebec villages at night, while nostalgic folkloric music is heard on the soundtrack. This lyrical moment in the film contrasts drastically with the scenes of torture and mayhem that follow. What is the purpose of this sequence?*

I wish I could give you a brilliant answer, but I cannot. The only thing I can say is that my first three fiction films are transposed illustrations of my two previous documentaries. For instance, when we were shooting *Quebec: Duplessis and After...* we were very often travelling outside Montreal in the evening, going from one church-basement election meeting to the next in the Eastern townships or around Trois-Rivières, and we would drive through small villages, late at night when all the lights were off, and we would see these small isolated houses only through the wan glow of the car's headlights. There is a kind of desolate beauty in these barren panoramas and I just tried to reproduce these images in *La Maudite Galette*. All I know is that these images haunted me and I put them in the film.

*I thought that by combining images of typical French-Canadian villages with folkloric music you were trying to suggest a nexus between traditional Quebec culture and the unbearable acts of violence that follow.*

Maybe that is what I was trying to do. There is an important portion of my fictional writing that is entirely unconscious and that demands to be elucidated by more competent critics than myself. I am too close to the material to give you a valid interpretation of my films. For instance, I have often been asked why 75% of the action in my films takes place at night. I had never even noticed that it was the case until a critic pointed it out to me. Maybe it is because when I was young I loved night-time. I used to get up very late, once the day was almost over, and I would live at night. Or maybe it is something even deeper than that, in my subconscious. My films are filled with elements that do not make sense to me, but nevertheless I put them there because they are part of my vision. It is your job to find out their meaning, not mine.

*And your feature documentaries offer clues to decipher the fiction films?*

Yes. I spent a total of five years on the two feature documentaries, at a time in my life [roughly between 25 and 30] when I was acquiring a great amount of knowledge, not only about filmmaking, but also about politics, society, life in general. Naturally I felt the need to prolong this learning process and reflect upon it in my fiction films. When I made *Quebec: Duplessis and After...*, for example, I witnessed a close connection between politics and organised crime. I would have liked to have shown this connection in the documentary but, as I said earlier, it is impossible to convince politicians and their acolytes to disclose anything in front of the camera. At one point, a Minister, who was escorted by his bodyguards from the Quebec Provincial Police, came to talk in favour of the candidate. The first thing you know, while the Minister and the candidate are giving their speeches in the assembly hall, the police officers and the candidate's mafiosi bodyguards are smoking a cigarette behind the scene, chatting. They are on a first name basis. And even we, the film crew, could mingle with them and talk about their jobs over a beer. But they would never allow us to take out the camera. So there is a whole world out there which you cannot possibly talk about in a documentary. That is the reason I made *Réjeanne Padovani*: in order to talk about that world. Of course, I transposed the situation, I gave it a dramatic form – even respecting the three neo-classical unities – but the whole thing comes from my experience as a political documentarist.

In the same manner *Gina* comes from my relationship with the exotic dancers that were giving their shows at the small-town hotels in which we were staying while shooting *On est au coton*. There was never anyone in those hotels, except for us and the strippers sent from some agency in Montreal. So after a while we got to know them, we would have breakfast with them, play pool. Again, over a beer, the girls would tell us about all the crap they had to put up with. But we could not get anything on film. So I had to use fiction to talk about the real world.

*One of the issues that recur in your three earlier fiction films,* La Maudite Galette, Réjeanne Padovani *and* Gina, *is violence, and especially violence against women. Does this also stem from your experience as a documentarist? Had you witnessed violence against women when you were shooting the documentaries?*

I witnessed violence against everyone! There was violence everywhere in the early 1970s. A lot of people saw violence as the only solution to their hopeless predicament, hence the blind, senseless brutality that culminated with the FLQ and the October Crisis. There was something in the collective unconscious of the Quebec nation around 1970 that led me to saturate my films with gory scenes.

You are right. It is true that women in my films are often victims of violence. But I was not trying to condone or condemn specifically violence against women. I was just portraying the atrocities of our society. At the end of *Gina*, for instance, it is the main female character who comes out a winner. The men who raped her have all been killed upon her order and she leaves for Mexico. Like everyone else, Gina resorts to violence because she lives in a horrific milieu immersed in a blood bath. Actually, Gina is the one who provokes the goriest death in any of my films, when she shoves a man in a snowblower.

*The snowblower death is indeed rather spectacular. Because of the sensationalist nature of this and many other sequences in* Gina *– the striptease scene, for example, or the chase scene involving a car and a snowmobile – it gives the impression that you were trying to exploit sex and violence to reach a broad audience, emulating the worst of Hollywood models.*

That is not at all what I was trying to do. To tell you the truth, I never try to do anything specific with my films. I never know where I am going; I am always in the dark when I shoot a film. I never know who my audience will be. I know the story that I am trying to tell, and that is about it. The film takes on its own shape as it is being made. Maybe *Gina* turned out to look like an exploitive film against my will. That might explain why it was so poorly received outside Quebec. *La Maudite Galette* and *Réjeanne Padovani* had been quite successful abroad, especially in Europe. And I was sure that *Gina* would interest the same audience. But it was not the case. *Gina* was not invited to any festival, everyone hated it. People who had praised *Réjeanne Padovani* were shocked by *Gina*. The director of the New York Film Festival, Richard Roud, found it atrocious. Yet it was my biggest financial success of the 1970s in Quebec.

In recent years, however, it seems that people outside Quebec are discovering the film. Last year, in a retrospective of my work at the Cinémathèque Ontario in Toronto, the film was received very enthusiastically by people who had never seen it before. And elsewhere viewers are starting to appreciate *Gina*, fifteen years after its release. I am happy about that because I always thought that the film was a failure. Now I am starting to think that maybe its lack of international success was just a matter of bad timing.

To return to your question, I was not trying to emulate the Hollywood model. But as a spectator I love action movies, with chases, fights and so forth. So I wanted to include that in *Gina*, to please myself, and I have the right to do that if I want to!

*Yes, you do. And* Gina *does bear witness to your increasing technical proficiency. The montage is far more effective than in* La Maudite

Galette *and* Réjeanne Padovani. *It is surprising, however, that after having acquired such mastery over the cinematic tools with* Gina, *you decided to abandon fiction filmmaking. Why did you choose, between 1975 and 1984, to work only on documentaries and television shows?*

I did not have the choice, actually. The failure of *Gina* on the international market depressed me immensely. I had no idea what kind of film I should make next. I felt totally lost. I did not have any encouragement from people in the industry, either. Furthermore, indigenous film production was virtually dead in Quebec at the time. Because of the federal tax-shelter policy, the Canadian Film Development Corporation [now Telefilm Canada] had elected to finance only third-rate co-productions, especially with the Americans; films that nobody remembers today. Between 1976 and 1980 – when Francis Mankiewicz's *Les bons débarras* [*Good Riddance*] heralded the renaissance of our cinema – there was basically nothing at all happening in the Quebec film industry. So my situation was pretty bad. I did not have a job, or any money. The only thing I did was to write the screenplay for the television series *Duplessis*. From 1976 to 1980 I also worked on *Le Confort et l'indifférence* [*Comfort and Indifference*, 1981], but that was just a part-time job, shooting once in a while over a period of four years.

In fact, between *Gina* in 1975 and *The Decline of the American Empire* in 1986, I did not work on any significant project. I did a lot of thinking, trying to find my own voice, but it led me nowhere. Producers were not interested in me. I was lost in a wasteland, and I cannot work in a wasteland! I cannot write a screenplay without having at least a faint hope that it will eventually be turned into a film. But nobody cared about the work I had done or the work I could do. That was a very painful period for me. Especially since I could see people in other countries making films and progressing in their career, while I was confined in my little province, where nobody gave a damn about me. Martin Scorsese, for instance, was as unknown as I was when he went to Cannes with *Mean Streets* in 1973, the same year I went there with *Réjeanne Padovani*. But while after 1975 his career sky-rocketed in New York, I remained trapped in Quebec, working on obscure documentaries, saying to myself "I was born in the wrong place!"

*But* Comfort and Indifference *is hardly an "obscure documentary". It is probably the most intelligent political film ever produced by the NFB.*

Yes. It turned out alright. But at first it was not satisfying at all. Initially I did not even want to make that documentary. It was Roger Frappier, producer at the NFB, who insisted. My association with Roger, which led to *The Decline* and *Jesus of Montreal*, actually dates back to 1976, when he convinced me to work on *Comfort and Indifference*.

When the Parti québécois won the election in 1976, the first item on their agenda was to hold a Referendum in 1980 on sovereignty-association. Roger Frappier told the people at the NFB that this crucial moment in our history had to be chronicled in a documentary and that Denys Arcand was the sole cinéaste in Quebec capable of making this film. So Roger came to my place in Deschambault with a few good bottles of wine, and tried to talk me into directing his documentary. At first I refused categorically. A documentary was the last thing I wanted to become involved in. I did not want to spend all my evenings in church-basement meetings, shooting political speeches, following politicians in a station-wagon to record their insipid statements... No thanks. It is the most boring thing in the world. But Frappier persisted, saying "imagine if we say 'OUI' [to sovereignty association], it will be a turning point. There must be a documentary on that event and you are the best person to make this film. There is nobody else. You must accept. The nation is counting on you, Denys!" Well, I am exaggerating a bit, but it was basically the tone of his argument. So eventually, at the end of the evening, after too much wine, I agreed reluctantly. After a while I started enjoying the work. But at first I had no enthusiasm whatsoever for the project.

*In* Comfort and Indifference, *you employ the character of Machiavelli as a raisonneur commenting on the events surrounding the Referendum. When did it occur to you that having an actor [Jean Pierre Ronfard] quoting Machiavelli would provide an enlightening perspective on Quebec politics?*

Actually it was not my idea. My brother Gabriel suggested it to me. After having agreed to work on the documentary, I started shooting a vast amount of footage without knowing where it would all lead me. That is always the way I work. Unlike what people may think, I am not a systematic filmmaker. I always start from scratch. So, several months into the shooting I had accumulated miles of film, but I could not see how to give a structure to that wide-ranging material. And then, in a conversation with Gabriel, who received his master's degree in philosophy from McGill University, he told me: "if you are making a film on politics, you must read Machiavelli. You cannot bypass him. He is the central thinker of occidental politics". Therefore, I read Machiavelli and everything started to fall into place. To understand the Referendum, I realised, it was necessary to expound Machiavelli's basic principles of politics: what is power, who holds power, how is power negotiated? In the light of Machiavelli's teachings, the defeat of the "OUI" makes perfect sense.

*Perhaps it even makes too much sense. Many reviewers criticised the*

*film vehemently, accusing you of scorning the people of Quebec, who naively fell into the trap laid by "the Prince".*
Yes. The film was criticised by many. But ironically, relatively few people actually saw it. CBC refused to broadcast it – as a matter of fact, CBC never broadcast any of my documentaries. It was shown only once, on Radio-Québec. Consequently, it was seen only by a limited audience, composed mainly of cinéphiles and political analysts.

I think the film should have been rebroadcast in October 1992, when we had the pan-Canadian Referendum on the renewal of the constitution. I think it would still have been a relevant reflection on the mechanism of politics. However, it was never shown again, except once in a while in some remote cinémathèque, to 50 film enthusiasts.

My documentaries have never enjoyed wide distribution because they aggravate those people in charge of controlling public opinion. One of the things that annoys them most is that all my documentaries are organised around the notion that there has been very little progression in political thought over the years. There is an incredibly slow movement in history that you cannot stop, but that you cannot accelerate either. There are only two or three truly novel ideas in politics over the course of a century. Of course, politicians like to think that they can come up with something brand new every other day, so they do not like being reminded that they are merely rephrasing old doctrines.

Another thing people hate about my documentaries is that I often include very amusing sequences in the midst of my analysis. You can make fun of politics and politicians only within the strict framework of official parody. As long as the audience is fully aware that they are watching a comic film or a variety show on television, then you can laugh at the authorities. But if you start making fun of the Government within the earnestly serious discourse of an NFB documentary on an election or a Referendum, then you make enemies; not only among politicians, but also in the media. Because the media are the politicians' acolytes in a massive fraud seeking to convince us that we are governed by people who know what they are doing. Have you ever seen anyone laugh in the middle of the news bulletin? It is like laughing in church. It is an attack on the sacred; it is sacrilege. From this perspective my films are certainly sacrilegious, for I am saying that our leaders are a bunch of clowns who do not have the slightest idea of what they are doing. Some of them are merely stupid, others are utterly demented, and my films are saying "beware of those who lead you and beware of their servile messengers – the petty media universe that gravitates around Ottawa and Quebec City".

*The most common complaint about your documentaries, I believe, is that they are not "objective".*

Absolutely! It is always the same excuse: my films cannot be broadcast because they are completely non-objective. The problem with this argument is that no one can tell me in what respect my films are non-objective. For instance, the federalists would have liked to accuse me of being the evil separatist, but simultaneously the separatists were condemning me for extolling the virtues of Pierre Elliott Trudeau. So I was caught between a rock and a hard place, with enemies on both sides. The only people who were defending my position were film enthusiasts who could appreciate the value of the work itself, apart from any political allegiance. My films have never defended a cause. I never made a militant film for or against the independence of Quebec, because I do not even know if I am for or against independence. It depends on the kind of independence and under which government. I do not want to live in an independent country dominated by a backward nationalism à la Maurice Duplessis. On the other hand, I am not a federalist either, because they cannot formulate a rational answer to the endless contradictions that permeate Canada. I have always been in this grey area. I say what I think to everyone. Most people are shocked, but some do appreciate the honesty and the incredible amount of work that goes into each and every one of my films.

*Your first important project after* Comfort and Indifference *was the television series* Empire Inc. *[1983], which was also your first production in English. Was your choice to work in English after the failure of the Referendum motivated by your political beliefs at the time?*

No. I worked for the English CBC because it was the only job I could get. It was well-made entertainment for the masses, very pleasant to work on, although it was really just an exercise in style. I had not worked on fiction for years. I wanted to work with actors again. *Empire Inc.* allowed me to do that and it was a good job.

*After* Empire Inc. *you worked on another non-personal exercise in style,* Le Crime d'Ovide Plouffe *[The Crime of Ovide Plouffe, 1984]. How did that come about?*

There is a bit of a story to that. When I was working on *Empire Inc.*, the producer Pierre Lamy, for whom I had made *Gina*, offered me the chance to make a film based on Louis Hémon's novel *Maria Chapdelaine* [1914] and I agreed. So, in the early 1980s I wrote a screenplay based on the novel. But somehow the word got out that I was working on this adaptation and, since the title was in the public domain, another group, with Gilles Carle as director, started working on a similar project. Now, my screenplay emphasized the darker side of the story, because Hémon's novel is actually very sad, very moving. It is the tale of a child who does not understand what is happening to her. I felt very close to the universe of Maria. I would have loved to have made the film. But at the time, in the early 1980s, I had no reputation, no one remembered my fiction films from the 1970s. So the producers chose Gilles Carle's project, which had far more glamour than mine, with Carole Laure as Maria. Moreover, Gilles was very much in vogue then, because of the success of *Les Plouffes* [1981].

Thus, I found myself without a job again. But since Gilles was now working on *Maria Chapdelaine*, he had to renounce making the sequel of *Les Plouffes*. So the producer, Denis Héroux, whom I had known since university, asked me to replace Gilles on *The Crime of Ovide Plouffe*. I needed a job and therefore I accepted, even if the novel on which it is based, Roger Lemelin's *Le Crime d'Ovide Plouffe* [1982] is not the best book I have ever read. I found it a very difficult film to make, actually, because I worked day and night trying to turn this novel into something...

*Did this film bring you anything other than excruciating pain?*

Yes. Like *Empire Inc.* it allowed me to work with actors and to employ 35mm equipment. I also used this opportunity to experiment with *mise en scène* techniques. Thanks to *The Crime of Ovide Plouffe* I became far more skilful at choreographing movements in a dramatic scene, and at articulating the narrative through the assemblage of small signifying units, rather than through endless takes. I also learned to work with far larger crews than ever before. While *Gina* was made with a crew of 15, *The Crime of Ovide Plouffe* involved over 100 people. I learned to work with production designers, costume designers and so forth. With *The Crime* I became a competent filmmaker. This technical expertise proved extremely useful when I moved on to work on *The Decline of the American Empire* and *Jesus of Montreal*.

*As you were working on* The Crime *were you already preparing* The Decline*?*

No. It is only after I had finished *The Crime* that Roger Frappier approached me and told me that films such as this were not for me, that I deserved better than this, that I should make my own films. He had managed to convince the NFB to support a group of cinéastes who would develop their own scripts in workshops, and would shoot them on a low budget with 16mm equipment. So he told me: "come up with a screenplay that can be realised with modest means, and we will produce it!" So that got me started. I tried to find a simple idea; something like Louis Malle's *My Dinner with André* [1981], a very interesting film made with next to nothing. So I decided to make a film of conversations. And the subject of conversation that always fascinates everyone is sex. Thus, I started to write dialogues revolving around sex, sometimes just a sentence or a few words picked up in a restaurant or told to me by a friend. I would ask questions to everyone concerning their sexual experiences and jot down their answers. On the basis of these scattered snatches of conversation I wrote some sort of screenplay that Roger found very interesting. So interesting in fact, that he thought we should produce it with a bigger budget, on 35mm, with professional actors, in nice locations, and so on. Roger found additional funds with the independent producer René Malo, who agreed to co-finance the film with the NFB. So I expanded the screenplay, situating it in a gorgeous country house, adding flashbacks that were not there in the original version...

*Were the characters academics from the start?*

It came sometime during the writing process, although I cannot tell you exactly at what stage. At first there were no characters, just conversations. But for that very reason I needed characters who could express themselves correctly. In Quebec, however, this poses a serious problem because of our endemic linguistic inabilities; we do not even speak a real language. The only people capable of expressing themselves clearly are individuals with a university education – everybody else is at the level of onomatopoeia, like the characters of my first three films, who speak with grunts rather than words. So my characters had to be educated. I could have chosen physicians or engineers, but it was easier for me to deal with history professors because it is a milieu that I know very well.

*The working title of* The Decline *was "Conversations scabreuses" (indecent conversations). When did the film become* The Decline of the American Empire, *and why did you choose that title?*

I always have a hard time finding titles for my films. I envy people who can come up with beautiful, evocative titles. In the case of *The Decline* I realised at one point that "Conversations scabreuses" was too narrow a title for what the screenplay had become. I started searching for a better one and eventually I noticed a line from the script, spoken by Dominique, which said "we are now experiencing the decline of the American empire", or something to that effect, and I thought it encapsulated rather well the issues at stake in the film. I had a hard time convincing the distributor to accept this title, however, because he was afraid the audience would mistake the film for a documentary on US history, the Vietnam war, or the disintegration of the inner cities.

*When you first approached Telefilm Canada for extra finance, I believe that the screenplay was vehemently criticised by the referees, was it not?*

Yes. Everyone at Telefilm Canada and at the Société Générale du Cinéma du Québec [now Société Générale des Industries Culturelles] considered that it was the worst thing ever written. One must admit, however, that on paper *The Decline* does not sound very promising: there is no action, the characters talk all the time. The screenplay goes pretty much against all the traditional laws of filmmaking. But I wrote it with a very small budget in mind and, as you know, there is nothing more expensive to film than action scenes. No wonder only the Americans make action films. It is not because they are less intelligent or less "profound" than the others. It is because they are the only ones who have the financial resources to make those films. In the old days, Kurosawa in Japan and, prior to that, Eisenstein in Russia, had big budgets so they made action films. But today, everywhere except in the United States, production budgets are infinitesimal.

*At any rate, the critical and commercial success of* The Decline *certainly proved those referees wrong. However, not everyone enjoyed the film in its final form. Some critics have attacked you for not taking a clearer stance in relation to your characters. It is impossible to know, some reviewers say, if you are criticising or glorifying the lifestyle of your characters.*

I am obviously not glorifying the characters. However, the first rule of dramatic writing is that you cannot scorn your characters. When you scorn your characters, there is no more drama, only caricature. So I am always ambivalent towards my characters. I find some of their witticisms amusing, and others contemptible. Sometimes they can express great insight into their own condition, and the next minute they prove incapable of seeing the blatantly obvious. That is the way human beings are. Writing a screenplay is not like writing an essay. In the latter form you can aspire to some measure of science, you adopt the point of view of Sirius, looking down on mere mortals. When you write drama you are among the mortals, you must accept their flaws as well as their qualities, you must put beauty and ugliness in the same basket. That is the only way to have living characters.

*The characters of* The Decline *seem to be very close to your own life. For instance, your characters have abdicated; they have forgone their social commitment, and now cultivate their "comfort and indifference". Could it not be argued that, having made engagé films in the 1970s, you have abdicated too, now concentrating on middle-class entertainment?*

Maybe you are right. But it is not the way I see it. I really do not like the word "abdicate". For me, to abdicate means to abandon a viable cause in order to devote oneself to comfort and indifference. I do not think that is what I did. All my films were made with honesty. I always invest myself completely in my work. Each of my films reflects my perception of who I am at the time of production. So obviously when I was 45, I was no longer exactly the same person as when I was 30. I had different interests, I had a different perspective on society.

I made a film on the working class when I was 30. I explored that theme with as much honesty as I could, and came to the conclusion that nothing would ever change for the workers in North America, except that factories would keep on closing and an increasing number of workers would be out of work. The notion of the proletariat as a distinct class able to find its own solution to its problems is erroneous. That was the conclusion I reached in 1970, and today I still agree with that deduction. If I were to make *On est au coton* today, I would come up with the same result. That is why I no longer make films such as *On est au coton*. That door is closed.

After that, I made films on politics. Those films convinced me that the political discourse in Quebec and Canada has been the same since Sir Wilfrid Laurier [Prime Minister of Canada 1896-1911]; that there are only cosmetic differences between Maurice Duplessis [Premier of Quebec 1936-39 and 1944-59] and René Lévesque [Premier of Quebec 1976-85]. And I do not foresee any major evolution for the next 25 years. I will be dead or very, very old before anything significant happens. So the door is closed on this as well. So, in 1986 I am 45, I have other interests. I am a professional filmmaker, I lead a comfortable existence, I have experienced certain failures in my personal life. What does all this mean? Where do I come from, where am I, and where am I going? That was what I wanted to explore at that time and it is my right, I believe, to ask questions about myself and try to answer them through the cinematic process. Because in fact *The Decline* does not deal with historians. It is not a comparative sociological study on the sexual habits of the professors of the Université de Montréal vs. those of the Université du Québec à Montréal. It is first and foremost a film about me. On the women in my life. It is obviously transposed, I am not writing my memoirs, yet. But my own life is at the centre of this film.

*So the lack of political ideology that those characters exhibit basically reflects a similar lack in your life?*

Exactly. Political ideology does not interest me at all anymore. Many of the collective movements in which I once took part, directly or indirectly, seem to lead to a dead end. Thus, I experience a feeling of disarray, and it is this feeling that suffuses the film.

*Is hedonism the only solution, then?*

Of course not. Hedonism is another dead end. It leads nowhere.

*Then where is the solution? Do you think that elsewhere, outside Quebec or Canada, things might be more promising?*
No. There probably are not any solutions elsewhere, either. The only difference is that at least things *happen* elsewhere. In Canada nothing ever happens. Canada has always been in the margin of everything. Firstly, it was in the margin of the French empire. Later it moved to the margin of the British empire. And now Canada is in the margin of the American empire. But there is nothing we can do about that. Canada is a northern country, with an enormous territory and a very small population. How can anything ever happen here?
But there are also advantages to living in the margin. The most insightful analysis of *The Decline* I have ever read is a comment published in *Saturday Night*.[2] The reviewer argues that critiques have focused too much on the spoken discourse of the film, at the expense of the visual and musical discourses. In his view, and I agree with him, these non-verbal enunciations convey that, while Canada might not have a very exciting history, there is a sense of peacefulness and serenity here; an immanent happiness that no one "talks" about, but that is communicated through images of the landscape, of nature, of the beautiful houses that the characters inhabit. It is also in the friendship that unites those people. Beyond differences of gender, of age, of sexual orientation, they are all friends. There is a certain gentleness, a certain civility about the characters that counter balances their cynicism. And it was part of the context of the production as well. Making this film was a very pleasant experience for me. We spent a month shooting in a wonderful location, with actors who were friends, and who enjoyed working on the film as much as I did, I think. During production we did not know if the film would have any success at all, and it was not really important. The pleasure of working together was what mattered. So the context and the subtext of the film converge and it is all part of the meaning of *The Decline*. But most people missed it. I am very happy that at least one reviewer perceived it, because that is part of what I wanted to say. One must admit that despite the global irrelevance of Canada, there are advantages to living here. If there were none, I would not live here and neither would you.

*The Decline has been compared to the American film* The Big Chill *[1983, Lawrence Kasdan]. Did this film influence your work?*
No. I saw *The Big Chill* only after having completed *The Decline* or very near the end of post-production. So Kasdan's film had no influence on mine. However, I realised, afterwards, that *The Decline* and *The Big Chill* belong to the same minor film genre, presenting

friends brought together, usually in a country house, where interactions among the characters form the core of the narrative. Buñuel's *The Exterminating Angel* [*El ángel exterminado*, 1962] and Jean Renoir's *The Rules of the Game* [1939] also belong to this genre. I am obviously not comparing *The Decline* to those masterpieces but they do share the same basic format. Kenneth Branagh's *Peter's Friends* [1992] also belongs to this category. These are films that depend entirely on the characters. If the audience does not care about the characters, there is no film.

*The psychological richness of the characters you created would then explain the success of* The Decline?

Maybe. However, one cannot really explain the success of a film. One can submit some hypotheses *a posteriori*, but there is something magic that cannot be rationalized. When the film premièred at Cannes during the Directors' Fortnight, there was a mini riot because everybody wanted tickets for my film. I do not know why. The actors were rather unknown. I was totally unknown, except for a few critics who remembered me vaguely from the early 1970s. But there was something magical in the air. And later, when the film travelled around the world, I met people in places as exotic as Rio de Janeiro who told me "Your film is a perfect depiction of academia in Brazil. How did you do it?" I have no idea!

*But you did it again with* Jesus of Montreal, *your second big international triumph. What gave you the idea of making a film about a modern-day Jesus?*

When I was doing the casting for *The Decline* a young actor came to audition for the role of Alain, the graduate student. When I asked him about his previous acting experience he told me he was playing the role of Jesus in a passion-play put on by the Oratoire St-Joseph on Mount Royal. This notion of an actor playing Jesus struck me as being a fascinating subject for a film. So I wrote a synopsis for my producer, Roger Frappier, who liked the idea. He actually proposed the working title "Jésus de Montréal" and we decided to keep it.

*Did you immediately perceive the symbolic potential of this situation – an actor playing Jesus in Montreal?*

No. And I am not sure that I perceive it now either. When I work on a screenplay I do not think about the broad symbolic implications of the film. I only deal with "micro-problems". I work on the structure of the narrative, on the *mise en scène*, on certain traits of character that are difficult to define. I never ask myself, "is this representative of Quebec society?" or whatever. Critics should ask these questions, not me. I carry with me 50 years of memory, unconscious things for the most part, and all this stuff works its way into my films. For instance, my mother was a Carmelite when she was young, and she raised us with the Gospel. When I started working on *Jesus of Montreal* I realised that, although I had not read the Bible for years, I could remember the Gospel by heart. I thought I had forgotten everything, but it all came back to me. The Catholic mythology that surrounded me when I was a child all resurfaced in my memory and I put it in the film because it allowed me to examine my own origins. I was a popular filmmaker in my late forties and I wanted to know what had happened to the religious ideals I had when I was 12 or 13. And what I explore in the film is this very personal relationship with my past. Of course, since I am from Quebec, my personal questioning is necessarily inscribed in the broader history of Quebec. But as I was making the film I was not thinking about that at all.

It is the role of the audience to decode all these signifying elements and to combine them into a coherent whole. When I read critical interpretations of my work, such as that of Heinz Weinmann, for instance [see bibliography], I am often very surprised to see all that critics can extract from my films. And I am not saying that to play the village idiot. There are things in my films that I am obviously aware of. But there is also a lot of material that is beyond my control.

*One aspect of* Jesus of Montreal *that seems to have been elaborated very consciously is the link between the theatrical ritual and the religious ritual as two forms of sensual and spiritual spectacle.*

Even that was not conscious. I make films about myself, and being an artist raised in a religious milieu, I carry with me traces of deeply rooted spiritual experiences that have affected my artistic expression. I know that this tension is present in the film, but it is not the subject of the film. There are no theses in my films. Their origin is far more mysterious than that. Firstly, there is an image, in the case of *Jesus of Montreal*, that of an actor playing Jesus. And this image begins to haunt me, and slowly other images crop up, that of an actor dubbing porno films, a visit to the planetarium, and eventually these images start assuming a certain structure, and the film emerges step by step. And it is the same process for the music. As I was starting to think about the film, I bought a recording of Pergolesi's *Stabat Mater* and somehow it became a part of my obsession. Because it is truly an obsession. When I am preparing a film I think only about my subject. I become a public menace. I forget my car everywhere. I lock myself out all the time. I become a monomaniac. Eventually it becomes a film. But during the creative process I never know what I am doing, never.

*Another element of the film which must have been consciously thought out is the death of Jesus/Daniel Coulombe at the end of the film. You create a modern-day metaphor for resurrection, namely, organ transplant. I always perceived this metaphor as a little ironic, inasmuch as there is no nexus between Jesus's artistic message and his medical "resurrection". Did you intend the audience to interpret the ending ironically?*

Not at all. I did not intend it to be ironic. I had decided from the start that Daniel Coulombe had to die. An individual longing for the absolute, unwilling to make any compromise, cannot survive in a world such as ours. Society crushes this type of person. So he had to die. However, I wanted to undermine somewhat the tragedy of his death because, in our age, tragedy has lost its importance. So I chose a rather grotesque death for the actor, having him fall under his cross, as if the performance itself killed the performer. But I still wanted his death to have some meaning. I wanted him to be rejected by everyone before his death, turned away at hospitals, supported only by the two actresses of the troupe. A physician had told me that there are certain types of cranial traumatism that allow a period of "resurrection" after the accident before the person actually dies. And the physician had also told me that people who die from such traumatism are "god sent", or something to that effect, because their organs are still in perfect condition for transplant. So I decided to go along with that. And there is no irony intended. The ending is absolutely plausible and functions very effectively as a symbol, I find. I believe in organ transplant. People survive thanks to it. It is an important, meaningful gesture to give your organs so that another may live. You probably see something in it that evades me, something deeper than what I intended. It is actually a very straightforward ending.

*Your outlook seems to have changed drastically between* The Decline *and* Jesus of Montreal. *At the end of the former, there is not much hope that any of the characters will ever find a way out of the hedonistic dead end. In* Jesus of Montreal, *on the other hand, there is much more optimism. The production of the passion-play gives meaning to the life of the actors. How do you explain this passage from cynicism to optimism?*

It is probably something very personal. What gives me hope, the solution I have found, is cinema. My goal in life is to make the best films I can and to enjoy myself while producing them. Through cinema I justify my existence to myself. Similarly, the actors in *Jesus of Montreal* find their purpose in life in the production of the play. Like me, they believe in the importance of what they are doing. They devote themselves completely to their art. Daniel even gives his life for his art.

*The success of the film is certainly due, in part, to the fact that you had a wonderful cast of actors: Lothaire Bluteau, Rémy Girard, Johanne-Marie Tremblay, Gilles Pelletier, Robert Lepage. What made you choose Bluteau to play the role of Jesus?*

I saw him in René-Daniel Dubois's play *Being at Home with Claude* [1985] and found him absolutely astounding. When I started thinking about *Jesus of Montreal* I immediately thought about him; so much so in fact, that I never imagined anybody else in the role. There was simply no one else in Montreal to play this part. So I went to see him and told him: "You must play the part of Jesus in my film, otherwise I do not make the film". He hesitated for a while before accepting. We saw each other every two months for about a year, to talk about the film. He read all the books that I read on Jesus to prepare for the role. He is a very intelligent actor. I am glad he accepted the part.

*What about Robert Lepage? As a very creative stage director himself, did he try to impose his vision on the staging of the play within the film?*

Not at all. It is very easy to work with Robert. Even if he is exceptionally talented, he is not at all egocentric. He is very generous, available, simple. I am grateful to him for suggesting the use of the Bulgarian Voices for some of the passion-play scenes. I had no idea what kind of music the actors would use on the mountain during the play. So Robert suggested the Bulgarian Voices and he was absolutely right.

*It is interesting that immediately after directing a film in which there is a theatrical production, you decided to move to the real theatre, directing your first stage play in 1990,* Les Lettres de la religieuse portugaise *[The Letters of the Portuguese Nun]. How did that come about?*

That was a bit of a fluke. Pierre Bernard, the artistic director of the Théâtre de Quat'Sous, asked me if I would be interested in directing a play, and of course I said yes; theatre had appealed to me ever since my college days. So we started looking for a play that I could direct and eventually Pierre gave me *The Letters*. Immediately upon reading the text, I agreed to do it not only because it is a wonderful drama, but also because it required only a very simple staging, with one set, one heroine and three peripheral characters. And since it was my first experience with professional theatre, I preferred to start with something easy to realise technically, exactly like when I began making fiction films in the early 1970s.

*The play deals with a religious subject, namely, a cloistered nun who writes to her lover. Was it just a coincidence that following* Jesus of

Montreal *you chose to work on another aspect of the Catholic mythology?*
Yes, just a coincidence. There was no conscious attempt on my part to carry on in the religious vein. It is just that an actress, Anne Dorval, wanted to have the play produced and asked Pierre Bernard to find a director, and he submitted it to me.

*Did you enjoy working in the theatre?*
Very much so, yes. I had always wanted to work in the professional theatre. However, no one ever offered me a chance to materialize this aspiration and since I am very timid, I would never dare to knock on doors to beg someone to give me a job as a stage director. But, you see, there are certain advantages to being famous, among other things, the fact that people think about you for a number of things, and it is actually very pleasant. Because when you are unknown people are unaware that you exist and that you have talent. But with the success of the films, I was often on television, so people saw me, and when something came up they thought about me. And I am very glad that it happened, because I loved working on *The Letters* and I am actually thinking about doing something else for the theatre in the near future. I thought about translating Eric Bogosian's *Sex, Drugs and Rock 'n' Roll* [1991], but after a while I realised that it would not come across very well in the Quebec dialect. However, I am keeping my eyes open and if anything strikes a chord, I will stage it. I am also thinking about putting on an opera. Robert Lepage, who recently staged a couple of operas at the Canadian Opera Company in Toronto, encourages me to do it. Opera is risky, though. But it is very tempting.

*After the play, you returned to film with* Seen From Afar, *a short contribution to the omnibus feature* Montréal vu par... six variations sur un thème *[Montreal Seen By..., 1991].*
Yes, but that was a rather small project. The producer, Denise Robert, came up with the idea of a making a film to celebrate the 350th anniversary of Montreal. So she approached me and since the other filmmakers involved in the project – Michel Brault, Atom Egoyan, Jacques Leduc, Léa Pool and Patricia Rozema – are all people that I know and whose work I enjoy, I accepted. At first I was supposed to write the screenplay, but I could not come up with anything. So at one point I thought I would have to abandon the project. In the meantime, however, Paule Baillargeon went to see the producer with a screenplay that she wanted to direct. So we decided that we would use her script but that I would direct it. And it did not present any problem, because Paule and I have known each other for decades, she had played in my early films, and actually had a small part in *Seen From Afar*. And it was

fun to make because it is a nice little story. It proved more time-consuming than I thought, though. Because some of the stages in the making of this short turned out to take as much time as with a feature. Location scouting, casting and so on, all this takes time. I must have spent 8 to 10 months working exclusively on that short. I do not regret having done it, but it was more laborious than I at first thought.

*After* Montreal Seen By..., *you went to work on an adaptation of Brad Fraser's play* Unidentified Human Remains and the True Nature of Love *[1989]. Was this project commissioned, like* The Crime of Ovide Plouffe*?*

No, it was a personal project. I was working on a screenplay that was leading me nowhere. And, by chance, I was invited to see the French-Canadian version of *Unidentified Human Remains* at the Quat'Sous [March/April 1991], in which my friend Yves Jacques played the main role. And I had also read a short note on the play, written by the director and translator André Brassard, that said "this is the best English-Canadian play ever written, and by far". So I was curious to see this phenomenon – an English-Canadian play praised by the Montreal theatrical community is a phenomenon – and I was very impressed by Brad's vision. He is truly a unique voice in Canadian theatre, something of an Albertan Michel Tremblay, but more hardcore. And I thought that it would make a wonderful film, because it is very cinematic in its structure, with several locations and quite a bit of action. And on the night I saw the play, I was with Roger Frappier. So I told him: "if you can get the film rights for this play, I will direct it". So Roger acquired the rights and Brad wrote the screenplay. I gave him a few indications as to what I thought should be developed, and other aspects that could be elided: the chorus, for instance, which I thought would not work on film. But by and large Brad did the adaptation himself. I worked with him just marginally, maybe 4 or 5 days every other month for 6 months, and by the summer of 1992 there was a final version. The process of adaptation itself was very easy because of the cinematic quality of the play. So the film is very close to the original.

*Does the fact that you shot the film in English have any political significance?*

No. It is simply because the play was originally written in English.

*What is next?*

I will probably return to the screenplay that I began before directing *Love and Human Remains*. I think I have found a way to improve it. But I am not sure that it will be my next film. Maybe I am still too close to the subject: it deals with my parents' death. They both died four or five years ago. And perhaps it is still too recent. I need a bit of distance to transpose it into a dramatic text. Because, as usual, although it is based on my experience, it is not my memoirs. It has to be transposed and maybe I will have to wait another two or three years before I can do anything with this material. Besides, I have always worked a lot. I needed to for financial reasons. Now that I can finally afford economically to slow down, I might decide to travel for a while. Leave filmmaking behind temporarily, and experience other things. I do not know.[3]

*Now that your work has been recognised at home and abroad, that a book is devoted to your films, that you have proved your talent on stage, as well as on the screen, do you have the feeling that you have "arrived"?*

Have I arrived?... You know, I was born and I grew up in Deschambault, a small village in Quebec, and there was not a single book in our house. At the school that I attended as a child, there was only one book, and I never managed to read it because it was always on loan. When I think that now there is a book devoted to my work, I feel very proud. Knowing where I come from, I think I can say that I have arrived. But, then again... I am always astonished and touched when people from other countries, sometimes very famous people, tell me that they enjoy my films, and would like to work with me. How do they know that I even exist? I have always worked in the very close vicinity of Montreal, except for *Love and Human Remains*, for which I went all the way to Toronto, 500 miles away. Is this a sign that I am leaning towards an "international" career? Will I ever leave my small country to work with the big people, with their big budgets? I just do not know.

I only know where I come from, not where I am going.

*Notes*

[1] *Copie Zéro* 34-35 (December 1987/March 1988): 7.

[2] Marshall Delaney, "The Joy of Sex", *Saturday Night* (October 1986): 71-72, 74.

[3] Since the interview, Arcand has embarked on another film project, provisionally entitled *C'est la Vie*. See Ray Conlogue, "English, the Language of Arcand's Love...", *The Globe and Mail* 27 January 1994: A13.

# Denys Arcand: filmography

*Compiled by André Loiselle*

The following abbreviations have been used:

| | | | |
|---|---|---|---|
| DA | Denys Arcand | *ed* | editing |
| *ad* | art direction | *ep* | executive producer |
| *anim* | animation | m | mins |
| bw | black and white | *m* | music |
| col | colour | *p* | producer |
| *comm* | commentary | *pc* | production company |
| *d* | director | *ph* | cinematography |
| *dist* | distributor | *sc* | scriptwriter |

[ ] around an English title indicates a literal translation in the cases where there is no official English title.

## A l'Est d'Eaton
[East of Eaton's]
Canada 1959 20m bw 16mm amateur film
*d* DA, Stéphane Venne
No remaining print.

## Seul ou avec d'autres
[Alone or with Others]
Canada 1962 64m bw 16mm feature docudrama
*ep* Georges Lefebvre *p* Denis Héroux *pc* Association générale des étudiants de l'Université de Montréal *d* DA, Denis Héroux, Stéphane Venne *sc* DA, Stéphane Venne *ph* Michel Brault, assisted by Jean Pierre Payette *m* Stéphane Venne, performed by François Cousineau *ed* Gilles Groulx, assisted by Bernard Gosselin
*main cast* Nicole Braün (Nicole), Pierre Létourneau (Pierre), Michelle Boulizon (Michelle), Marie-José Raymond, Marcel Saint-Germain, Carl Mailhot.
First Quebec film shown at the Critics' Week at the Cannes Film Festival, 1963.
Not distributed

**Champlain**
[working title: "Samuel de Champlain, une réévaluation"]
Canada 1964 28m colour 16mm documentary
*pc* National Film Board *d* DA *sc* DA *ph* Bernard Gosselin, assisted by Gilles Gascon *illustrations* Frédéric Back *anim ph* Doug Poulter, James Wilson, assisted by M Fallen, J Chouinard *m* Kenneth Gilbert, the Quintette de cuivres de Montréal *ed* Werner Nold, Bernard Gosselin *comm* Gisèle Trépanier, Georges Dufaux
*dist* National Film Board
A 14-minute version of this film, entitled **Québec 1603 (Samuel de Champlain**), was adapted and edited by Réjane Charpentier.

**Les Montréalistes**
Ville-Marie
[working titles: "Pour l'amour du ciel" and "Mysticism"]
Canada 1965 27m colour 16mm documentary
*ep* Fernand Dansereau *p* André Belleau *pc* National Film Board *d* DA *sc* Andrée Thibault *ph* Bernard Gosselin, assisted by Jacques Leduc *m* Donald Mackey and the Renaissance Singers of Montreal *ed* Monique Fortier *comm* Gisèle Trépanier, Gilles Marsolais
*dist* National Film Board

**La Route de l'Ouest**
The Westward Road
[working titles: "L'Ere des découvreurs" and "Découvreurs"]
Canada 1965 28m colour 16mm documentary
*p* André Belleau *pc* National Film Board *d* DA *sc* DA *ph* Bernard Gosselin *m* Kenneth Gilbert, Olav Harstad, Sorcha ni Ghuairim, Société de Musique d'Autrefois *ed* Werner Nold *comm* Christian Delmas
*dist* National Film Board

**Montréal un jour d'été**
Montreal on a Summer Day
Canada 1965 12m colour 35mm documentary
*ep* Raymond-Marie Léger *pc* Office du film du Québec *d* DA *ph* Bernard Gosselin *m* Stéphane Venne *ed* DA
*dist* Office du film du Québec

**Volleyball**
Canada 1966 13m bw 35mm documentary
*ep* Guy L Côté *p* Jacques Bobet *pc* National Film Board *d* DA *ph* Jean-Claude Labrecque, Jean Roy, Thomas Vamos *m* Claude Léveillée, Les Pharaons *ed* DA
*dist* National Film Board

**Parcs atlantiques**
Atlantic Parks
Canada 1967 17m colour 35mm documentary
*p* Jacques Bobet, André Belleau *d* DA *based on an idea by* Jacques Bobet *ph* Gilles Gascon, assisted by Roger Rochat *m* François Cousineau *ed* DA, assisted by Pierre Bernier
*with the participation of* Marie-José, Jean, and Jérôme Décarie.
*dist* National Film Board

**On est au coton**
[We're Fed Up]
[working title: "Les Informateurs"]
Canada 1970 159m bw 16mm documentary
*ep* Guy L Côté *p* Marc Beaudet, Pierre Maheu *pc* National Film Board *d* DA *research* Gérald Godin *ph* Alain Dostie, Pierre Mignot *ed* Pierre Bernier
*with the participation of* Georges Vaillancourt, Edward F King, Claude Lemelin, Madeleine Parent, Jacques Girard, Carmen Bertrand, Bertrand Saint-Onge etc.
*dist* National Film Board (available on video)

**La Maudite Galette**
[The Damned Dough]
[working title: "Calibre 45"]
Canada 1971 100m colour 35mm feature
*ep* Pierre Lamy *p* Marguerite Duparc *pc* Cinak, Les Films Carle-Lamy, France Film *d* DA, assisted by André Corriveau, Monique Gervais *sc* Jacques Benoit *ph* Alain Dostie *m* Michel Hinton, Gabriel Arcand, Lionel Thériault *ed* Marguerite Duparc *ad* Jacques Méthé
*main cast* Luce Guilbeault (Berthe), Marcel Sabourin (Ernest), René Caron (Roland), J-Léo Gagnon (uncle Arthur), Jean Pierre Saulnier (Rosaire), Gabriel Arcand (Ti-Bi) [DA appears in a small part as a detective].
*dist* Québec-France Film

**Québec: Duplessis et après...**
Quebec: Duplessis and After...
[working title: "Duplessis est encore en vie"]
Canada 1972 115m bw 16mm documentary
*p* Paul Larose *pc* National Film Board *d* DA *research* André Théberge *source* Pierre Maheu (original idea) *ph* Alain Dostie, Réo Grégoire, Pierre Letarte, Pierre Mignot *ed* DA, Pierre Bernier
*cast/narr* Gisèle Trépanier, Robin Spry.
*dist* National Film Board (available on video)

**Réjeanne Padovani**
[working title: "La Mort de Lucie Patriarca"]
Canada 1973 94m colour 35mm feature
*p* Marguerite Duparc *pc* Cinak *d* DA *sc* DA, assisted by Jacques Benoit *ph* Alain Dostie, assisted by Louis de Ernsted, Michel Caron *m* Gluck, Walter Boudreau, interpreted by Margot MacKinnon *ed* Marguerite Duparc, DA *ad* Robert Scheen, Louis Ménard
*main cast* Luce Guilbeault (Réjeanne Padovani), Jean Lajeunesse (Vincent Padovani), Pierre Thériault (Dominic Di Muro), Frédérique Collin (Hélène Caron), Roger Lebel (J-Léon Desaulniers), Margot MacKinnon (Stella Desaulniers), Hélène Loiselle (Jeannine Biron), Thérèse Cadorette (Aline Bouchard), Jean Pierre Lefebvre (Jean Pierre Caron), René Caron (Jean-Guy Biron), J-Léo Gagnon (Georges Bouchard), Céline Lomez (Manon Bluteau), Paule Baillargeon (Louise Thibaudeau), Gabriel Arcand (Carlo "Lucky" Ferrara) [DA appears in a small part as Sam Tannenbaum's bodyguard].
*dist* Criterion
*award* Canadian Film Award – best original screenplay (DA, Jacques Benoit) – Canadian Film Academy, 1973.

**Gina**
Canada 1975 94m colour 35mm feature
*ep* Luc Lamy *p* Pierre Lamy *pc* Productions Carle-Lamy *d* DA *sc* DA, assisted by Jacques Poulin, Alain Dostie, Jacques Benoit *ph* Alain Dostie, assisted by Louis de Ernsted, Michel Caron, André Gagnon *m* Michel Pagliaro, Barbara Benny *ed* DA, assisted by Pierre Bernier *ad* Michel Proulx, assisted by Jacques Chamberland
*main cast* Céline Lomez (Gina), Claude Blanchard (Bob Sauvageau), Frédérique Collin (Dolorès), Serge Thériault (the assistant cameraman), Gabriel Arcand (the director), Louise Cuerrier (Carole Bédard), Jocelyn Bérubé (Andy Titel), Paule Baillargeon (Rita Jobin), Jean Pierre Saulnier (Marcel Jobin), Roger Lebel (Léonard Chabot).
*dist* Criterion

**La Lutte des travailleurs d'hôpitaux**
[The Struggle of Hospital Workers]
Canada 1976 28m bw 16mm documentary
*pc* Productions Prisma, Confédération des syndicats nationaux
*p, d* DA [direction], Jacques Blain [sound], Ronald Brault, Alain Dostie [cinematography], François Gill [editing]
Not distributed

**Le Confort et l'indifférence**
Comfort and Indifference

[working title: "Québec et après..."]
Canada 1981 109m colour 16mm documentary
*p* Roger Frappier, Jean Dansereau, Jacques Gagné *pc* National Film Board *d* DA *ph* Alain Dostie, additional images by Pierre Letarte, André Luc Dupont, Martin Leclerc, Roger Rochat, Bruno Carrière, Jean Pierre Lachapelle, Pierre Mignot *ed* Pierre Bernier, assisted by France Dubé
*cast* Jean Pierre Ronfard (Niccolò Machiavelli)
*dist* National Film Board (available on video)
*award* Prix L.E. Ouimet-Molson (best feature film) – Association québécoise des critiques de cinéma, 1982.

**Empire, Inc.**
Canada 1983 51m/episode colour 16mm 6 episode television drama
Episode II: Brother, can you spare $17 million?
Episode V: Titans Don't Cry
Episode VI: The Last Waltz
*ep* Mark Blandford *p* Paul Risacher, Stefan Wodoslawsky *pc* Canadian Broadcasting Corporation with the collaboration of the National Film Board *d* DA *sc* Douglas Bowie (assisted by Jacques Benoit on episode II) *ph* Alain Dostie *m* Neil Chotem *ed* Pierre Bernier, Alfonso Peccia, France Dubé, Antonio Virgini *ad* Pierre Garneau
*main cast* Robert Clothier (Percy), Lyn Jackson (Violet), Charles Jolliffe (Metcalfe), Alexander Knox (Atholstan), Pamela Redfern (Helen), Tony Van Bridge (Arthur), Mitch Martin (Amy).
*dist* Canadian Broadcasting Corporation

**Le Crime d'Ovide Plouffe**
The Crime of Ovide Plouffe
[working title: "Les Plouffe II"]
Canada/France 1984 107m colour 35mm feature
*ep* Denis Héroux, John Kemeny, Jacques Bobet *p* Gabriel Boustani, Justine Héroux *pc* International Cinema Corporation, Société Radio-Canada, National Film Board, Filmax, Film A2 *d* DA *sc* Roger Lemelin, DA *based on the novel by* Roger Lemelin *ph* François Protat *m* Olivier Dassault *ed* Monique Fortier *ad* Jocelyn Joly
*main cast* Gabriel Arcand (Ovide Plouffe), Véronique Jannot (Marie), Jean Carmet (Pacifique Berthet), Anne Létourneau (Rita Toulouse-Plouffe), Donald Pilon (Stan Labrie), Pierre Curzi (Napoléon Plouffe), Juliette Huot (Joséphine Plouffe), Denise Filiatrault (Cécile Plouffe), Serge Dupire (Guillaume Plouffe), Louise Laparé (Jeanne Plouffe), Nathalie Vachon (Arlette Plouffe).
*dist* Les Films René Malo

*award* Genie Award for best actor (Gabriel Arcand) – Academy of Canadian Cinema and Television, 1984.

## Le Déclin de l'empire américain
The Decline of the American Empire
[working title: "Conversations scabreuses"]
Canada 1986 102m colour 35mm feature
*ep* Lyse Lafontaine, Pierre Gendron *p* René Malo, Roger Frappier *pc* Corporation Image M & M, National Film Board *d* DA *sc* DA *ph* Guy Dufaux, Jacques Leduc *(nature images) m* François Dompierre on themes from Handel *ed* Monique Fortier *set design* Gaudeline Sauriol *costume design* Denis Sperdouklis *main cast* Dominique Michel (Dominique), Dorothée Berryman (Louise), Louise Portal (Diane), Pierre Curzi (Pierre), Rémy Girard (Rémy), Yves Jacques (Claude), Geneviève Rioux (Danielle), Daniel Brière (Alain), Gabriel Arcand (Mario).
*dist* Les Films René Malo (available on video)
*awards*
Prix de la Critique Internationale, quinzaine des réalisateurs/Directors' Fortnight – Cannes Film Festival, 1986.
Laurentienne Award (public's award) – Quebec Film Festival, 1986.
Georges Brassens Award (best film) – 3rd International Georges Brassens Colloquium, 1986.
Brazilian Press Award – Rio Film Festival, 1986.
Italian Press Award – 27th Taormina Film Festival, 1986.
Toronto City Award (best Canadian production); Labatt Award (most popular film) – Festival of Festivals, Toronto, 1986.
Public's Award – 3rd Vichy Film Festival, 1986.
Silver Hugo – 22nd Chicago International Film Festival, 1986.
New York Film Critics Circle Award (best film in a foreign language) – 1986.
Prix L.E. Ouimet-Molson (best feature film) – Association québécoise des critiques de cinéma, 1986.
Academy Award® (Oscar) nomination (best foreign language film) – Academy of Motion Picture Arts and Sciences, 1986.
Genie Awards: best motion picture; best supporting actor (Gabriel Arcand); best supporting actress (Louise Portal); best director (DA); best original screenplay (DA); best overall sound (Richard Besse, Jean Pierre Joutel, Adrian Croll); best sound editing (Paul Dion, Diane Boucher, Andy Malcolm); Golden Reel Award – Academy of Canadian Cinema and Television, 1986.
Grand Prize – Société générale du cinéma du Québec, 1987.

**Jésus de Montréal**
Jesus of Montreal
Canada/France 1989 119m colour 35mm feature
*p* Roger Frappier, Pierre Gendron, Doris Girard, Gérard Mital, Jacques-Éric Strauss *pc* Max Films, Gérard Mital Productions *d* DA *sc* DA *ph* Guy Dufaux *m* Yves Laferrière, François Dompierre, Jean-Marie Benoît *ed* Isabelle Dedieu *ad* François Séguin
*main cast* Lothaire Bluteau (Daniel Coulombe), Johanne-Marie Tremblay (Constance Lazure), Gilles Pelletier (Father Raymond Leclerc), Rémy Girard (Martin Durocher), Robert Lepage (René Sylvestre), Catherine Wilkening (Mireille Fontaine), Yves Jacques (Richard Cardinal), DA (judge), Cédric Noël (Pascal Berger), Monique Miller (Denise Quintal).
*dist* Max Films (available on video)
*awards*
Prix L.E. Ouimet-Molson (best feature film) – Association québécoise des critiques de cinéma, 1989.
Prix du Jury – Cannes Film Festival, 1989.
Prix du Jury Œcuménique/Ecumenical Jury's Award – Cannes Film Festival, 1989.
Le Permanent Award – Montreal, 1989.
International Critics' Award – Festival of Festivals, Toronto, 1989.
Award for Best Feature Film – 5th Atlantic Film Festival, Halifax, 1989.
Award for Best Cultural Film – Premio San Remo, Italy, 1989.
Public's Award – 25th Chicago International Film Festival, 1989.
Public's Award – 8th Abitibi-Témiscamingue International Film Festival, Rouyn, 1989.
Critics' Award – 1st Puerto Rico International Film Festival, 1989.
Academy Award® (Oscar) nomination (best foreign language film) – Academy of Motion Picture Arts and Sciences, 1989.
Genie Awards: best motion picture; best actor (Lothaire Bluteau); best supporting actor (Rémy Girard); best director (DA); best cinematography (Guy Dufaux); best art direction (François Séguin); best editing (Isabelle Dedieu); best costume design (Louise Jobin); best music (Yves Laferrière); best overall sound (Patrick Rousseau, Jocelyn Caron, Hans Peter Strobl, Adrian Croll); best sound editing (Diane Boucher, Marcel Pothier, Antoine Morin, Laurent Levy); best original screenplay (DA); Golden Reel Award – Academy of Canadian Cinema and Television, 1990.

**Les Lettres de la religieuse portugaise**
[The Letters of the Portuguese Nun]
Canada 88m colour video (1 inch) television programme
*broadcast* 19 November 1991, Radio-Québec

*p* Daniel Harvey *pc* Spectel Vidéo Inc [now Les Productions Sphinx (1992) Inc.] *d* DA, adapted for television from his stage production of a play by the same title [Théâtre de Quat'Sous, November/December 1990] *sc* DA [screenplay and playscript] from a 17th century text attributed to Guilleragues *ph* Alain Dostie *ed* Alain Baril *set design* François Séguin *costume design* Marc-André Coulombe *main cast* Anne Dorval (Marianne, the Portuguese Nun), Luc Picard (the lieutenant), Johanne-Marie Tremblay (Dona Brites), Jean-François Casabonne (Rodrigue, Marianne's brother).
*dist* Alliance Vivafilm (VHS)

**Montréal vu par... six variations sur un thème**
Montreal Seen By... Six Variations On a Theme
*aka* Montreal Sextet
DA's episode: Vue d'ailleurs (Seen From Afar)
Canada 1991 123m (DA's episode: 20m) colour 35mm omnibus feature
*ep* Michel Houle, Peter Sussman *p* Denise Robert *pc* Atlantis Films, Cinémaginaire
*Credits for DA's episode: sc* Paule Baillargeon *ph* Paul Sarossy *m* Yves Laferrière *ed* Alain Baril
*main cast* Domini Blythe (old lady), Rémy Girard (consul), Paule Baillargeon (consul's wife), Guylaine Saint-Onge (young woman), Raoul Trujillo (the lover) [DA appears as himself in Rozema's film].
*other individual episodes directed by:*
Patricia Rozema: Desperanto / Let Sleeping Girls Lie
Jacques Leduc: La toile du temps / A Canavas in Time
Michel Brault: La dernière partie / The Last Period
Atom Egoyan: En passant / Passing Through
Léa Pool: Rispondetemi
*dist* Melenny Distribution (available on video)
Certain prints in circulation on the international market do not include Jacques Leduc's film and present the five remaining episodes in a different order. In this version, DA's segment is entitled **Seen From Elsewhere** and opens the film.

**Love and Human Remains**
Canada 1993 98m colour 35mm feature
*ep* Roger Frappier, Pierre Latour *p* Roger Frappier, Peter Sussman *pc* Max Films, Altantis Films *d* DA *sc* Brad Fraser, from his play "Unidentified Human Remains and the True Nature of Love" *ph* Paul Sarossy *m* John McCarthy *ed* Alain Baril *pd* François Séguin
*main cast* Thomas Gibson (David), Ruth Marshall (Candy), Cameron Bancroft (Bernie), Mia Kirshner (Benita), Joanne Vannicola (Jerri), Matthew Ferguson (Kane), Rick Roberts (Robert).
*dist* Max Films

# Denys Arcand: selected bibliography

*Compiled by Brian McIlroy*

The intention of this selected bibliography is to provide a list of major resources written in English and in French. A comprehensive listing of material written and published in French can be found in the Quebec journal *Copie Zéro* 34-35 (1987/1988): 71-74. More recent scholarship may be found in the *Annuaire du cinéma québécois* (1988-), published by the Cinémathèque Québécoise.

**Primary bibliography**

*A: published screenplays*

*Jésus de Montréal*. Montreal: Boréal, 1989; translated by Matt Cohen in *Best Canadian Screenplays*, edited by Douglas Bowie and Tom Shoebridge. Kingston: Quarry Press, 1992: 339-429.

*Le déclin de l'empire américain*. Montreal: Boréal, 1986.

*La maudite galette: dossier établi par Pierre Latour sur un film de Denys Arcand*. Montreal: Le Cinématographe: VLB, 1979.

*Duplessis*. Montreal: VLB Éditeur, 1978. [television series]

*Gina: dossier établi par Pierre Latour sur un film de Denys Arcand*. Montreal: L'Aurore, 1976. [available for inspection at the Cinémathèque Québécoise]

*Réjeanne Padovani: dossier établi par Robert Lévesque sur un film de Denys Arcand*. Montreal: L'Aurore, 1976. [available for inspection at the Cinémathèque Québécoise]

B: *interviews and statements*

*(i) in books*

Arcand, Denys. "Speaking of Canadian Film", in André Pâquet (ed), *How to make or not to make a Canadian film*. Montreal: Cinémathèque canadienne, 1967: 17.

Arcand, Denys. "L'Historien silencieux", in Robert Comeau (ed), *Maurice Séguin, historien du Pays québécois*. Montreal: VLB, 1987: 256-257.

Arcand, Denys. "Denys Arcand", in Marie-Christine Abel et al. (eds), *Le cinéma québécois à l'heure internationale*. Montreal: Stanké, 1990: 109-115.

Bonneville, Léo. "Denys Arcand", in *Le Cinéma québécois (par ceux qui le font)*. Montreal: Éditions Paulines & A.D.E., 1979: 33-52.

Coulombe, Michel. *Denys Arcand: la vraie nature du cinéaste*. Montreal: Boréal, 1993. [a collection of interviews with Arcand, and a few introductory comments by Michel Coulombe]

Hofsess, John. "Denys Arcand", in *Inner Views: Ten Canadian Filmmakers*. Toronto: McGraw-Hill Ryerson, 1975: 145-157.

Wright, Judy and Debbie Magidson. "Making films for your own people: An Interview with Denys Arcand", in Seth Feldman and Joyce Nelson (eds), *Canadian Film Reader*. Toronto: Peter Martin Associates, 1977: 217-234.

*(ii) in journals*

"Denys Arcand: le confort sans indifférence", *Séquences* 171 (April 1994): 14-16.

"Des évidences", *Parti Pris* 7 (April 1964).

"Le réalisateur d'un film est-il un auteur?: une bataille pour le respect de l'auteur du film et de ses droits", *Lumières* 16 (November-December 1988): 5-7.

"Le cinéma et l'argent", *Lumières* 12 (March-April 1988): 6-7.

Amiel, Mireille. "Denys Arcand", *Cinéma 73* 180 (September-October 1973): 102-105.

Andrew, Geoff. "Messiah's handle", *Time Out* 1011 (3-10 January 1990): 22-23.

Barker, Adam. "Actors, magicians & the little apocalypse", *Monthly Film Bulletin* 57: 672 (January 1990): 4.

Bergeron, Johanne. "Denys Arcand, scénariste", *Séquences* 153-154 (September 1991): 80-83.

Bonneville, Léo. "Entretien avec Denys Arcand", *Séquences* 74 (October 1973): 5-11.

——————. "Interview Denys Arcand", *Séquences* 140 (June 1989): 15.

Bouthillier-Lévesque, Jeannine. "Entrevue avec Denys Arcand", *Positif* 187 (November 1976): 20-22.

Chabot, Jean. "Cheminements d'une écriture", *Lumières* 22 (spring 1990): 17-21.

Chabot, Jean and Paul Tana. "Le cinéma et l'argent (5): la face cachée de Jésus", *Lumières* 19 (summer 1989): 44-48.

Charbonneau, Alain. "Entretien avec Denys Arcand", *24 Images* 72 (spring 1994): 6-11.

Ciment, Michel. "Entretien avec Denys Arcand: sur Le déclin de l'empire américain", *Positif* 312 (February 1987): 16-20.

Corbeil, Norman. "Ma solitude diminue", *Philosopher* 3 (1987): 7-17.

Demers, Pierre. "Denys Arcand, cinéaste", *Mouvements* 4: 1 (September-October 1986): 46-50.

Dorland, Michael. "Renaissance Man", *Cinema Canada* 134 (October 1986): 15-19, 21.

Fortin, Marie Claude. "Denys Arcand chasseur d'images", *Vous* (September 1989): 28, 30, 32-33.

Hennebelle, Guy. "Brève rencontre ... avec Denys Arcand", *Écran* 72: 9 (November 1972): 26-28.

—————————. "Entretien avec Denys Arcand", *Écran* 19 (November 1973): 61-63.

Lachance, Micheline. "Saint Denys Arcand", *Châtelaine* (August 1989): 29-30, 32, 34.

Lionet, G and N Ghali. "Denys Arcand: le chemin d'un cinéaste québécois", *Jeune Cinéma* 73 (September-October 1973): 23-26.

Marcorelles, Louis. "Entretien avec Denys Arcand", *Image et son* 270 (March 1973): 81-94.

Marsolais, Gilles and Claude Racine. "Entretien avec Denys Arcand. A propos de Jésus de Montréal", *24 Images* 43 (1989): 4-9.

McSorley, Tom. "Between Desire and Design: The Passionate, Sceptical Cinema of Denys Arcand", *Take One* 4 (winter 1994): 6-13.

Nuovo, Franco. "Denys Arcand un an après le déclin...", *Hommes* 5 (spring 1987): 50-51.

Racine, Claude. "Denys Arcand: le confort après l'indifférence", *24 Images* 28-30 (autumn 1986): 27-32.

Ramasse, François. "Être tendre malgré tout: entretien avec Denys Arcand", *Positif* 340 (June 1989): 12-17.

Rousseau, Yves. "*Jésus de Montréal*, c'est aussi l'histoire de ma vie", *Ciné Bulles* 8: 4 (June-August 1989): 4-7.

Sklar, Robert. "*Decline of the American Empire*: An Interview with Denys Arcand", *Cineaste* 15: 2 (1987): 50.

—————————. "Of warm and sunny tragedies: an interview with Denys Arcand", *Cineaste* 18: 1 (1990): 14-16.

Tadros, Jean Pierre. "The second coming of Denys Arcand?: *Jésus de Montréal* in official competition at Cannes", *Cinema Canada* 162 (April-May 1989): 11-12.

—————————. "Un film dramatique pour provoquer une série de

sentiments: *Réjeanne Padovani*", *Cinéma/Québec* 3: 1 (September 1973): 17-23.

Toumarkine, Doris. "Post-Decline satire and drama in Arcand's *Jesus of Montreal*", *The Film Journal* 93: 5 (June 1990): 14, 28.

Vigeant, Louise. "Adaptation des lettres écrites, jouées, filmées: entretien avec Denys Arcand", *Cahiers de théâtre Jeu*, 60 (1991): 93-99. [interview concerning Arcand's staged adaptation of *Les lettres de la religieuse portugaise*" (text attributed to Guilleragues [1669] performed at the Théâtre de Quat'Sous in Montreal from 12 November to 8 December 1990)]

**Secondary bibliography**

*a: special journal issues devoted to Arcand*

*24 Images* 44-45 (autumn 1989)
Contents: "Denys Arcand", by Marcel Jean (39); "Du Spirituel dans l'art. Critique de *Jésus de Montréal*", by Gilles Marsolais (40-43); "Jésus des médias. Critique de *Jésus de Montréal*", by André Roy (44-45); "Entretien avec Denys Arcand", by Marcel Jean (46-53); "Homo Ludens", by Michel Euvrard (54-55); "Quand le cinéma devient un spectacle", by Louis Goyette (56-59); "Cet obscur objet du documentaire", by Henri-Paul Chevrier (60-61); "L'éternel retour", by Marcel Jean (62-63); L'éloquence contre la forme", by Michel Beauchamp (64-65); "Le metteur en scène, par ses acteurs" [interview with Rémy Girard, Paule Baillargeon and Johanne-Marie Tremblay from *Jesus of Montreal*], by Claude Racine (66-68).

*Copie Zéro* 34-35 (December/March 1987/1988)
Contents: "Présentation", by Pierre Véronneau (3); "Entretien. Conversation autour d'un plaisir solitaire", by Pierre Jutras, Réal La Rochelle and Pierre Véronneau (4-12); "Denys Arcand: la tentation du lyrisme", by Réal La Rochelle (13-17); "Fin de siècle" [synopsis of unperformed opera] (18-19); "La fin du voyage" [extract from a sketch] (20-21); "Maria Chapdelaine" [extract from unproduced film project written by André Ricard and Denys Arcand] (22-23); "De l'incertitude au paradoxe: De l'histoire, ou la singularité originelle d'Arcand", by Pierre Véronneau (24-26); "L'histoire chez Denys Arcand: la marque du passé sur les temps présents", by Marcel Jean (27-28); "Le Québec, Machiavel et Arcand...", by Roger Bourdeau (29-31); "De *On est au coton* à *Gina*", by Michel Larouche (32-33); "La lucidité et le désespoir", by Henri-Paul

Chevrier (34-36); "La série Duplessis dix ans plus tard", by Claire Dion (37-39); "Denys Arcand et le ressentiment canadien ou (petite) lecture machiavélique d'Arcand", by Michael Dorland, (40-41); "Arcand ou la vie d'artiste", by Marc DeGryse (42-44); "Les origines: *On est au coton*", by Gérald Godin (45); "I lost it at *La maudite galette*", by Luce Guilbeault (46); "Le pré-vu et l'imprévu ou les charmes discrets du montage", by Monique Fortier (47); "Du comportement du cinéaste", by André Pâquet (48); "*Le Déclin*: une stratégie filmique oscillant entre le cliché et l'ironie", by Denise Pérusse (49-51); "Retournement et duplicité", by Denis Bellemare (52-54); "La vérité perdue", by Fulvio Caccia (55); "La critique féministe et *Le déclin de l'empire américain*", by Véronique Dassas (56-57); "Réflexion sur un succès", by Marguerite Lemay (58-59); "Les hauts et les bas d'un scénario devenu diva. Rapports de lectures du scénario du *Déclin de l'empire américain*" (60); "Textes critiques de Denys Arcand" (61-63); "Filmographie", by Pierre Véronneau (64-70); "Repères bibliographiques", compiled by Nicole Laurin and Carmen Palardy (71-74).

Denys Arcand. *Cinéastes du Québec 8*. Montreal: Conseil québécois pour la diffusion du cinéma, 1971.
Contents: "Présentation", by Réal La Rochelle (3-9); "Points de Vue" [extracts from Arcand's writings] (10-11); "Entretien" [interview with Arcand by Michel Houle, Jacques Leduc and Lucien Hamelin] (12-31); "Post Scriptum: *On est au coton*" [interview with cinematographer Alain Dostie, researcher Gérald Godin and textile worker Bertrand St-Onge by Michel Houle, Jacques Leduc and Lucien Hamelin] (32-39); "Paroles" [extracts from *On est au coton*] (40-46); "Filmographie" (47-48); "Bibliographie" (49).

*b: chapters or sections on Arcand and his work in books*

Collins, Richard. "Duplessis", *Culture, Communication, and National Identity: The Case of Canadian Television*. Toronto: University of Toronto Press, 1990: 318-326.

Hoven, Adrian Van Den. "The Decline of the American Empire in a North-American Perspective", in Joseph I Donohoe, Jr (ed), *Essays on Quebec Cinema*. East Lansing, Michigan: Michigan State University Press, 1991: 145-155.

Jean, Marcel. "Denys Arcand", in Michel Coulombe and Marcel Jean (eds), *Le dictionnaire du cinéma québécois*. Montreal: Boréal, 1991: 9-12.

Jean, Marcel. "L'histoire chez Denys Arcand: la marque du présent sur les temps passés", *Cinéma et histoire: bilan des études en cinéma dans les universités québécoises*. Montreal: Association québécoise des études cinématographiques, 1987: 49-53.

Larose, Jean. "Savoir et sexe dans *Le déclin de l'empire américain*", *La Petite Noirceur*. Montreal: Boréal, 1987: 9-17.

Major, Ginette. "*Réjeanne Padovani*", *Le cinéma québécois à la recherche d'un public: bilan d'une décennie, 1970-1980*. Montreal: Presses de l'université de Montréal, 1982: 91-97.

Pérusse, Denise. "Analyse spectrale autour de la représentation des femmes", in Claude Chabot, Michel Larouche, Denise Pérusse and Pierre Véronneau (eds), *Le cinéma québécois des années 80*. Montreal: Cinémathèque Québécoise, 1989: 22-37.

Posner, Michael. "The Big Chill with a Ph.D.: *The Decline of the American Empire*", *Canadian Dreams: The Making and Marketing of Independent Films*. Vancouver/Toronto: Douglas & McIntyre, 1993: 213-234.

Testa, Bart. "Denys Arcand's sarcasm: a reading of Gina", in Pierre Véronneau, Michael Dorland and Seth Feldman (eds), *Dialogue: cinéma canadien et québécois/Canadian and Quebec Cinema*. Montreal: Mediatext Publications and la Cinémathèque Québécoise, 1987: 203-222.

Véronneau, Pierre. "Quebec Documentary in Perspective", in Ian Lockerbie (ed), *Image and Identity: theatre and cinema in Scotland and Quebec*. Stirling: The John Grierson Archive: University of Stirling, Dept. of French, 1988: 109-119.

Weinmann, Heinz. *Cinéma de l'imaginaire québécois: De la petite Aurore à Jésus de Montréal*. Montreal: L'Hexagone, 1990: 139-255. [chapters on *The Decline of the American Empire* and *Jesus of Montreal*]

c: articles in journals and magazines

Beaulieu, Janick. "*Jésus de Montréal*", *Séquences* 141-142 (September 1989): 67-72.

Bellemare, Denis. "Les négativités", *Revue belge du cinéma* 27 (autumn 1989): 55-58.

Bombardier, Denise. "Le succès a-t-il changé Denys Arcand?", *L'Actualité* 13: 4 (April 1988): 176-179.

Garel, Sylvain and Michel Coulombe. "Denys Arcand: prophète en son pays", *Cinéma 90* 465 (March 1990): 11-12.

Garneau, Michèle. "Du pays de rêve au Québec prêt-à-porter", *24 Images* 52 (November-December 1990): 32-35.

Goyette, Louis. "L'opéra revisité: *Réjeanne Padovani* et *Au Pays de Zom*", *Copie Zéro* (October 1988): 27-30.

Harkness, John. "The improbable rise of Denys Arcand", *Sight & Sound* 58: 4 (autumn 1989): 234-238.

Lamontagne, Gilles G. [untitled] *City Magazine International* 30 (March 1987): 124-125.

Leblond, Daniel. "Symbolisme retrouvé, mais .....", *Relations* 553 (September 1989): 213-214.

Montal, Fabrice. "Histoire d'absence", *Revue belge du cinéma* 27 (autumn 1989): 17-21.

Patar, B. "Denys Arcand: le refus de la ligne juste", *24 Images* 22/23 (autumn/winter 1984/1985): 70-71.

Rochais, Gérard. "Dire Jésus au présent: point de vue d'un exégète", *Relations* 553 (September 1989): 209-212.

Shek, Ben-Z. "History as a unifying structure in *Le déclin de l'empire américain*", *Québec Studies* 9 (autumn 1989-winter 1990): 9-15.

Warren, Paul. "Le style de Denys Arcand", *Québec français* 75 (autumn 1989): 94-95.

*d: selected reviews*

**Love and Human Remains**

Castiel, Elie. "*De l'amour et des restes humains*", *Séquences* 171 (April 1994): 38.

Charbonneau, Alain. "La guerre du faux", *24 Images* 72 (1994): 4-5.

Groen, Rick. "The State of the Alienation", *The Globe and Mail* 1 April 1994: A10, A12.

Johnston, Trevor. "*Love and Human Remains*", *Sight and Sound* 4: 8 (1994): 44-45.

Loiselle, André. "*Love and Human Remains*", *Reverse Shot* 1: 2 (summer 1994): 45.

Roberge, Huguette. "Arcand et le choix de Toronto: pas un pied de nez au Québec", *La Presse* 13 September 1993: A8.

## Montreal Seen By...

Petrowski, Nathalie. "Le désespoir a une ville", *Le Devoir* 9 November 1991: C3.

Von Kursk, Harold. "Montreal Stories", *The Globe and Mail* 8 November 1991: A12.

Arcand's staged adaptation of **Les Lettres de la religieuse portugaise**

Lazaridès, Alexandre. "*Les lettres de la religieuse portugaise*", *Cahiers de théâtre Jeu* 58 (1991): 152-155.

## Jesus of Montreal

Alioff, Maurie. "Denys Arcand's *Jésus de Montréal*", *Cinema Canada* 164 (June-July 1989): 16-17.

Barker, Adam. "*Jésus de Montréal*", *Monthly Film Bulletin* 57: 672 (January 1990): 3-4.

Gay, Richard. "Le troublant Jésus de Denys Arcand", *L'Actualité* (July 1989): 81.

Moore, Suzanne. "*Jesus of Montreal*", *New Statesman & Society* 3: 85 (26 January 1990): 43.

Ramasse, François. "Un personnage tout à fait à la mode (*Jésus de Montréal*)", *Positif* 339 (May 1989): 32-34.

## The Decline of the American Empire

Barrowclough, S. "*Le déclin de l'empire américain*", *Monthly Film Bulletin* 53: 632 (September 1986): 268.

Baxter, Brian. "*The Decline of the American Empire*", *Films and Filming* 384 (September 1986): 32-33.

Dorland, Michael. "*Le déclin de l'empire américain*", *Cinema Canada* 134 (October 1986): 20.

Sarris, Andrew. "Films in Focus: Arcand and his academics", *Village Voice* 31 (2 December 1986): 99.

Sklar, Robert. "*Decline of the American Empire*", *Cineaste* 15: 2 (1987): 46-47.

## The Crime of Ovide Plouffe

Bonneville, Léo. "*Le Crime d'Ovide Plouffe*", *Séquences* 118 (October 1984): 34-36.

Dorland, Michael. "Denys Arcand's "*Le Crime d'Ovide Plouffe*"", *Cinema Canada* 112 (November 1984): 24-25.

Lever, Yves. "Nostalgie, quand tu nous (re)tiens...?", *Relations* 505 (November 1984): 307-308.

Masson, Alain. "*Le Crime d'Ovide Plouffe*", *Positif* 289 (March 1985): 71.

Patar, Benoît. "*Le Crime d'Ovide Plouffe*: l'étonnant crime d'un cinéaste", *24 Images* 22/23 (autumn/winter 1984/1985): 70-71.

## Comfort and Indifference

Bissonnette, Lise. "Denys Arcand and *Le confort et l'indifférence*", *Cinetracts* 16 (1982): 74-76.

Bonneville, Léo. "*Le confort et l'indifférence*", *Séquences* 108 (April 1982): 18-20.

Bourdeau, Roger. "Le Québec, Machiavel, et Arcand...", *Copie Zéro* 34/35 (December 1987/March 1988): 29-31.

Dorland, Michael. "Denys Arcand's *Le confort et l'indifférence*", *Cinema*

*Canada* 82 (March 1982): 32-33.

Lazarus, C. "Arcand's pic another Québécois politics fuss for national Film Board", *Variety* (17 February 1982): 5 +[2p].

**La Lutte des travailleurs d'hôpitaux**

"*La Lutte des travailleurs d'hôpitaux*", *New Canadian Film* 8: 4 (1977): 34.

**Gina**

Beaulieu, Janick. "*Gina*", *Séquences* 80 (April 1975): 21-22.

Gay, Richard. "Notre condition de violés: *Gina* de Denys Arcand", *Cinéma/Québec* 4: 2 (April 1975): 11-14.

Handling, Piers. "*Gina*", *Cinema Canada* 19 (May/June 1975): 61.

Jeancolas, Jean Pierre. "*Gina*", *Positif* 171/172 (July/August 1975): 64-65.

Marsolais, Gilles. "Denys Arcand: un pessimisme justifié?", *Vie des arts* 80 (autumn 1975): 64-65.

**Réjeanne Padovani**

Ciment, Michel. "Cinéma, politique, plaisir et jouissance", *Positif* 156 (February 1974): 49-53.

Haskell, Molly. "Bedding Down with power", *Village Voice* (18 October 1973): 82.

Miller, Mark. "*Réjeanne Padovani*", *Cinema Canada* 13 (April/May 1974): 75-76.

Vallières, Pierre. "Le refus de l'imposteur: *Réjeanne Padovani*", *Cinéma/Québec* 23 (November/December 1973): 7-9.

Vanasse, Michael L. "*Réjeanne Padovani*", *Séquences* 74 (October 1973): 26-27.

## Quebec: Duplessis and After...

Beaulieu, Janick. "*Québec: Duplessis et après...*", *Séquences* 70 (October 1972): 23-24.

Godard, Barbara. "*Québec: Duplessis et après...*", *Take One* 3: 7 (September-October 1971): 32-33.

Johnson, William. "Nothing's changed since Duplessis maker of banned film says", *The Globe and Mail* 27 December 1972.

McKensie, Robert. "Documentary film shows Duplessis-style politics still thriving in Quebec", *Toronto Star* 12 July 1972.

Scully, Robert Guy. "Maurice Duplessis de retour (au cinéma) l'espoir du film documentaire...", *Le Devoir* 23 June 1972.

## La Maudite Galette

Beaulieu, Janick. "*La maudite galette*", *Séquences* 70 (October 1972): 26-27.

Gay, Richard. "Notre condition interrogée: *La maudite galette*", *Cinéma/Québec* 2: 3 (November 1972): 25-27.

Jeancolas, Jean Pierre. "Denys Arcand: *La maudite galette*", *Jeune cinéma* 70 (April/May 1973): 18-19.

Niogret, H. "*La maudite galette*", *Positif* 47 (February 1973): 75-76.

Shek, Ben Z. "En français: cinema from Quebec", *Performing arts in Canada* 10: 1 (spring 1973): 34-35.

## On est au coton

Burnett, Ron. "The crisis of the documentary and fictional film in Quebec", *Cinetracts* 16 (1982): 29-35.

Godin, Gérald. "Les origines: *On est au coton*", *Copie Zéro* 34/35 (December 1987/March 1988): 45.

Gwiazda, Wojtek. "Workers' film now on screen: forced underground", *The Gazette* 9 December 1975.

Hennebelle, Guy. "Le cinéma québécois change de cap: *On est au* coton", *Écran* 72: 1 (January 1972): 22.

Houle, Michel. "*On est au coton*, la censure de la presse", *Champ Libre* 2 (November-December 1971): 54-60.

**Volleyball**

Brodeur, P. "Sport, idéologie et cinéma", *Cinéma Québec* 4 (autumn 1977): 33-42.

**Seul ou avec d'autres**

Basile, Jean. "Seul ou avec d'autres au Cinéma Orpheum", *Le Devoir* 21 April 1962.

Leduc, Jacques. "Cul-de-sac", *Objectif* 62: 14 (July 1962): 26-30.

# Index

*20 ans express [Twenty Year Express]* 11
*24 heures ou plus (24 Hours or More)* 15
*24 Hours or More* see *24 heures ou plus*

*A l'Est d'Eaton [East of Eaton's]* 11, 136
*A tout prendre (Take It All)* 10
academia 73, 74, 77, 79, 84, 107, 116, 120, 151, 155
Achbar, Mark 31n37
advertising 25, 26, 91, 92, 97-99, 129
AGEUM see Association générale des étudiants de l'Université de Montréal
AIDS 25, 78, 84
allegory 5, 7, 41, 45, 90-92, 95, 97-109, 111n13, 114, 120, 127-129
Allen, Woody 74, 121
*Alone or with Others* see *Seul ou avec d'autres*
*ángel exterminado, El (The Exterminating Angel)* 155
Ansen, David 124
Antonioni, Michelangelo 139
Appaduri, Arjun 131
Arcand, Gabriel 62, 65, 78, 111n15, 141, 147
art 47, 48, 50, 52, 53, 63, 74, 78
Association générale des étudiants de l'Université de Montréal (AGEUM) 11, 27n4

Atelier de Conception Sonore 32
*Atlanta Journal* (magazine) 126
Atlantic Parks see Parcs atlantiques
Atwood, Margaret 117, 118
*Au Pays de Zom [In Zom's Country]* 50n7
Auf der Maur, Nick 31n35
Augustine, Saint 107
Bach, Johann Sebastian 48
Back, Frédéric 14
Bailey, Peter 68n12
Baillargeon, Paule 64, 159
Balzac, Honoré de 33
Barre, Raymond 42
Baudrillard, Jean 128
Beauchemin, Serge 45
*Being at Home with Claude* (play) 158
Bel, François 50n6
Bell, Daniel 106
Benoit, Jacques 18, 19, 55, 60
Benveniste, Emile 110n4
Beresford, Bruce 92
Bergman, Ingmar 106, 139
*Berlin: Die Sinfonie einer Großstadt (Berlin: Symphony of a Great City)* 32
*Berlin: Symphony of a Great City* see *Berlin: Die Sinfonie einer Großstadt*
Bernard, Jami 121, 122, 128
Bernard, Pierre 158, 159
Bernier, Pierre 36, 45
Berryman, Dorothée 71
Bérubé, Jocelyn 64

Bible, The
    39, 91, 97-99, 101-104, 107, 109, 125, 127, 156
"Big Bang" 47, 48
big business
    30n29, 90, 95, 96, 99, 103, 104, 107-109
*Big Chill, The* 154
Bigras, Jean-Yves 10
Bissonnette, Lise 22
*Black Robe* 92
Blackburn, Maurice 32
Blanchard, Claude 64
Bluteau, Lothaire 90, 92, 158
Bogosian, Eric 159
Bonneville, Léo 9n5
*bons débarras, Les [Good Riddance]* 146
Book of Job, The 35
Bordwell, David 110n6
*Boston Herald* (newspaper) 126, 127
Bourassa, Robert 16, 29n17, 41, 42
Bourdieu, Pierre 24
Bowie, Douglas 110n3
Branagh, Kenneth 155
Brassard, André 160
Braudel, Fernand 74, 79
Brault, Michel
    10, 27n3, 27n4, 45, 137-140, 159
Brecht, Bertolt
    22, 55, 57, 58, 62, 63, 65, 102, 103
Bresson, Robert 106
Brother André 28n15
*Brothers Karamazov, The* (novel) 90, 97-99
Brunet, Professor Michel 12, 27n5, 88n20
Bryson, Scott 110n10
Bulbulian, Maurice 28n14
Bulgarian Voices 158
Buñuel, Luis 19, 54, 63, 139, 155
Burns, Robert 42
Caccia, Fulvio 22
Cadorette, Thérèse 60
Caligula 44

Canadian Broadcasting Corporation (CBC) 116, 148, 149
Canadian Centennial (1967) 14
Canadian Film Development Corporation (CFDC) 146
Canadian Opera Company, Toronto 159
Canby, Vincent 121, 124
Candid-Eye movement 11
Candy, John 115
Cannes Film Festival
    1, 18, 20, 44, 124, 146, 155
"Can't Help Falling In Love With You" (song) 47
*Cap d'espoir (Cape Hope)* 15
Cape Hope see *Cap d'espoir*
Caravaggio, Polidoro Caldara da 47, 74, 78
Carle, Gilles 18, 26, 149, 150
Caron, René 55, 60
Carpenter, John 105
Carrière, Louise
    28n14, 30n30, 86n1
Carrière, Marcel 27n3, 27n4
*Cat in the Bag, The* see *Le Chat dans le sac*
Catholicism
    10, 17, 29n16, 33, 40, 42, 91, 105, 119, 124, 156, 159
CBC see Canadian Broadcasting Corporation
censorship
    1, 15, 16, 32, 33, 45, 100, 138-141
*C'est la Vie* (film project) 161n3
CFDC see Canadian Film Development Corporation
"Challenge for Change/Société nouvelle" (series) 16
*Champlain* 2, 13, 14, 35, 37, 137
Champlain, Samuel de
    2, 13, 31n41, 37, 38, 137, 138
Charest, Nicole 28n6
*Charme discret de la bourgeoisie, Le (The Discreet Charm of the Bourgeoisie)* 19, 63
Charpentier, Gustave 35

184

Charpentier, Réjane 14
*Chat dans le sac, Le [The Cat in the Bag]* 50n7
Chatman, Seymour 110n4
Chevrier, Henri-Paul 62
*Chicago Sun Times* (newspaper) 128
*Chicago Tribune* (newspaper) 121
*Christian Century* (magazine) 125
*Chronicle of a Summer* see *Chronique d'un été*
*Chronique d'un été [Chronicle of a Summer]* 137
*Cineaste* (magazine) 116, 119
Cinéastes Associés 140
cinéma direct (direct cinema) 11, 12, 14, 27n3, 45, 93, 137
Cinémathèque Ontario 145
*City of God, The* (book) 107
*Clockwork Orange, A* 37
Collin, Frédérique 60, 64
Comeau, Robert 51n13
comedy 125
*Comfort and Indifference* see *Le Confort et l'indifférence*
Commission Supérieure Technique de l'Image et du Son (CST) 50n6
communism 15
*Confort et l'indifférence, Le (Comfort and Indifference)* 1, 6, 21-23, 26, 35, 37, 39, 40, 42, 43, 85, 106, 107, 146, 147, 149
Congregation of Notre-Dame 38
Conlogue, Ray 161n3
Conseil des Universités 111n14
Conseil québécois pour la diffusion du cinéma 44
consumerism 37, 41, 107
*Contempt Will Last But a Time* see *Le mépris n'aura qu'un temps*
Coopératio (production company) 140
*Copie Zéro* (magazine) 11
Coppola, Francis 62, 63

Corneille, Pierre 35
Costa-Gavras, Constantin 19
*Crime d'Ovide Plouffe, Le (The Crime of Ovide Plouffe)* 23, 149, 150, 160
*Crime d'Ovide Plouffe, Le* (novel) 150
*Crime of Ovide Plouffe, The* see *Le Crime d'Ovide Plouffe*
Cronenberg, David 1, 115
CST see Commission Supérieure Technique de l'Image et du Son
Curzi, Pierre 71
*Dallas Times Herald* (newspaper) 124
*Damned Dough, The* see *La Maudite Galette*
"Daniel Coulombe Theatre" 6
Dansereau, Fernand 28n14
Darwin, Charles 7, 53
*Day for Night* see *La nuit américaine*
*Déclin de l'empire américain, Le (The Decline of the American Empire)* 1, 4, 5, 7, 8, 23, 27, 27n5, 35, 36, 43, 44, 46, 47, 69-89, 91, 93-95, 103, 104, 106, 107, 113-126, 130, 131, 143, 146, 150-155, 157
*Decline and Fall of the Roman Empire, The* (book) 115
*Decline of the American Empire, The* see *Le Déclin de l'empire américain*
*Decline of the West* (book) see *Untergang des Abendlandes*
Delaney, Marshall 161n2
Denby, David 121, 122, 124, 128, 129
*Denver Post* (newspaper) 124, 127
Descartes, René 39
*Detroit Free Press* (newspaper) 119
DeVine, Lawrence 119

*Dictionnaire latin-français du baccalauréat* 35
direct cinema **see** cinéma direct
*Discreet Charm of the Bourgeoisie, The* **see** *Le Charme discret de la bourgeoisie*
Dominion Textile 140
*Don Juan* (play) 35, 78
Dorland, Michael 68n15, 110n8
Dorval, Anne 159
Dostoyevsky, Feodor 90, 98-100
Drapeau, Jean 21, 29n21
Dreyer, Carl Theodore 106
*Drifting Downstream* **see** *Entre la mer et l'eau douce*
Dubois, René-Daniel 158
Duparc, Marguerite 36, 44
*Duplessis* (television series) 23, 30n29, 146
Duplessis, Maurice 2, 3, 8n3, 16, 17, 28n15, 29n16, 30n29, 31n41, 33, 40-42, 88n16, 149, 153
Dupond, Patrick 74
Durham, Lord 2, 8n3, 29n19, 41, 42, 51n10
Durham Report **see** Report on the Affairs of British North America
*East of Eaton's* **see** *A l'Est d'Eaton*
Ebert, Roger 128, 129
*école des autres, L'* *[The School of Others]* 28n14
Egoyan, Atom 159
Eisenstein, Sergej 17, 110n12, 152
Elizabeth II 42
*Empire, Inc.* 30n29, 149, 150
*Entre la mer et l'eau douce [Drifting Downstream]* 139, 141
*Entre tu et vous* 50n7
*Esprit du mal, L' [The Evil Spirit]* 10
Euvrard, Michel 21
*Evil Spirit, The* **see** *L'Esprit du mal*
*Exterminating Angel, The* **see** *El ángel exterminado*
Fano, Michel 34, 43, 50n6
*Father Chopin* **see** *Le Père Chopin*

Feldman, Seth 68n15, 110n8, 111n19
Fellini, Federico 106
FEMIS **see** Institut de Formation et d'Enseignement pour les Métiers de l'Image et du Son
Fennario, David 49
*Film Comment* (magazine) 120
film noir 18, 55, 57-59
*Film Quarterly* (magazine) 125
*Films in Review* (magazine) 126
Fletcher, Angus 103, 110n9, 111n13
FLQ **see** Front de Libération du Québec
Folkways Records 39
Fonda, Jane 64
Ford, John 139
Fortier, Monique 36, 45
Fournier, Claude 11, 26
FRAP **see** Front d'Action Politique
Frappier, Roger 146, 147, 150, 155, 160
Fraser, Brad 8, 46, 47, 49, 160
Freedman, Richard 127
Friday, Nancy 79
Front d'Action Politique (FRAP) 29n21
Front de Libération du Québec (FLQ) 29n20, 142, 144
Fukuyama, Francis 106
Gagnon, J-Léo 55, 60
Garcia, Maria 126
Garde Républicaine 42
Gelmis, Joseph 122
*génération lyrique, La* (book) 24
Genette, Gérard 110n4
Géricault, Theodore 47, 74, 78
Gibbon, Edward 115
*Gina* 3, 4, 6, 8, 20, 22, 23, 30n27, 35, 36, 44-46, 51n17, 52-54, 63-66, 69, 92-95, 111n15, 141, 143, 144, 145, 146, 149, 150
Girard, François 48
Girard, Rémy 71, 96, 158

Gluck, Christoph Wilibald 3, 44, 45
Godard, Jean-Luc 6, 7, 22, 52, 54-59, 61-68, 138
*Godfather, The* 62
*Goldberg Variations* 48
*Golden Gloves* 50n7
*Good Riddance* see *Les bons débarras*
*Gospel According to St Matthew, The* see *Il Vangelo secondo Matteo*
Gosselin, Bernard 59
Gould, Glenn 48
Greer, Germaine 79
Grierson, John 112n19
Groulx, Gilles 15, 26, 27n3, 36, 45, 138
GROUPE μ 89n26
"Groupe de recherches sociales" 16
Guilbeault, Luce 55, 60
Halimi, Serge 26
Handel, George Friederic 46
*Hands Over the City* see *Le mani sulla città*
*Hartford Courant* (newspaper) 129
Hawks, Howard 139
Hegel, Georg Wilhelm Friedrich 112n21
Hémon, Louis 149
Henderson, Brian 59, 67n4, 67n6, 110n4
Henry, Pierre 36
Herchberg-Pierrot, Anne 89n24
Héroux, Denis 11, 26, 27n4, 137, 150
Herrmann, Anne 2
"History Makers, The" (series) 13
Hitchcock, Alfred 59, 66
Hite, Shere 78
*Hite Report* 78
Hoberman, J 119, 121
Hofsess, John 54
Hollywood 20, 52, 57, 62, 67n1, 92, 125, 131, 145

homosexuality 78, 82, 122
"Hymnen" (music) 43
IBM 33
*Imitatio Christi (The Imitation of Christ)* (treatise) 105
*Imitation of Christ, The* (treatise) see *Imitatio Christi*
*In Zom's Country* see *Au Pays de Zom*
Institut de Formation et d'Enseignement pour les Métiers de l'Image et du Son (FEMIS) 50n6
Jacobs, Tom 128
Jacques, Yves 71, 104, 160
James, Caryn 126, 127
Jameson, Fredric 130
Janzen, Elizabeth 68n13
Jennings, Peter 115
*Jésus de Montréal (Jesus of Montreal)* 1, 5, 7, 23, 25-27, 35, 44, 46, 47, 49, 90-114, 123-136, 143, 146, 150, 155-159
*Jesus of Montreal* see *Jésus de Montréal*
Jewison, Norman 115
Johnson, Malcolm L 129, 130
Johnson, Virginia 78
*Jonah qui aura 25 ans en l'an 2000 (Jonah Who Will Be 25 in the Year 2000)* 121
*Jonah Who Will Be 25 in the Year 2000* see *Jonah qui aura 25 ans en l'an 2000*
Juneau, Pierre 28n11
*Jusqu'au cou [Up to the Neck]* 27n4
Jutra, Claude 10, 11, 45, 68n16, 138, 139
Jutras, Pierre 28n13
Juvenal 20
Kael, Pauline 120, 122
Kaplan, E Ann 135n57
Kasdan, Lawrence 154
Kauffmann, Stanley 117, 118
Kehr, Dave 121, 122, 130

187

| | | | |
|---|---|---|---|
| Kellogg-Briand Pact | 84 | Liberal Party | |
| Kempis, Thomas à | 105 | 16, 17, 29n16, 29n17, 40-42, 88n16 | |
| *Killers, The* | 58 | Lipovetsky, Gilles | 27 |
| King, Allan | 55 | *Little Burgundy* see *La p'tite* | |
| King, Edward | 140 | *Bourgogne* | |
| *Kino-Eye* | 32 | Loiselle, Hélène | 60 |
| Koenig, Wolf | 11 | Lomez, Céline | 64 |
| Kroitor, Roman | 11 | *Los Angeles Daily News* | |
| Kronke, David | 124, 126 | (newspaper) | 128 |
| Kubrick, Stanley | 37 | Lotringer, Sylvère | 135n52 |
| Kundera, Milan | 74 | *Love and Human Remains* | |
| Kurosawa, Akira | 139, 152 | 1, 6, 8, 35, 43, 44, 46, 47, 115, 160, 161 | |
| La Rochelle, Réal | 6, 28n12, 28n13 | | |
| La Tour, Georges de | 74 | Lully, Jean-Baptiste | 35, 50n1 |
| Labrecque, Jean-Claude | 27n4 | *Lutte des travailleurs d'hôpitaux,* | |
| Laferrière, Yves | 47 | *La [The Struggle of Hospital* | |
| Laing, R D | 74 | *Workers]* | 30n28 |
| Lajeunesse, Jean | 60 | Lyotard, Jean-François | 103 |
| Lamothe, Arthur | 16 | Macartney-Filgate, Terence | 11 |
| Lamothe, Willie | 28n15 | Machiavelli, Niccolò | |
| Lamy, Pierre | 149 | 12, 21-23, 39, 40, 43, 140, 147 | |
| Landry, Bernard | 42 | MacKinnon, Margot | 60 |
| Larose, Jean | 70, 75, 88n21 | MacNeil, Robert | 115 |
| Lasch, Christopher | 89n28 | Magidson, Debbie | 111n19 |
| *Last Temptation of Christ, The* | 105, 124, 125 | Mahar, Ted | 132n4 |
| | | Malle, Louis | 150 |
| Laure, Carole | 150 | Malo, René | 151 |
| Laurier, Sir Wilfrid | 153 | *Mani sulla città, Le (Hands Over* | |
| Lebel, Roger | 60 | *the City)* | 19 |
| Leduc, Jacques | 15, 159 | Mankiewicz, Francis | 146 |
| Lefebvre, Jean Pierre | 18, 19, 26, 60, 68n16, 142 | *Manufacturing Consent: Noam Chomsky and the Media* | 31n37 |
| Lefebvre, Martin | 111n17 | Maoism | 32 |
| Lemelin, Roger | 150 | Marcuse, Herbert | 30n32, 33, 37 |
| Leninism | 15 | *Maria Chapdelaine* (film) | 150 |
| Lepage, Robert | 48, 95, 158, 159 | *Maria Chapdelaine* (novel) | 149 |
| Lesage, Jean | 29n16, 88n16 | *Married Couple, A* | 55 |
| *Letters of the Portuguese Nun, The* (play) see *Les Lettres de la religieuse portugaise* | | Marxism 3, 4, 13, 15, 24, 28n8, 29n18, 29n22, 56, 63, 74, 112n21, 140 | |
| *Lettres de la religieuse portugaise, Les* (play) | 158, 159 | Masters, William | 78 |
| Lévesque, René | 9n4, 16, 17, 21, 29n17, 40, 42, 87n3, 153 | *Maudite Galette, La [The Damned Dough]* 3, 6, 7, 18, 19, 22, 52-60, 62, 66, 141-146 | |
| | | McGill University | 27n2, 147 |

McLaren, Norman 45
McPherson, Hugo 28n11
*Mean Streets* 146
melodrama 10, 23, 56, 130
*Men's Club, The* 122
*mépris n'aura qu'un temps, Le
[Contempt Will Last But a
Time]* 16
Metz, Christian 110n5
Meyers, Mike 115
Michel, Dominique 71
Miller, Monique 97
Mills, David 51n10
Milne, Tom 68n14
*Minute, papillon* (series) 30n29
Molière 35
Montand, Yves 64
Montreal (city)
   4, 5, 8, 10, 19, 38, 40, 44-46,
   49, 53, 54, 60, 63, 74, 78, 90,
   91, 96, 105, 107, 115, 116, 123,
   124, 131, 139, 143, 144, 155,
   158-161
Montreal International Film
   Festival 38, 125
*Montreal on a Summer Day* see
   *Montréal un jour d'été*
*Montreal Seen By... Six Variations
On a Theme* see *Montréal vu
par... six variations sur un
thème*
*Montreal Sextet* see *Montréal vu
par... six variations sur un
thème*
*Montréal un jour d'été (Montreal
on a Summer Day)* 14
*Montréal vu par... six variations
sur un thème (Montreal Seen
By... Six Variations On a
Theme)* 159, 160
*Montréalistes, Les (Ville-Marie)*
   14, 35, 37, 38, 137
*Moontrap, The* see *Pour la suite
du monde*
Movshovitz, Howie 124, 126, 127
Mozart, Wolfgang Amadeus 53
Murray, Steve 126
music (use of)
   6, 54, 57, 59, 71, 94, 143, 156, 158
*Music for the Funeral of Queen
Mary, The* 37
musique concrète 32, 34, 36
*My Dinner with André* 150
Narboni, Jean 68n14
NASA 48
National Assembly of Quebec 16
National Film Board (NFB)
   1, 2, 6, 10-16, 28n10, 30n27, 32,
   36, 37, 39, 43-46, 50, 51n17, 52,
   64, 115, 136-141, 146-148, 150,
   151
*National Review* (magazine) 116
Nazism 53, 63
Nelson, Joyce 111n19
*New Republic, The* (magazine) 117
*New York* (magazine)
   121, 124, 128
New York Film Festival 145
*New York Post* (newspaper)
   121, 122, 128
*New York Times, The* 118, 126, 127
*New York Tribune* (newspaper)
   125, 126
New York World's Fair 39
*New Yorker, The* (magazine) 120
Newman, Sydney 32, 139
*Newsday* (magazine) 122
*Newsweek* (magazine) 124
NFB see National Film Board
Nichols, Bill 67n4
Nietzsche, Friedrich Wilhelm
   32, 39
Niles, Fred A 91
Noël, Cédric 90
Nold, Werner 27n4, 36, 45
*Notre passé, le présent et nous*
   (book) 27n5, 88n20
Nouvelle Vague 139
*nuit américaine, La (Day for
Night)* 46
"O Canada" (Canadian national
   anthem) 37, 42, 45, 66

O'Brien, Tom 124, 134n37
October Crisis
   17, 29n20, 29n21, 142, 144
*On est au coton [We're Fed Up]*
   1, 3, 6, 15-17, 20, 26, 30n32,
   32-35, 45, 64, 93, 103, 111n15,
   139-142, 144, 153
opera
   1, 3, 32, 34, 35, 45, 50n1, 53,
   60, 63, 136, 159
Oratoire St-Joseph 5, 47, 155
*Orfeo ed Euridice (Orpheus and
Eurydice)* (opera) 3, 44
*Orpheus and Eurydice* (opera)
   **see** *Orfeo ed Euridice*
*Out of the Past* 58
Owens, Craig 101
Ozep, Fédor 10
Pally, Marcia 126
Pâquet, André 27n1
*Parable* 91
*Parcs atlantiques (Atlantic Parks)*
   14
Parent, Madeleine 33, 34
Parizeau, Jacques 88n16
*Parti Pris* (magazine) 28n8, 29n22
Parti québécois (PQ)
   3, 9n4, 16, 21, 29n17, 40-42,
   86n3, 147
Pasolini, Pier Paolo 105, 125
*Passion de Jeanne d'Arc, La (The
Passion of Joan of Arc)* 106
*Passion of Joan of Arc, The* **see**
   *La Passion de Jeanne d'Arc*
Patry, Pierre 11, 140
*pays sans bon sens!, Un (Wake
up, mes bons amis)* 15
Pei, I M 40
Pelletier, Gilles 90, 158
*Père Chopin, Le [Father Chopin]* 10
Pergolesi, Giovanni Battista
   5, 47, 156
Perrault, Pierre 10, 15, 18, 26
Pérusse, Denise 7
*Peter's Friends* 155

*petit catéchisme des électeurs, Le
(The Voter's Handbook)*
   17, 41, 45
Place Ville Marie 40
*Plouffes, Les* 150
Pool, Léa 159
Portal, Louise 71
*Postmodern Condition, The* (book)
   103
postmodernism
   7, 36, 45, 106, 114, 125, 126,
   128, 130, 131
*Pour la suite du monde (The
Moontrap)* 10
PQ **see** Parti québécois
Presley, Elvis 47
*Prince, The* (book) **see** *Il principe*
*principe, Il (The Prince)* (book) 21
Prix du Jury Œcuménique/
   Ecumenical Jury's Award 124
Provincial Liberal Party 3, 40
*p'tite Bourgogne, La [Little
Burgundy]* 28n14
Purcell, Henry 37
*Québec 1603* 14
*Quebec: Duplessis and After...* **see**
   *Québec: Duplessis et après...*
*Québec: Duplessis et après...
(Quebec: Duplessis and After...)*
   2, 6, 16, 17, 20, 21, 23, 26, 27,
   30n29, 35, 37, 40, 41, 43, 45,
   51n10, 141-144
Quebec Provincial Police 144
"Quiet Revolution" **see**
   "Révolution tranquille"
Quinault, Philippe 50n1
Rabine, Henry 30n25
Racine, Jean 35, 106
Radio Canada 72
Radio-Québec 148
Rameau, Jean Philippe 35
Ray, Nicholas 47, 48
*Reader's Digest* (magazine) 25
Reagan, Ronald 119
*Rebel Without a Cause* 47

Referendum (1980)
    4, 9n4, 21, 37, 40-42, 70, 85,
        87n3, 147-149
Referendum (1992)    148
Règle du jeu, La (The Rules of the
    Game)    19, 61, 155
Régnier, Michel    28n14
Réjeanne Padovani
    1, 3, 5, 6, 19, 22, 25, 35, 43, 44,
    47, 52-54, 59-64, 66, 69, 136,
        142-146
religion
    8n3, 14, 24, 26, 38, 91, 98,
    102-104, 106, 111n17, 123-126,
        128-131, 156, 158, 159
Rembrandt (Harmenszoon) van
    Rijn    62, 74
Renaissance    39
Renoir, Jean    6, 19, 26, 61, 155
Report on the Affairs of British
    North America (Durham
    Report)
    2, 3, 8n3, 17, 29n19, 41, 51n10
"Révolution tranquille" ("Quiet
    Revolution")
    8n3, 10, 11, 17, 26, 29n16, 78,
    79, 84, 85, 87n3, 88n16
Ricard, François    24, 88n16
Richard, Maurice    28n15
Rioux, Geneviève    76
Robbe-Grillet, Alain    50n6
Robert, Denise    159
Rocher, Guy    12
Rochereau, Jean    20
Roman Empire    19, 38, 44, 115
Romanticism    111n13
Ronfard, Jean Pierre    21, 40, 147
Rosi, Francesco    19
Rossellini, Roberto    106
Rouch, Jean    137
Roud, Richard    145
Route de l'Ouest, La (The
    Westward Road)
        14, 32, 36, 38, 39, 137
Rozema, Patricia    159

Rules of the Game, The see La
    Règle du jeu
Ruttmann, Walter    32
Sabourin, Marcel    55
Sacramento Bee (newspaper)
        117, 121
Saint-Jérôme    28n14
San Francisco Examiner
    (newspaper)    129
Sartre, Jean-Paul    19, 24
Saturday Night (magazine)    154
Schaeffer, Pierre    36
Schoenberg, Arnold    36
School of Others, The see L'école
    des autres
Scorsese, Martin    105, 124, 146
Seen From Afar see Montréal vu
    par... six variations sur un
    thème
Séguin, Maurice    12, 41
Sénéchal, Father Henri Paul    38
separatist movement
        11, 119, 120, 149
Séquences (magazine)    38
Seul ou avec d'autres [Alone or
    with Others]    12, 136, 137
Sex, Drugs and Rock 'n' Roll
    (book)    159
Shakespeare, William    35
Shek, Ben    54, 91, 105, 107
Shoebridge, Tom    110n3
Shulgasser, Barbara    129
Simon, John    116-119
Siodmak, Robert    58
Sir George Williams University
        27n2
Sirius    152
Sisyphus    26
Sklar, Robert
    113, 116, 119, 120, 132n2
soap opera    25
Social Credit Party    16, 41
Société Générale des Industries
    Culturelles    152
Société Générale du Cinéma du
    Québec    152

Sontag, Susan 74, 87n6
Sophocles 35
sound (use of)
    6, 11, 12, 32-51, 57, 64, 66, 94,
    95, 142, 143
sovereignist movement
    16, 17, 21, 24, 40, 42, 147
sovereignty-association 9n4, 87n3
Spengler, Oswald 115, 117
Spry, Robin 41, 51n10
St John the Baptist
    41, 98, 99, 101, 102
*Stabat Mater* (1736) 5, 47, 156
*Star Ledger* (newspaper) 127
*Starman* 105
Stein, Elliott 120
Stockhausen, Karl-Heinz 43
*Struggle of Hospital Workers, The*
    see *La Lutte des travailleurs*
    *d'hôpitaux*
Suetonius 19, 44
Surrealism 63
Tacitus, Publius 12
*Take It All* see *A tout prendre*
Tanner, Alain 121
*Tartuffe* (play) 35
Telefilm Canada 115, 146, 151, 152
television
    4, 7, 10, 11, 20, 25, 45, 75, 104,
    113, 115, 121, 127, 129, 146, 148,
    159
Testa, Bart 7, 55, 67
textile industry, Quebec
    1, 3, 4, 15, 16, 20, 32-34, 45,
    64, 65, 92, 94, 111n15, 139, 140,
    141
theatre
    6, 29n18, 36, 46, 50, 90, 91, 95,
    97-100, 102-105, 107-109, 128,
    129, 136, 137, 156, 158-161
Théâtre de Quat'Sous
    158, 160, 174
*Thirty-Two Short Films About*
    *Glenn Gould* 51n18
Thompson, Kristin 57, 58
THX 34

Toronto 8, 115, 145, 159, 161
Tourneur, Jacques 58
*Tout va bien* 57, 63
Toynbee, Arnold 74, 79
tragédie en musique 6, 32-51
Tremblay, Johanne-Marie 92, 158
Tremblay, Michel 30n24, 160
Trépanier, Gisèle 36, 37, 41, 42
*Trouble-fête [Trouble Makers]* 11
*Trouble Makers* see *Trouble-fête*
Trudeau, Pierre E
    21, 29n20, 40, 43, 87n3, 149
*True Nature of Bernadette, The*
    see *La vraie nature de*
    *Bernadette*
Truffaut, François 46, 138
*Twenty Year Express* see *20 ans*
    *express*
*Unidentified Human Remains*
    *and the True Nature of Love*
    (play) 8, 46, 160
Union nationale
    16, 17, 40, 41, 88n16
Université de Montréal
    2, 12, 27n2, 36, 46, 85, 136, 153
Université du Québec à Montréal
    153
*Untergang des Abendlandes*
    *(Decline of the West)* (book)
    115, 117
*Up to the Neck* see *Jusqu'au cou*
*Vangelo secondo Matteo, Il (The*
    *Gospel According to St*
    *Matthew)* 105, 125
Varèse, Edgar 37
Venne, Stéphane 11, 27n4
Verniere, James 127
Véronneau, Pierre
    6, 28n13, 29n20, 68n15, 110n8
Vertov, Dziga 32
Vienne, Gérard 50n6
Vietnam war 151
Vikings 38, 39
*Village Voice* (magazine) 119
*Ville-Marie* see *Les Montréalistes*
Volleyball 14

192

Voltaire, François Marie Arouet de 20
*Voter's Handbook, The* (book) **see** *Le petit catéchisme des électeurs*
Voyager space probe 48
*vraie nature de Bernadette, La [The True Nature of Bernadette]* 18
*Vue d'ailleurs* **see** *Montréal vu par... six variations sur un thème*
*Wake up, mes bons amis* **see** *Un pays sans bon sens!*
Wall, James M 125
Walz, Gene 6, 7
War Measures Act 29n20
*Wayne's World* 115
*Weekend* **see** *Wochende*
Weinmann, Heinz 71, 81, 85, 156
*We're Fed Up* **see** *On est au coton*
*Westward Road, The* **see** *La Route de l'Ouest*
Wilkening, Catherine 96
Wilkins, Peter 7
Williams, George 117, 118, 121
Wintonick, Peter 31n37
Wittgenstein, Ludwig Josef Johann 74
*Wochende (Weekend)* 32
World War II 88n16
Wotan 39
Wright, Judy 111n19
Yourcenar, Marguerite 48
Ziolkowski, Theodore 111n18

# Notes on contributors

**Réal La Rochelle**, a film critic and professor at Collège Montmorency, received his doctorate in communications from the Université Stendhal in Grenoble. He has recently edited a special issue of *CinémAction* on the teaching of cinema in Quebec and Canada, as well as a special issue of *Cinémas* on film and "musicality". His other publications include several works on the relationship between images and music.

**André Loiselle** is presently completing a doctoral dissertation on the cinematic treatment of Canadian and Quebec drama at the University of British Columbia, where he also teaches the history and comparative analysis of the cinemas of Canada and Quebec. He has published articles in such journals as *L'Annuaire théâtral*, *Canadian Journal of Film Studies*, *Essays in Theatre* and *Québec Studies*.

**Brian McIlroy** is Assistant Professor of Film Studies in the Department of Theatre and Film at the University of British Columbia. He has contributed articles on film to such journals as *Film Criticism*, *Canadian Journal of Film Studies* and *Literature/Film Quarterly*. He is the author of books on Swedish cinema (1986) and on Irish cinema (1989).

**Denise Pérusse** received her PhD in film studies in 1989. She is a specialist in Quebec cinema, the cinematic representation of women, and the sociological analysis of the reception of French-Canadian films. Co-founder of the journal *Cinémas (Montreal)*, she has published many articles and has co-authored and co-edited numerous books, including *Le Cinéma québécois des années 80* (1989) and *Les Films québécois en France: Dix ans de cinéma* (1991).

**Bart Testa** teaches cinema studies and semiotics at the University of Toronto. He is the author of *Spirit in the Landscape* (1989), a study of landscape motifs in Canadian experimental film, and *Back and Forth: Early Cinema and the Avant-Garde* (1992). He has also co-edited, with Patrick Rumble, *Pier Paolo Pasolini in Contemporary Perspective* (1994), a collection of critical essays.

**Pierre Véronneau** holds a PhD in history and is responsible for publications and historical research at the Cinémathèque Québécoise. He also teaches film studies at the Université de Montréal and Concordia University, and since 1973 has published several books and articles on Canadian and Quebec cinema.

**Gene Walz** is the author of a book on François Truffaut and has edited two collections of articles on Canadian film. He has also written many essays on film and several film scripts (including *The Washing Machine* which he also directed). Currently the President of the Film Studies Association of Canada, he was formerly on the board of directors of the Manitoba Motion Picture Industry Association and the Winnipeg Film Group. He teaches film at the University of Manitoba.

**Peter Wilkins**, a Canadian, is a graduate student in the Department of English and Comparative Literature at the University of California, Irvine. He is currently writing his PhD dissertation on apocalyptic narratives by North American writers.